ON TWO FRONTS

The story of a soldier deployed to Afghanistan—
and the friend he left behind.

by

SGT Adam Fenner & Lance Taubold

From

Adam Fenner

To

Honey Duprey Smith

and

Rick Taubold

To the two people, who, without a doubt, have made the greatest impact on my writing: Honey, the best English teacher in the state of Nevada, also the only one whose class I saw fit to take, who never let me turn in anything other than my best, despite how many times I tried to do just that. Rick, whose thoughtful encouraging critiques and edits turned the raging stream of conscious style writings of a former Marine infantryman into something fit for consumption by the public.

As with all great teachers, your impacts are immeasurable, and will be felt by my readers and myself, until I finally hate editing my works so much, I quit writing.

From

Lance Taubold

To

Every soldier and every loved one of a soldier from time immemorial. Over the course of writing this book, I have come to realize the wide-reaching scope and impact of just one soldier on so many lives. War is a devastating and life-changing experience for those abroad and at home.

Note to Reader

Integrated throughout this book are links to photos and videos taken by SGT Fenner while on deployment to Afghanistan. The hyperlinks may be utilized directly, while your e-book device is connected to the Internet. Simply click on the hyperlink at the end of the chapter, or use the link below.

http://www.13thirtybooks.com/#!on-two-fronts/cbdf

In addition, QR codes, may also be used to access the photos and videos. A QR reader is needed and can be downloaded for free, on any "smart phone" or Internet capable device. Once installed, use the QR reader to "scan" the QR code and you will be directed to Internet site.

INTRODUCTION

~Lance~

The genesis of this book did not come from divine inspiration, but rather through my abject desperation.

My best friend, Adam, is being deployed to Afghanistan. He is an Army medic in the National Guard and a former Marine, having served in the first two tours of the Iraq invasion.

Adam told me a couple of years ago, while he was in Iraq and before he met me, that he hadn't kept in contact with anyone back home. He said he'd just wanted to do the job and come home.

Well, I'm not anyone and things work differently with me. There is no way I'm not going to talk to him for a year—war or no war! I've never had anyone close to me go off to war. To say that I'm upset is the understatement of my life. It's like losing a limb—or worse, my heart.

With Adam being somewhat intractable and recalcitrant, (speaking of understatements) I knew I needed a great plan. When it was finally formed, I presented the book idea to him.

I'm sure I'm not the only person back home who has a friend or loved one overseas and wonders exactly what is going on over there.

The idea: A book chronicling my life here in Las Vegas with all the emotions and fears, and Adam's life in Afghanistan, relating all of his events and feelings as they happen, then sending the book back and forth, through the miracle of e-mail, to write as the story unfolds.

He agreed.

Which then presented me with another dilemma. I am an entertainer and writer in Las Vegas, and an avid reader of romance stories. As such, I always want a happy ending. The difficulty with writing about things as they happen is... you don't know what's going to happen. Of course, my ending would be him getting off the plane and running into my open arms, which may sound gay, but... I am. Adam's straight. As for the happy ending, I'll settle for the realistic one of him getting off the plane safe and sound.

Please, God, (or even Allah in this case) let there be a happy ending.

~Adam~

I'm not a writer. I'm a grunt. This book was not my idea. It was an obligation... to a friend. Like my deployment, I took it and ran with it, forging it into more than I ever expected, or perhaps I was just swept along for the ride.

Lance wanted a chance to keep in touch. I needed a way to vent. However, the book became more than just a target for my frustrations, it became: my story, their story, and our story.

This book is my attempt to show the world that we are more than faceless boys and men, crammed into uniforms, sent to fight America's war against the elusive and bestial Taliban forces, and that our families are more than unknown martyrs mourning their absent sons, fathers, and brothers. We really are somewhere that really exists, and we really do walk among you, silently carrying our burdens.

~Lance~

So this is our story, told from two fronts, Adam's from Afghanistan, and mine from Las Vegas.

Let the show begin...

BOOK I

It Begins

1

Another Beautiful Day

~Adam~

I strolled through the double doors of the Drill Hall. The sun had set behind me on the forty-five minute ride across town. My digital-patterned uniform was dusty from hanging in my closet all month, and my hair was barely within regulation length.

"Hey, sir, what is up?" I said to the young, thin LT as he walked past me.

"Not much, how you doing?" He greeted me with a half-smile.

"Another beautiful day, sir." I smiled at him as we passed each other, our combat boots knocking on the tile floor.

"Yeah, we will see," he replied from behind me, the life taken out of his voice.

"Who shit in his cover?" I asked Davey Crockett (Yes his name is David Crockett), my red-headed, pale-faced friend.

"He might be mad he had to come in on a Friday night too," Davey offered.

Outside, the last bits of the sun highlighted the mountains surrounding the Las Vegas valley. Our formation was lit by the giant lights hanging above us now, the heat of the day still noticeable as it rose off the blacktop.

"Company..." First Sergeant started the movement with a preparatory command.

"Platoon," Staff Sergeant Khan said, looking back at us in the traditional Army way.

"Attention"!" First Sergeant finished the command.

We casually went from pushing each other and joking around to feet together and eyes locked forward.

The officers moved around the formation in rehearsed movements, while the First Sergeant traded places with the Company Commander.

"Gentlemen, I look forward to serving with you in Afghanistan," he yelled across the formation.

Through the corner of my mouth I whispered to the soldier to my left, "Hmm. He said that like Afghanistan isn't Afghanistan."

The evening was a mess of questions.

"When?"

"Where in Afghanistan?"

"Did you know?"

The tough guys, without right shoulder patches signifying prior combat tours, feigned excitement and puffed their chests out.

Those few of us who had seen combat tours kept silent, knowing this was all part of the cycle.

Davey drove me home. I sat in the passenger seat. He asked me questions. This would be his first tour. We kept the tone casual, as he stressed on how to tell his wife Kaitlyn. I sent Grant a text message: "I'm going to Afghanistan."

Grant, who rode with me in an AAV (Amphibious Assault Vehicle) during the Iraqi invasion, had been nineteen at the time, and I was eighteen, one of the most junior Marines in the invasion. That was seven years ago.

"I hate you. I'm so jealous," he texted me back.

We had done a second tour to Iraq as well. I missed his third deployment. This would be my third and my first deployment as an Army Medic, instead of a Marine Rifleman.

I thanked Davey for the ride and went up to my second-story apartment. I kissed Angela, my girlfriend, after I took my boots off. She had a friend over from across the country, leaving her distracted.

"How was drill?" she asked.

"Good," I told her. I would wait to tell her the rest after the weekend. I didn't want a scene while her friend was in town. She was already planning to move out anyway, no reason to sweat the details now. I made myself a drink. "You girls want a drink?" I yelled across the apartment.

"Oh, yes, please," Angela replied, excitement in her voice as the two of them giggled on Angela's and my bed, playing with coloring books for some obscure reason.

"Captain and Cokes it is."

2

A Lousy Day

~Lance~

There he is.

Looking fit in his T-shirt and jeans. Short dirty-blond hair spiked up.

He smiles, stands up from the table, and gives me my hug. It feels good. It always feels good. He knows how to hug and mean it.

My best friend. Adam.

"I ordered you an iced tea," he says.

"That's fine. So, what's new?"

"Let's order first."

Uh oh. My alarm goes off. Lunch for us has never been a great idea, well, for me really. Adam has this annoying idiosyncrasy, better yet, aberration, of dropping bombshells on me at lunch, such as: "I have to go train in Texas to be a medic for four months." Or more recently: "Angela and I have decided to move to North Carolina next year." That one I put down to impulse.

"What are you having?" I ask.

"A burger. Do you want an appetizer?"

"Sure, whatever you want. I'll get a burger, too." We often get the same things to eat.

We order, talk about the show I perform in at The Venetian, have some fried chicken-fingery things, and I say, "So, what's up?"

"Do you want the good news or the bad news?"

Here we go.

"Good news?"

"Angela and I broke up."

"Oh. Wow. I'm sorry. Are you okay about it?" (Guess moving to North Carolina is off.)

He shrugs. "There's nothing I can do about it. It's fine. I knew it was coming. We talked about it."

"Ok. And that's the good news?"

"Well, I thought you would think so." He half-smiles at me.

"No, I don't. I want you to be happy. I do like her." And I really do. She might be a little rough around the edges, talks like a truck driver at times, and looks like Mary Martin in Peter Pan, but I like her. She and I have always gotten along, for the year they've been together. And, coincidentally, she always refers to me as Peter Pan, because of my penchant for never growing up. (Which is a good thing.)

The burgers arrive. I start to eat. He is waiting for me to ask.

I swallow—just in case. "And the bad news?"

"My unit's been deployed to Afghanistan."

My mouth goes dry. My head gets a little buzzy. I know I didn't hear him right. Right? That horrible feeling of when I lost my mom returns. I think I can feel my face blanch a couple of shades.

"It'll be all right," he assures me. "It's not that long. I've done this before."

Somehow the words formulate. "Not with me around, you haven't. How long you going for?"

"Nine months."

Months? Why not just make it years? I want to leave. I want to cry. I want to make believe he never said this. I know he reads it all on my face. I make a lousy poker player.

He says, "I'll be fine."

Oh, okay then. Let's have dessert.

3

BAD DAYS

~Lance~

"I can't believe Adam's being deployed again!" I told my husband, Richie, as soon as I got home.

Oh yeah, I'm married. To a great guy. (Most of the time) Richie. We've been together over twenty years.

"He's leaving for a year!" I tell him. "Three months of training at some bases around the country in addition to the nine months, in country. (A new phrase added to my vocabulary.) The fucking Army.

Actually, I have nothing against the Army. I appreciate all they do, but... Give me a break. This is a big deal.

"Where's he going?" Richie, says, almost casually.

"Fucking Afghanistan! It's not fair."

"He did sign up for it. Of course it's fair. You shouldn't be surprised. This is what happens when we're at war."

Richie can be so irritating and unsympathetic. I'm all for pragmatism, but this is different. "He's going to be in danger and fighting, and what if something... happens?"

"That's all part of it. Do you want to go with him and hold his hand and make sure he doesn't get hurt?"

Yes. "No, but he's already served his country twice. I don't care if it was with the Marines and this is the Army. Serving is serving."

"That's not the way it works."

"Well it should. It's not fair."

"You said that. Anything else?"

Grrr. I was not getting anywhere here. "Yes. I'm probably not even going to get to talk to him. When he was in Iraq, he didn't keep in touch with anybody. Not even his family. He said he just wants to do the job, get paid, and come home. Like it's nothing and it's that easy."

"Maybe it is for him."

"Well it's not for me. He's my best friend. What am I going to do without him for a whole year?" I think I may have just gone too far.

"Obviously he doesn't think the same thing."

Yep. Too far. Shit. "Yes, he does. He's just not as vocal as I am."

"Fine. You deal with it."

"I will. I'll think of something."

The wheels started to turn.

Light bulb!

4

For Real?

~Adam~

I sat in the leather chair in the lobby waiting. As formally dressed as I ever got: a shave, some paste in my hair, and a button-up shirt. I looked at my phone. Yup, late.

"Adam, you can have a seat if you want," the hostess said.

"Yeah, I guess."

She smiled at me, grabbed two menus and guided me to the booth. She set the menus on opposite sides of the booth and asked if there was anything else I would need.

I thanked her as I took my seat, pulling my phone out of my pocket and placing it on the table. The room was modestly lit, a mix of deep browns and reds with plants lining the walls. Tuscan statues and decor filled the open areas.

The busboy came by and cleared the table of the extraneous sets of silverware and dishes.

"Thank you."

He nodded.

The waiter, a short, older Latino man, made his way slowly to the table.

"Gilberto! Good to see you my friend. How are you?" I said, shaking his hand.

"I am good. Lance is coming?"

"Yeah, Lance is coming. He is late as always."

"Ok, very good. Is there anything I can get for you?"

"Of course. Could I get him a double Maker's Mark, with a splash of soda... on the rocks—and a Jack and Coke—and two shrimp cocktails?"

"Very good, I will get those for you."

The busboy brought some bread and dipping oil.

I thanked him with a nod.

"Hey!" Lance said, wearing an unnecessarily tight, yellow tank top and denim pants, hailing to decades past.

I stood to greet him. We exchanged one of his excited hugs and I returned to my seat.

Lance sat across from me and began to awkwardly slide along the edge of the curved seat, until he was beside me.

I rolled my eyes.

"Ok. I have been thinking," Lance said.

"Uh oh."

Gilberto shuffled over with our drinks.

"Gilberto!" Lance smiled and leaned across me to shake his hand. "How are you?"

I leaned against the soft back of the booth to avoid him.

"I am good. I am good. Your shrimp cocktails are on the way," Gilberto said with a smile before moving along to his other tables.

Lance looked at me. A grin spread across his face. I spun the straws around the bottom of my glass and took a sip. "You were thinking."

"Yes, ok. I know you don't like to keep in contact with people while you are over there, but I want you to talk to me."

"I'm sure you do." I brought the straws, again, to my mouth.

"I want to write a book about our experiences over there."

I looked at him over the brim of my glass, slowly letting the hickory flavor warm me.

"My experience here, and your experience over there, and our relationship."

"It sounds like a big gay adventure to me."

"No, it is not."

"Lance, I'm not a writer, and even if I was, I wouldn't have anything to write about except staring at the wall and jacking off."

"I have seen some of the stuff you have written—it's good. And it has never been done. I could even comment on what you've written writing, say how I feel about what you are going through. We could really help people with this."

I took another deep pull of my drink. I let the air in my lungs slowly escape through my nose. "And I get to comment on yours?"

"No, why would you comment on mine?"

"Why wouldn't I be able to? That is bullshit."

"I'll think about it."

"You'll think about it? This is ridiculous, a non-fiction, written as it happens. I hope I die, just to make sure you don't get your happy ending."

"AHHH! You asshole..."

"That's right, no riding off on a yellow motorcycle into the sunset for you."

"What? I..."

"Ooohh, I want an open bar at the funeral."

"You're not going to die."

"I could. The Taliban are a wily bunch."

"Over my dead body."

"Well, at your age, that may not be too far away." My straw found the bottom of my glass empty. "I have to piss. Can you get me another Jack and Coke?"

"Yes. Ass-hole."

I smiled, slid my phone into my pocket, and walked out the back entrance to the bathroom.

~Lance~

I told Adam tonight, over dinner and some decent champagne, about a whole e-mail exchange thing between us and my idea to turn it into a book. He balked at first, until I explained that this wouldn't be just for me. I am certainly not the only person with a friend or loved one overseas who wants to know what's going on day to day over there. It gives one a sense of being there and being connected, and comforted. I know I'll feel better, even if he is in danger. I would rather know than not know. But he really does care about me and would keep in touch anyway. Our friendship matters to him.

I said, "This could be something good for a lot of people."

He saw the possibility of it and agreed.

At least I've convinced him to e-mail me as often as possible, since that will be the only way we can really communicate. He says there should be a phone on base, but it'll be hard to use.

As for cell phones? Ha! It's Afghanistan. What do sheep and Sherpas need cell phones for, let alone cell sites, if they even know what they are. Afghanistan's literacy rate is well below thirty percent. I looked it up. [Adam: Some areas are as low as five percent. That doesn't mean they don't have technology, just not a lot.]

~Adam~

I returned home. My bed sat empty and cold, consuming the majority of the available floor space of my bedroom. The world gently rocked, and my buzz gently tickled my cheeks.

I awkwardly turned my computer on and let the glow fill the room.

"Nope. Not doing it."

I turned the monitor off and climbed over the footboard of my bed, shedding clothes lazily, letting them fall where they might along my path.

The blue light from my wireless router spread across the spinning ceiling above me, while my eyes adjusted to the low light. Quotes and dialogue floated around my brain. My brain whispered little ideas into my ear, keeping me awake.

An hour slipped by.

Fuck.

I slowly climbed out of bed. My buzz having left me, I turned my monitor on and clumsily maneuvered through the very bright menus to the word processor.

The click of keystrokes echoed off the room and carried me into the early morning.

5

NOT MY IDEA

~Adam~

I had spent four years of fighting to be able to go to college, literally. The National Guard was kind enough to accept me and pay for what the GI Bill would not, allowing me the education my family was unable to provide.

I was three semesters into my degree.

In addition to my three semesters working toward a diploma, I had spent the last two and a half years trying to build a life, surrounding myself with people who, in a strange way, had become my family.

If someone had told me when I walked into that massive tent in Kuwait and shook hands with the guys I would be invading a country with, that in five years my family would include: Grant's ugly ass, his fat heterosexual life-mate Ed, and a gay Las Vegas entertainer, I would have—

I probably wouldn't have done anything, except not believe them. But here they are, splattered all over my life. Family. The difference between family and friends: you can't get rid of family, even if you want to.

I missed the third deployment that Grant went on. We had spent our first two together. During the Iraq invasion, his fighting hole was right next to mine. Our common personalities kept us as roommates in and out of the Marines even after our time was up.

~Lance~

Monday. I've hopped onto my computer for a little research and writing. I figured I needed to be as forewarned and forearmed as I could. I've studied the area he's going to in Afghanistan. It's a province called Laghman, in the northeast sector, kind of by Pakistan and China. He says it's not a real war zone—whatever that is—and has been pretty calm over the last few years.

He tells me where he will be has seen very little action over the past five years, with only one KIA (killed in action) during that time. One is more than enough, as I'm certain his family will attest.

However... I was finishing up my show at The Venetian today, (I sing and dance in my own show there.) and a guy from the audience came up to me.

"Hey, you were great. I just got back from Afghanistan and this is the first place I've been. You been doing this long?"

Clang! The Afghanistan word.

"A couple of months," I answered. "What were you doing over there?"

"I was a contractor for a year. Did the job. They paid me a lot. Now I'm back." Adam had told me that contractors make a shitload of money.

"I've heard it's great money, but there's got to be a better, or at least safer, way of making a living." I subtly probed. "How was it?"

"I really didn't like being there. It was ugly and barren, you know, a typical third-world country where people pee in holes dug in the ground in the streets."

Nice. [Adam: I'm lazy. I don't dig holes to pee.]

bad she can't be waiting at my cot when I get back from patrol. That would be nice.

I'm hardly old, but old enough to have learned the lesson that, unless you have been there, you can't understand. Don't try to, just listen.

After I'm done venting, a hug is all I need. (Lance, as you read this, that is not an invitation.) It is more for the mothers and girlfriends I spoke of. Guy hugs are less fun. Words can't communicate the feelings that one wishes to express in regard to a great many things that body language will always make up for. And a hug says, "I don't understand, but I'm here for you."

~Lance~

What Adam doesn't realize is that when I hug him, it's not a sexual thing—most of the time. It's a love thing. I'm going to tell him that, when I hug him, I'm not hugging his body, I'm hugging his soul. That ought to change his impression of my hugs.

But I do mean it.

I put love into my hugs. Why bother if it's only perfunctory?

Soul hugs.

I like it. [Adam: Ugh.]

7

FROZEN SHELLFISH AND LIBATIONS

~Lance~

Gilberto had already brought our "tails" to the table—cock and shrimp, as usual. And, as usual, we waited before ordering our entrees. I'd probably let him order for both of us. It's kind of fun. He'd probably order us surf and turf. It's pretty much a staple for us—with our special sides of penne with vodka sauce. We liked to dine together and have conversation like civilized folk. Besides which, I didn't know how many more of these we had left.

"Are you okay with going?" I ask, while he takes a swig of his Jack and Coke.

"Yeah, I'm fine. I don't have a choice. It bothers you more than it does me."

"I can't help it. It's—"

"I know. It's your first time."

"I guess I have mentioned this before."

He gives me one of those quelling Adam faces. I'm duly berated. A quirk of a smile comes to his face.

"It's my job. I'll be fine."

"Some job."

"Nothing's going to happen to me. I'll be careful."

This all sounds fine. But the reality still looms. "I know you're okay with it. I'm trying to be, too. Pragmatism must run in your family." I think about his mother and feel slightly chastised.

"Have another drink. It'll help," he says.

Gilberto has arrived to take our order.

"I'll have the steak and lobster, medium rare," he says.

Gilberto nods. "And penne vodka?"

"Of course. And Lance needs another drink."

"And I'll have the same," I say.

Emphasis on needs. "What about you?" I look at his half-empty glass.

"I'll wait a few minutes. I don't need to be hurting tomorrow. And you don't either."

I'm hurting now.

He can come off as unemotional and uncaring at times, but not to me. I see through it to that other thoughtful side. He understands where I'm coming from. He might not agree, but he understands.

And he's not perfect either. He's not exactly humble, for instance. He knows he's good-looking and intelligent and will use it to his advantage. He's not obnoxious about it, and it does make me laugh, probably because I'm not so humble all the time either.

Also, his laissez-faire, non-committal attitude can drive me crazy.

I smoothly change topics.

8

HOLDING ON

~Adam~

"The only thing that would have made that shower better was a blow job," I told my roommate last night after I finally meandered out of the bathroom, a half-drunk beer, cold with heavy condensation from collecting steam within the shower, in hand.

That was last night. This morning I woke up exhausted from strange dreams and terrible sleep. The Sonar ringtone on my phone began pinging.

Lance.

Four pings. Then, I waited. A fifth ping. One new voicemail. What followed was a message, in which he, again, tried to guilt-trip me into spending as much time with him as possible before I leave. [Lance: I was desperately trying anything. I don't know why I tried the guilt thing. That never works with him.]

Lance. He would rather I place an exclamation point at the end of his name. It's much more exciting that way. As he reads this, my assumption is that he is not wearing sleeves, mostly because he doesn't own any shirts that have sleeves, unless it is required for work. He likes to show off his muscles. (I must note that I was wrong. He read this sitting next to me. He was wearing a normal shirt. He might have borrowed it from Richie.)

Adam, once again, is taking the illnesses of his father and grandfather in stride. My mom was also like that, very practical about life and death. I try to be like her, but that doesn't stop the hurt of missing her. I personally would like to see Adam let out his feelings more. I think it would help him, and I would be there for him if he did.

All of this is by way of saying that this past year has been shitty, with the adjustment of losing my mom and now losing my best friend for the next year. This is not a "woe is me" complaint at all. That's not me. I always try to be optimistic and positive. (Thanks, Mom.) I know things will work out fine. It's just such a long time.

It's not only the year thing. These preceding four months, before Indiana, he has to go out of town twice to bases in California, then to Wisconsin for more pre-training training. He is leaving in a couple of days for the first of these. Great.

We have been trying to get together as much as we can, but we both have other obligations: my new job/gig as the entertainer at the Venetian hotel, and his bouncer job at the Paris hotel nightclub on weekends.

We were involved in a D&D campaign. For those of you who aren't in the know, this is Dungeons and Dragons, a role-playing game. We have been ensconced in it with a couple of other guys for the past year or so. The game is usually associated with the nerd set, and justifiably so. But occasionally non-nerd types, like Adam and me, get involved. I confess, though, we both are a little nerdy because we are playing, but we do also have other interests in our lives, so that doesn't qualify us as complete nerds.

Ed, a rather large guy, and a true nerd is in our group. The others pick on him mercilessly about his weight and his difficulties with the opposite sex, at least as far as the sex is concerned. Adam keeps telling him he's gay and that he's just waiting for our other D&D buddy, Grant, Ed's best friend since grade school, to come out of the closet and get together. We all love to zing one another. My zinging is usually sarcastic. I guess I don't have to state that.

* * *

Richie likes Adam and, usually, understands our friendship. I say "usually" because I can sometimes go overboard with Adam, presents, etc. He never blames Adam, just me. Oh, well. At least I'm not sleeping with Adam.

No comment.

All right. I will comment.

Adam and I have talked about this, which makes it easier. Everything's in the open, and we're both fine with it. We joke about it and move on. I really am glad he's straight. Otherwise, I don't even want to think of the possible problems. I love them both and would not want to lose either one or have to make a choice. Either choice would be wrong. So, in this respect, I have the best of both worlds. I'm a pretty lucky guy.

Most of my guy friends are straight. I do have gay friends, too, and Adam gets along with them all. I have a lot of friends, always have. Adam, not so many. He's more discerning, like Richie. I'm like my mom. I've never met a stranger. A sore point with Richie. And I have to admit it sometimes, justifiably so. But my argument is: "Look at all the great people I've met along the way." I think I've made Richie gun-shy.

Adam is off to California for his first training. Fort McCoy— I'm pretty sure. There are so many forts it's hard to keep them straight. He'll be gone about three weeks. He's always 'ish 'ish about the times. Aggravating. But now I'll start to get an idea of what the next year will be like, getting his daily (I hope) e-mails and commenting on them, and really learning how this whole deployment thing works. Except I get to find out (almost) as it happens. Goodie.

10

THE GAUNTLET

~Adam~

We had arrived in Camp Roberts, California, just south of Fort Hunter Liggett. It was bright and sunny, as California tends to be, but the buildings rotted around us. A section had been renovated to house us while we trained in preparation for Pre-mobilization training in Camp Atterbury, Indiana. For the time, we were taking care of the bulk of our army required Warrior tasks and drills. The hope would be that by the time we got to Indiana we wouldn't be bogged down by mandated training and could focus on more mission-specific training. Time would tell, however.

* * *

It's pissing out there.

My blouse is hanging from the rafters of this wooden building that hails back to WWII. I like it in here. It reminds me of my grandpa's house in northern Wisconsin. It isn't concrete and brick and has a cold white paint that turns yellow over time, like so many other military billeting. The floors are a linoleum tile 'ish, thing. The walls are wooden, and in the NCO's room, light shines through the cracks in the walls. There are small metal lockers—which the Kids upstairs insist on constantly moving around—to hold our various gear in something that resembles security. (Our Kids are our subordinates, the younger, or in some cases older, junior soldiers.)

I step into the bathroom, a towel wrapped around my waist and hygiene gear under my arm. I place my black bag onto the metal rack above the sinks. I am not looking forward to shaving. The faucets show their age—or price—and don't like to stay on when the handle is turned.

Behind me is the pisser. It is a trough with a hole at the bottom to drain off urine, rocks, and dip. To flush, a copper pipe has had holes drilled into the bottom to allow water to pour out at such pressure as to blast your own urine back out at you when you are finished pissing. Above the urinal, for our viewing pleasure, is a hole that was, more than likely, a knot in the wood that has been removed. The view through the hole is unimpressive. Trash fills it, and possibly a mouse. The mystery of what lies beyond prevents the curious from sticking his penis in there.

It's a safety issue.

Around the hole is what is worth looking at. Quite a long time ago, lips and legs were drawn to give the illusion of a vagina spread beyond normal limits, the kind of thing one would see in a video involving baseball bats. Nonetheless, I miss vagina.

The toilets are to the left of the pisser, set lower than the traditional, comfortable toilet, with curtains in place of doors, allowing a little privacy.

To my right, I hear laughter. All the shower heads are already taken in the Meat Locker. Four shower heads line the left wall of what would appear to be a metal-lined hallway with concrete floors. And right now, this small hallway is filled with naked, laughing soldiers.

One of my fellow medics in the far back end is finished. I laugh as he walks The Gauntlet. He leaves the water running for me as I hang up my towel on the exposed pipes outside the shower. He slides against the sheet-metal wall along the rear side, attempting to avoid the soaking wet backside of the first soldier he must squeeze past.

"Excuse me."

"Oh, my bad," he says, stepping back toward the back wall, reducing the space available to pass.

"You mother fucker." His voice carries the joking tone out into the bathroom.

A step forward, and the required space to pass is granted.

The next guy he passes is facing with his back to the shower head and his front side to the soldier attempting to pass. As he tries to make it past, Mac makes mock attempts to tackle or block his path. His hands are filled with his shower supplies, making self-defense difficult.

"Goddamnit. What are you doing? Ahhh."

More laughter.

He nervously dodges the advances and easily makes it past the last man who is just laughing. We are all laughing. I spank him on the ass.

A loud crack fills the bathroom followed by laughter.

"Do I at least get a good game?"

I smile in return.

I step into the same peril.

More laughter. [Lance: All right. Let me get this straight (pun intended). I'm the one who's gay and I've never encountered a situation like this. What's wrong with this picture?]

* * *

"Hey guys, just letting you know, if it sounds like I have a leg cramp in the middle of the night, just leave me alone. I'll work it out myself," Joey, the oldest and fattest, said before bed the first night in.

Thanks, Joey.

I laughed over my laptop screen. I slowly organized the events of the day and splattered them across the screen. I'll just give this to Lance when I get back to Vegas.

* * *

The California sky continues to piss on us. All of us left outside, digging the small culverts away from the supply area to prevent it from flooding, are drenched. Not entirely to the bone, but we are thoroughly wet. The Kids tried. They dug random, ineffectual paths leading in varying directions. Mac and I remain, adding the needed direction to the veritable Amazon River they created. The massive puddle no longer threatens our supply area. It has already overtaken the one across the way.

Our tasks complete, I eye the large puddle just to the left, outside the massive sliding door into the supply building.

"Mac, you up for some mud wrestling?"

He looks at me, takes off his glasses, looks at the puddle next to us, and proceeds to remove the articles from his pockets that he doesn't want to get wet.

Wrestling with a devout Mormon generally would not seem like a good time. That's a lie. Mac is the type who enjoys this Army thing as an escape from the general proper behavior around his wife and two daughters. He may not necessarily take part in the debauchery that his church frowns upon, but he does enjoy having a chance to watch it.

Within minutes, my boots are in four inches of water. Mac and I are squaring off. He weighs about the same as me but is a little softer around the edges. Those few years he has on me, along with the family life, have taken their toll.

Mac throws coins down in the water.

We are soon rolling around, both attempting to gain the dominant position.

I notice his notebook is still in his pocket. Too late now.

Mac's head lands too close to the building.

My options are limited. I lean back.

His hands move to my shoulder blades.

I grab hold of his wrist, plop a squat on his chest, pull a foot around his head, and drop back.

Lift up with my hips, and the arm bar is complete.

We go a few more rounds while a fellow medic coaches and the supply sergeant films us. We decide to finish and head back to the barracks.

My boots now hang from the air vents in a vain attempt to air them out.

* * *

Before I left for Cali, I broke down and told Mom. She asked almost all the right questions about the coming school semester and my plans. I was a chicken-shit at first and dodged the questions. I hung up the phone, took a shower, had a rum and Coke, mostly rum, and called her back.

She is better at this than I thought she was. I worked myself up too much, and by the time I said it, she took it like any other news. Way better than Lance took the news, for sure. [Lance: As I've said, this is my first time with this. His mother has done it several times before.]

Since I told her, Lance and she have been corresponding via e-mail and telephone.

* * *

We have continued to train today in preparation for this deployment. Today was the land navigation course. It was a fun little adventure. They gave us a map, compass, and a list of places that we needed to find. More fun than you would think.

My boots are caked with mud and are showing the beginning signs of rotting due to how often they have been wet since our arrival. I have not trained in anything aside from desert conditions for quite a few years, and the rain is a welcome change. Mud is not in itself bad. It is, though, bad when it tries to steal my boots off my feet and when it creates slick hillsides for me to lose footing on and slide down the hill.

Odie, my partner, is more nimble than me, at least until he started to get blisters. He is referred to as a dark-green soldier, or as a dark-green Marine only a few years earlier. This is a politically correct way of referring to his African heritage, which, although noticeable, is significantly less noticeable than his stature or lack thereof. His height is a fact that few comment on for fear of the quiet rage that builds within his very little body. I have only been able to get away with making references to his height because we share a common background in the Corps. Both he and I participated in the Iraq invasion, I in a basic infantry capacity, while he was a member of a sniper platoon.

Odie and I spent a good portion of the time looking at a map, scratching our heads, and looking again at the map.

This we did while confidently making more wrong decisions that consistently led us up and down hills in a northward direction. Luckily, a combination of accidental and pseudo-intentional actions led us to one of our points.

Smooth sailing from there, but we were sweating it for a bit.

The rest of the day was ours to relax, thankfully. I have been getting exhausted with these constant classes. A little time in the gym, some food, and a lot of Spades have been occupying my afternoon.

Okay, that's not really going to work. I'll keep the emotional level down, but as for not thinking about it...

Well, I'll figure it out. He's a different person now.

Hell, I'm a different person now.

[Adam: I hope he takes that advice to heart. I'm getting stressed out hearing about me getting maimed or killed.]

[Lance: This is something I have not mentioned—and will not ever mention. The insensitivity of a couple of his other friends sometimes appalls me. If I were the violent type or if I thought it would do any good, I would do something about it. However, Adam knows how to adjust to it for what it is and whom it's coming from. But it obviously does bother him. It bothers the hell out of me.]

12

LONG DRIVES

~Lance~

I just reviewed a couple of things Adam had written, and I sit here trying to not let tears drop onto my keyboard. Richie would not be happy if I short-circuited the computer (especially if he knew why). But how could Adam say that he felt he could not measure up in the friendship department? He doesn't realize what he does for me as a friend, even though I tell him.

Last year, for three months, Adam was in San Antonio attending medic school. Two months in, I got booked to perform at a convention in Houston. I told him I would be there for the weekend, and he immediately said he would try to make it, without my asking. I said that would be great, or some equally ebullient word.

It turned out he got assigned to guard duty on Saturday, the day he was going to come. He said he would still try, but he could only stay a short time. I think I hid my disappointment fairly well, and I understood. It was a fluke I was there anyway.

Saturday came, he called and said, "I'm going to drive over, but I can only stay a couple of hours."

"It's three or four hours away," I said.

"I know. I can probably do it faster. I'll call when I'm close."

I couldn't believe it. He'd drive all that way just to see me for a couple of hours?

He knew how much it would mean to me.

And still does.

Doesn't measure up as friend? Bah!

* * *

After talking to his mom (Oh yeah, I talked to her today—I promised I would—for an hour.), she told me that growing up he used to be a more private type of guy, kind of a wallflower. He had only a couple of friends, but they were close friends.

It seems, since being with me and my coterie of friends, he has come out of his shell. He really has become quite gregarious.

I hope I haven't created a monster.

So, I talked to his mom today. She was very pleasant and seemed glad to talk to me. I thanked her for her e-mail words of advice. Adam had told her quite a bit about me, all good it seemed. Go figure. She expressed her concerns over Adam's leaving and, more than once, told me she hoped I would keep her apprised of how he was doing. I assured her I would. I know she has so much going on with her husband and his care, as well as moving back to Wisconsin since she lost her job. If I can help her in any way by reassuring her that her son is okay—I pray to God—then I'm glad I can do it.

She also freely told me about Adam's personality and how he had been affected by his first two tours. The first he had come back from fine, not much had happened. The second, he had come back angry and had had some disturbing experiences. He'd seen more death and destruction, actual war. She said it took a while for him to come back to himself and thanked Adam's then soon-to-be wife for helping to bring that about.

I hope sometime, if he wants, he'll relate some of his stories to me, certainly not because I want to hear about man's inhumanity to man, but because maybe I can help share his feelings by listening. I tell him that verbally airing problems can often bring a release and an easing of the mind. Keeping things bottled up can be very bad.

Maybe someday. I'm there for him.

~Adam~

I watch as the sand swirls into the drain. My day washes down the crack of my ass, along with my stress.

Battle drills, as they are called, involve a variety of infantry tasks that are deemed necessary to be trained in prior to deployment. Movement under fire seems to be the main issue in a variety of conditions. Inside of my various nooks and crannies, the sand and dirt collects. I can't figure out where it all came from, maybe from the various dives I took during imaginary fire during mock patrol lanes.

Ambush left, fire-maneuver-kill.

Far ambush. I dive into another pile of dirt. Sand spills into my shirtsleeves, but stops at my forearm where the elbow pads that I wear—despite a great deal of protest—squeeze against my forearm, providing a sand-proof barrier. We maneuver, fire, maneuver, fire, and finally withdraw.

"INCOMING!" We dive for cover again. My newly issued elbow pads are beginning to show wear.

"Twelve o'clock. Three hundred meters," my squad leader shouts.

"Twelve o'clock. Three hundred meters." Our echoes fill the training area. Heavy breathing and the stomping of feet fill the air around me as we rush to the designated rally point.

"LACE REPORT!"

The dirt gathers too high around my collar and spills in. I continue to shoulder-walk my way past more wire, a single strand, followed by open sky.

The stars aren't as bright in the wooded area as in the desert, I notice. California may have too many lights.

I roll and the dirt settles. Gravity guides it along a journey down my shirt, past my belts and into my underwear and trousers.

We set more security.

I dive over a wall, tactically.

My squad leader face plants. Legs up, face down. I move up, slide over, and continue forward, plant myself in the dirt several more times. The dummy/target finds itself, too, now lying in the dirt. Tackled and elbow-dropped, it lies motionless.

"INDEX!"

* * *

It is time for me to turn the lights off for the evening. A fellow medic is heckling Joey, who attempts to read with a headlamp.

13

OLD MAN IRONS

~Adam~

In the traditional fashion to which all military members had become accustomed, we were waiting. Sixteen-hundred sharp applied to us, not to our ever-professional instructors. So, there we stood, outside the trailers/classrooms to receive some other pieces of training that we would fight to stay awake during. And after we grew tired of throwing rocks into our hats, we turned on each other, and Irons was standing there. What started as one well-placed joke, and ultimately ended up going to the point of just being annoying, is chronicled here.

Points to understand about Irons:

He is younger than Joey, who came up with a lot of these.

He is also a bit of a ghost. We know he is always around; we just don't know where.

And he is never directly involved in any of our shenanigans.

Irons is so old:

They carbon date his farts.

He named it the Achilles Heel.

He knows what frankincense and myrrh are.

He burnt down the Library at Alexandria to avoid an overdue book fee.

He appears twice in the fossil record.

He remembers calling the Virgin Mary a prude.

When he first joined the military, they didn't throw grenades, they threw Greek fire.

He reappears repeatedly in his own family tree.

He "begat" children.

He remembers when incest was the only option.

When he was in field artillery, he was a loader on a trebuchet.

He remembers when Sun Tzu was a lieutenant.

He took alchemy for a science credit.

He was a member of the Whig party.

He doesn't get crabs, he gets trilobites.

He remembers how to use an abacus.

He predicted Nostradamus. [Lance: My personal favorite.]

Whenever someone says "fuck," he gets a residual check. [Lance: My second favorite.]

One of his ex-wives actually was a Neanderthal.

His accent is from before the Tower of Babel.

He has Adam and Eve's e-mail address.

He still writes B.C. on all of his checks. [Adam: Joey passed out laughing on this one.]

He is still living off his insurance payoff from Pompeii.

He remembers whatever the hell they had before 8-track tapes.

He still thinks that talking motion pictures are a fad.

He remembers the real reason the Hindus and the Muslims hate each other.

14

CLICHÉS

~Lance~

It's been two weeks. He's been so busy with training, I barely get texts. It would be nice to talk. I miss his voice. I've been thinking about Adam a lot. It's kind of disturbing, but I guess, with writing this, I have to think about him.

Shit!

I need to stop this.

Grin and bear it.

I love clichés. I feel like a walking one sometimes. [Adam: *Rolling eyes*]

He said that, yesterday, he'd been on the shooting range from 5:30 A.M. until about 7:00 P.M.

When I say, "said," I mean text. Of course, this is a warm-up for the Big Leave. Then it's just e-mails. I can't wait.

I'm really going to try to curb my sarcasm as this year progresses. It helps to keep things light—for me anyway.

15

CHASING MY PILLOW

~Adam~

The days at the various ranges seemed to stretch on. These eighteen-hour days are ridiculous: twenty minutes of training preceded by four hours of waiting and followed by fourteen hours waiting for transportation.

* * *

We are beginning to figure it out. The guys who know are leading the way, showing the less experienced soldiers and guiding us into this deployment. The patch on my shoulder suddenly has weight—other than general trash talking.

Military leaders are like no others on the planet. Currently, I have to present myself at all times, all day, and in a manner in which I want my subordinates to behave. It is like living with your boss. You may hate it, but your boss, if he is worth his weight in salt, will behave at all times professionally. This is hard when you shower, eat, and shit next to each other. There is no time when you get to relax and not be professional. They are always watching, and it is hard to discipline that same guy when you are borrowing porn mags from him and critiquing the physical features of the fine young ladies in various magazines.

* * *

Joey, Mac, and several other guys were randomly piled onto two beds and flipping through a large stack of pornos.

There was a discussion that had a strong comparison between the movement from a swimming pool to a hot tub and from the "big girl magazine" to the "pretty girl magazine," as Joey put it. Apparently, the ladies in the "pretty girl magazine" look better if you spend some time looking at the "big girl magazine" first.

I save, close my laptop, and walk over. "All right, let me see."

16

COLD LITTLE PIGGIES

~Adam~

I have recently rediscovered that few people, barring skiers and cold weather survivalists, understand what cold toes honestly means. I thought about this for several hours while I sat in a HMMWV (Highly Mobile Multi Wheeled Vehicle, pronounced "Humvee") watching a range as a support role. I was enjoying a good book in a vain attempt to distract myself from the pain in my feet.

The pain goes through a variety of stages. The first can be described simply as, "My toes are fucking cold." This is the stage where your toes are cold. This is when the temperature is bearable. Almost.

In a cold weather situation, your body has a series of safety precautions it takes to ensure that its important functions can continue, by sacrificing the less mission-essential equipment. What the body does, in the event the temperature begins to drop, is to begin to pull blood from the extremities into the core of the body mainly the head, core organs, and genitals.

I am driving around. My body is cold, but not that cold. I try to ignore the cold and it works 'ish.

Here is where I begin to move into the second phase of my toes being cold. This phase is called, "This isn't so bad. I'm fucking awesome!"

I have effectively reached this phase. My toes just feel hard. Not bad and not good, just nothing.

I can live with that. I continue to enjoy my little story and try to flex my feet, to no avail. My fingers are gloved. I have a beanie on my head. I am in the driver's seat watching my breath collide with and move about my book as I listen to static and the random conversations on the radios.

My complacency will strike as it always does.

Fierce. And in a way I don't expect. (Well, I expect it, lesson not learned and all.)

Warmth. This is third phase, aptly called "I am so fucking bad ass. My little toes feel wonderful."

This is the shortest lived of all the cold-little-toe phases, because soon that pleasant warmth is replaced by a fierce heat.

This brings us into the fourth phase, the "Okay, too fucking hot" phase.

Now, my toes feel like they are on fire. Blood is no longer needed in my core. My penis can rest easy until the next cold spell strikes. The true command center of the male body releases the life giving fluid that it has been hoarding for its own selfish needs and desires. That is right. My penis is a jerk, and not just because of how selfish it is. But because, when push comes to shove, my body will make an honest effort to ensure that my penis is safe, completely neglecting my hands and feet. I guess my body didn't consider the dire ramifications of a situation in which I lost my hands. "Then what would you do, penis, you little fucker. Who will play with you then? Dick."

So, the "Okay, too fucking hot" phase passes, with a significant amount of me cringing and pretending nothing is wrong.

Now, I am in the "I like my toes. I should invest in some better socks" phase. The pain has passed. I am enjoying my little story and continuing on with my day. I may find myself lulled to sleep by the random bursts of machine-gun fire.

I did.

I was happy to enjoy a small nap lying in the middle board of my HMMWV, an MRE as a pillow, and random military-related noises to keep me company.

17

SPADES

~Adam~

In the center of our little bay, on a storage box, Hunt the platoon sergeant and a couple other medics are all playing Spades. Khan, the Medical platoon sergeant is enjoying teaching the other medics in a style that is akin to verbal abuse. Khan has the advantage of being exceedingly tall, a compliment to his Mexican and Pakistani heritage, or Mexistani as it has come to be referred to. Khan, although being the platoon sergeant, is not immune to the verbal abuse, which we throw around at every meal, offering up varieties of pork products to him. His Muslim beliefs lead to his most common rebuttal, "Thanks, I'm trying to quit."

Sounds of spitting, texting, and verbal abuse fill the air around them, along with the smell of Copenhagen and farts. Khan issues out constant abuse/advice, but only after the hand has been played. And only to prove his superiority over his competitors, while shifting blame away from himself for poorly played hands.

Days have been dragging along. The military lifestyle is exactly that. There remains no separation between work and home. I'm living my job. It adds value to my moments of silence and little bits of privacy that I may be able scrounge up. Those instances are not actual privacy, but brief chances to enjoy the warm water on my skin in silence. I enjoy these moments, attempting to zone out Roberts so I can hear Nickelback songs that I don't particularly like, and just write.

I originally selected the job of medic because I wanted to be a surgeon, after watching the effect on my family a couple years ago when a team of surgeons took a kidney from one human body and placed it into my father to buy him a couple of years out of the dialysis center. I wanted to give families that feeling.

I started my time in the Army with that intention. I picked Combat Medic with the idea that it would help me along the path to transplant surgery, while satisfying my need to go get dirty. After completing Whiskey school, (MOS code for Medic is 68W, and W in the phonetic alphabet is whiskey), I started college.

I was twenty-three when I started school, and I wanted it bad. It wasn't until my second semester that I realized why not everybody is a transplant surgeon. Chemistry is hard. I didn't like all the memorization, and while I did pass with relative proficiency, my refusal to memorize the periodic table—or study—proved to be my downfall. That was the end of my aspirations for a medical career. I remain a medic though. I enjoy my job for the most part. There is a lot of down time, and I like being in a group of people who need to be above average intelligence, as it is required for the job.

I have found through my studies that I am a bit of a wayward spirit. I want to travel a lot, and I want to be paid to do it.

18

OUT OF THE MEAT LOCKER

~Adam~

After a month and a half I was finally free 'ish, finally back in Vegas. I managed to get my shower to myself, to enjoy the little things: plastic floor, no fear of foot bacteria, tile walls, the soulless white that fills the walls, and everything that is within the traditional "modern" American apartment bathroom. My red—matching—department store shower curtain, towels, and bathmats invite me in. And the poster print of Escher's "Eye" stares at me while I piss out my first beer of the evening, a beer that accompanied some much deserved "Me" time.

The beer I carry into the shower has already begun to gather condensation from the air around my excessively hot shower. As if I had not taken one in a month, I finally feel clean.

My month washed away, invisible dirt that only I can see.

I remain in long enough to finish the better part of my beer and for red streaks along my back and chest to form.

I enjoy the fit of my blue jeans and take my time selecting a T-shirt. The selection is minimal. It is the process that is important. I enjoy my first chance in some time to choose what I want to wear, and where to go while wearing it.

I relish this feeling as I try desperately to fall back into my normal, now alien, surroundings. My apartment is strangely soft, colorful, pleasant, and inviting.

It is empty, despite the area being so filled. Aside from my first foray into the military, the transition into it is never the hard part. It is the transition out. I'm driving my car—alone. I'm at the store—alone. I'm not in a rush, but moving like I am.

Conscious awareness is the first step to defeating the abnormal behavior that carries over from the military setting into the real world. I stress the word "real." The military is an imaginary lifestyle, desperately trying to reach an unreachable standard, and is always angry at itself for that. I slow my pace and peruse the aisles, gathering supplies for my few days ahead. It is still uncomfortable to be around so many people.

I am the only one who is driving out to Wisconsin for this training. As such, I have less time to enjoy home compared to everyone else. Sunday we got released, finally, after staring at our weapons and willing them clean for enough hours that eventually they met the standard. A few of us hurry across town to go see the wedding of one of my soldiers.

After the festivities I met up with Odie—a fellow former Marine—for a few drinks before we headed off to Fort McCoy for Medic-only training. He was as single as I was, and we were both bored.

We enjoyed a conversation about the nuances of missing "beer and pussy" and the reset that occurs when it arrives—like it was never gone in the first place. I had had my beer. He needed his. We had both been lacking in the second department.

We eventually went our separate ways. We had warmed our bellies with some bar food, in that we had succeeded, and if the gods smiled upon us tonight, we would find a place to warm our genitals.

19

BEING A BOY

~Adam~

I went to get my hair cut, needed because it looked dumb. My platoon sergeant kept saying something about regulations. I don't know what that is all about. My normal guy, who I really like, was out of town. I followed his recommendation of one of his co-workers. [Lance: I was there for all of this. He handled it with great aplomb.]

She did a great job, but that is beside the point.

She asked about what I do.

I dodged the question a bit, explaining that I'm a bouncer at a club, but mainly a student. Eventually, my military activities became known, something about which she had a large number of questions.

"What is your job?"

"Medic. I put people back together outside the wire, and wipe their noses inside." (The wire separates one from inside and outside of base—a.k.a. the idea of safety.)

"What part of that do you prefer?"

"Outside."

"So you are some kind of an adrenaline junkie or something?"

"No, I just hate the idea of going someplace like Afghanistan and feeling like I didn't do my part."

Adrenaline junkie. I'm twenty-four years old. All I want to do is fuck and fight, neither of which I get to do as often as I would like.

Joey likes to quote Nietzsche on this one, "Man shall be framed for war, woman for the recreation of the warrior; all else is folly." Beside the point, it does seem that the general population doesn't understand the idea of putting oneself into direct danger.

Self-preservation is important, but so is being aware of what is truly important.

My bed feels softer, knowing what it felt like to sleep without it.

I couldn't appreciate a nice meal if I hadn't had some really bad ones, or missed a few.

I wouldn't love a nice hot shower if I didn't know what it felt like to finish up two months with a shower under a garden hose.

I appreciate my life because I honestly, with every cell in my body, thought I might lose it.

20

SOFT LIGHTING AND COLD DRINKS

~Adam~

Tuesday night, after running around all day, I ended up again at the same restaurant that birthed the idea for this little book I'm attempting to write with Lance. His partner, Richie, and another friend joined us. We made gay jokes and heckled Lance. (In case you don't know, gay jokes are funnier around gay guys.)

He brought up interesting points though. In the end, it boils down to two different struggles: his and those like him to take the greatest advantage of the time spent with me, and mine to hide from that fact. I am becoming less a person and more a symbol. My time spent around those who care about me is the same. The fact that we did it is less important than the activities themselves. I would rather spend my time with those I am less close to. It is less important. I am not reminded about leaving constantly. I get to escape and don't have to stress over this impending deployment.

There is no escape around Lance. I am constantly being reminded that I am leaving and that we don't have much time left together. [Lance: Uh huh.]

When I spend time with the people who care about me, I know that they will care when I am gone. They will be worrying. I will be worrying about that when I'm gone. I would rather be looking at porn and pleasuring myself in the porta-shitter.

There was a sobering realization that I was reminded of when I returned to the real world after my short time away.

The world doesn't need me to turn. I realized that the first time I came back, and it was hard. The second time, not so much, and I won't pretend like I mind now. But it was a fact that I forgot, something that my time away has reminded me. This last month was a like a little mini-deployment, a chance to warm up and practice the things that I will be experiencing again during this deployment.

* * *

Tuesday night after drinks, I shot out a text.

One last chance.

The gods smiled.

Reset.

21

ROAD TRIPPING

~Lance~

Adam is in Wisconsin for four weeks of more training, mostly classes, long boring days, wherein he is free to text me. I could use a couple of calls though. There is nothing like hearing the sound of a voice on the other end. You know, inflections and all. This is really hard to do in text. Sometimes, I have gotten into trouble because of it. I'll text something, meaning to be sarcastic, and sometimes the sarcasm doesn't translate. I'll have to recant and explain. It's annoying. Also, certain things that I would like to tell in detail get the expurgated version. Again annoying. [Adam: Like the word "expurgated."] [Lance: Hey, one of the best places to use the vocabulary I've gleaned over the years is in writing. Get used to it. You've got another ten months or so of it coming. So comment all you want. Besides which, I know you have quite the plethora of verbiage in your cerebrum just waiting to spew forth.]

I can tell he is starting to get anxious to come home. He texts me more often and talks about things we'll do when he's here—for a lousy two weeks—before he's gone for the Big Leave.

* * *

He was here for three and a half days between trainings. It went by like three-and-a-half minutes. And he'd gotten a cold of sorts and was feeling lousy the first day-and-a-half.

"Are these work people really going to care after you're gone?"

"Probably not," he admitted.

"I don't mean to tell you how to spend your time, but don't you think it would be better if you spent time with people who really do care about you. I've hardly seen you at all these past couple of months, and when you do have a couple of days, you book up solid with people you barely know, and when I ask you if you want to get together, all I get back from you is, 'I'll see.' or 'I'll let you know.' I have to tell you, I'm really hurt."

"I'm sorry." He seldom says this. I'd gotten through to him, for a change. He can be incredibly stubborn.

I try to rationalize my feelings, but that's an oxymoron. Should I feel guilty for caring? I know it makes it hard for him, but what can I do? This is new for him, somebody caring. I'm not sorry, quite the contrary. I think we're sorting it out.

22

IT'S COLD AND YOU SHOULDN'T HAVE BEEN TEXTING

~Adam~

Fort McCoy, Wisconsin is not the most hospitable of bases I have lived on. It is a harsh reminder of why I don't visit Wisconsin nearly as much as my family would like. I've had enough of this weather.

Prior to mobilization, the medics are required to complete additional training in preparation for this deployment. They fill our days with classes and practical applications designed to dummy-proof even the most complex of simple tasks. My nights are spent typing until my fingers are too cold to continue.

* * *

Wisconsin is still cold. Frozen ground and unaccustomed feet have guaranteed me a sore ass.

I attempt to choke down the remaining pieces of a country-fried meat disk covered in a gravy-like substance. My attempts are thwarted by my gag reflex, and I dive into my bowl of chili, which for the last nine days has become a staple of my lunch and evening meals—in the absence of anything better to eat.

My heart rate returned to normal about ten minutes ago, and now the last bit of hormones that kept me warm, or simply deadened the nerves on the surface of my skin, to help me on my run back from the gym is running out.

It wasn't the two plus miles—approximately—that I covered, or the backpack full of my uniform that made this run particularly difficult. It is fifteen degrees outside right now.

The last of my hormones wash out, and all that remains are raised hairs and a shiver that is beginning to ride through my body.

A quick run back to my barracks—very quick—the temperature is dropping rapidly.

* * *

Now I'm cold.

* * *

The last of my energy gets ripped out of me by the showerhead, which must be the end cap of a sandblaster. I slump against the back wall of what is now a personal shower—with a shower curtain—and attempt to gather my breath and pull some energy together to make it through my shave and climb into bed. I also need to give the water time to coax my scrotum out from inside of me, where it seems to have decided to hide. These are the times I am glad that sometimes my nervous system dulls itself so I can accomplish a given task.

Our new barracks is still open bay, similar to our last home, slightly more modern, with relatively clean, white walls and a distinct lack of graffiti. The bathroom is cleaner in appearance, but smaller and less accommodating to the number of guys living on this floor. It is not just my platoon here. Medics from all over the country have come here to train and are living with us, ultimately making Joey's nude stroll from one end of the bay to the bathroom significantly funnier.

We fill what free time we do have with movies. "Role Models" has been on for three days in a row.

The quotes that have carried over into class at random and often inappropriate moments are a pleasant break from the monotony of the day.

Turns out some parts of the Army take themselves seriously. They will have to either learn to deal with our shenanigans or figure out a way to correct them.

* * *

One of the often-left-out considerations for medical training is the role players. It is one of my favorite activities. Well, except when I am being butchered with a needle, and I become the pincushion for the guy who is the "don't be this guy" guy.

Whether or not one's patient will actually be screaming obscenities and wishing for death is a moot point. What was important, in this case, was the motivation that came with it. Energy in its own way is contagious. Like yawns, if everyone is in a bad mood, everything looks like shit out there, and everyone acts like it. All it takes, sometimes, is one person who is willing to not let the world get down on him to make the training not any more valuable, but significantly more fun. Because, really, why can't this be fun? Aside from the fact that it is thirty-five degrees outside, drizzling, and I'm sitting on the moist cold ground in a T-shirt, leaning up against a concrete bunker, and bleeding like a stuck pig all over my uniform.

I really do like that stuff: cold, wet, miserable. And I can't complain. Well, I don't mean it. There is something inherently motivating about horrible conditions.

* * *

"I want to die, this hurts so bad," I yelled as the Medic threw me against the concrete barrier and began his assessment.

"You are so fucked up. Just stop attempting to treat me and put a bullet in my mouth," I continued to scream.

"I hope that mortar lands right here, so that it kills me and takes all you fucks with me." The fake artillery exploded in the distance as I harassed my medic.

"If I had the choice between you living with this pain, and dying, I choose death." The medic working my imaginary injuries still hadn't given me a valid reason to stop yelling.

"I will sue you and take your boat." I was unable to hide my smirk.

"Lyrik, I blame you. This accident was your fault. We flipped that stupid fucking vehicle. It's because you were fucking texting," I yelled at the beautiful young, dark-skinned soldier, who was also a patient in this exercise.

"You didn't complain when I was texting you," she said calmly.

Silence.

"He's blushing," the medic supervising the exercise pointed out.

"Touché." I dropped out of character and raised my eyebrow with a smile.

23

NICE GIRLS

~Adam~

While my MP3 player attempted to lull me into a depression-induced slumber, I was suddenly smacked with an epiphany.

I'm lonely.

Laughter filled the air around me; a warm feeling accompanied a chilling feeling as I realized that this will be my new temporary family. Some guys will fill the deployment with their incessant bitching. Some will constantly repeat movie quotes. And Joey will be loud, gigantic, and will entertain us with a combination of intelligent and hilarious antics.

This is my deployment.

This is why everyone has such a hard time transitioning. This is where they are accepted and understood. Through the constant threats of sodomy and degenerating remarks, this becomes home. It is warm, comfortable, and inviting.

Soon, nothing else is.

I have been making an honest effort to keep those who want to be close to me away, to make it easier on them. And here I am. Lonely. Missing human companionship in a way that it seems these fuck-offs will provide. [Lance: So, it's really not easier on anybody.]

The rule that women throw themselves at you only when you are romantically involved (and mean it) is the same for deployments.

Memories race through my head as I fight for some semblance of reasoning and order in my life. I stare at the computer screen. Its light illuminates my face, the only source of light in the long, dark room. The others and I now thoroughly exhausted from a ten-hour day in the classroom, where we fight our repeated urges to disrupt class with our antics or to fall asleep.

The instructors have been making active efforts to keep us away from the other students. They explained that our little crew has outperformed the bulk of the class and made the others feel inadequate while they attempt to learn the basic skills that every medic learns in his initial training. This means we often are pulled out of class for various tasks around the schoolhouse, which we are more than happy to perform.

* * *

Christmas is different away from what I grew up with. I fake the funk now. There are no white Christmases out here in Vegas.

I found myself at a small burger joint with my favorite college professor, and a select few students. The casual ambiance invited us in and wrapped around us: friendly conversation among students and their favorite teacher. She only invited her "Threepeaters," as she called them. Three semesters are the requirement to be invited to this occasion. The room was full, a testament to the love this teacher has for her students and us for her.

Kayla, a fellow student, and a delicious little creature who once sat in front of me during class, now stood in front of me.

"The girls have a bet," Kayla said.

I tried hard not to lose myself in her green eyes filled with golden specks. A wisp of blue in her hair danced just about her shoulders. [Lance: Have you been reading too many romances?]

[Adam: Too much time drinking around the gay community, I guess.]

"Oh, really, what is that?" I asked.

"They think the two of us will end up dating."

"Oh, really." I smiled.

That would be nice. Stupid Afghanistan.

"I don't think I could drag you through a deployment," casually I spoke the words. She received them with the same casual demeanor.

We were texting later that night, discussing the complications, and dancing around the something that we both seemed to want. Too complicated. It wasn't worth it. I couldn't do it to her.

* * *

The day before I was to report in for this medical pre-deployment thing I found myself sitting in a room, in a house that held a great deal more memories than I was comfortable with, the home of my ex-wife, Susan. The beautiful black bulk of Ryah, my Doberman Pinscher, which I left with Susan after our divorce, now lay across my feet. I was scratching her ears. I missed that little girl. Her confusion was spread across my boots in the form of little coarse black hairs. She recognized the tone of voice her mom and I were using as the conversation shifted to heavier topics.

"What happened, Susan?"

"What do you mean?"

I looked at Ryah. She was no longer looking at me. Her head rested on the floor.

"We were talking. It looked like we might take another stab at it."

"I can't miss you for a year."

It all changed with that text message "I'm going to Afghanistan."

Suddenly, we weren't close.

"I understand."

Suddenly, she didn't take my calls anymore.

My heart didn't skip. There was no lump in my throat.

Nothing.

Across from me she sat, once my beautiful bride.

Then... not.

Then, for a period of time, she unknowingly held my heart in her hands.

Now, nothing.

I fucked up again.

It hit me on the car ride home, doing eighty-five down a country back road.

* * *

I had finished my advanced training in California, and was making my rounds briefly before heading out again in a couple days.

Julie's office seemed empty with the rest of her ducklings absent. Julie and I enjoyed a pleasant conversation while her class watched a movie, as we used to do after class. A professional, teacher-student relationship had turned into a friendship that I greatly enjoyed.

"Did you hear that? That stupid shit got engaged?" Julie told me.

"No, I didn't hear that."

"Yeah, Kayla went up to Alaska to see him before he deploys, and he proposed. And she accepted."

"Hmm. Sounds about right. Girls are dumb," I said.

Conversation drifted aimlessly.

"Hi, Julie." Tight jeans caught my attention. Golden-flecked eyes peeked through dark hair, with a pleasant smile below it as she looked at me sitting next to the door.

Her ring finger was naked.

We all exchanged our general pleasantries as she took a seat catty-corner to me.

"How is the fiancé?" Julie asked Kayla.

Kayla covered her hand. "Julie, we broke up."

"What? When did this happen? What happened?" Julie asked.

"Didn't you notice, Julie, she isn't wearing her ring?" I chimed in.

"No, I didn't notice. So what happened? He is about to deploy. How did he fuck it up?" Julie asked again, while shooting me one of her teacher glares.

Julie probed. (She cares about her students so much. It is hard not to open up when she has you under the light and is asking you questions.)

"He leaves tomorrow. He got drunk about a week ago. We got into a fight. He said a lot of mean things, and then broke up with me," Kayla continued.

The room was quiet; I realized I couldn't stop smiling. I stifled my amusement and just listened.

"He called the next morning to apologize and tried to take it back. I didn't let him. That was the last time I let him do that to me," Kayla said.

"Boys are dumb," I said. It seemed like an appropriate response.

"Good for you. Now, you need to find a really good guy." The part of Julie that remembers holding a newborn while the rest of the girls her age burned bras suddenly becomes apparent.

"I just don't get why guys are like that," Julie said, her eyes glancing my way. She didn't know that I didn't have any real answers.

I faked it. "He is scared. He doesn't want to be alone, and even if he doesn't feel right in the relationship, he would rather have an impossibly difficult one than nothing. It is comforting knowing that someone is waiting for you, no matter how twisted it is."

"Military guys suck," Kayla said, knowing I agreed.

He doesn't want to be lonely. She won't be there to hold him or keep his legs warm at night in Iraq. But the idea that she might when he gets home is enough. His knowledge that she is waiting for him, and that someone is thinking about him, is what is important.

24

TEN DAYS

~Lance~

I can always sleep. But not tonight. My head is too busy thinking about his coming home for the last time. So here I am at 4:00 A.M., fingers tickling the keyboard and praying Richie doesn't miss me in bed and come to find out what I'm doing. Maybe I should have the porn screen ready to switch to. He'd be less irritated at me for that.

I'm just getting anxious, and I have to say, if it wasn't for texting, this would be extremely difficult. Adam and I have talked twice, but he's not really in a private confine when we do. Still, the chatting and verbal contact is good. This is all getting me prepared for when e-mail will be the only contact.

He'll be back in ten days. We'll have his party; we'll hang out and laugh and talk and drink. I hope it'll be exactly what he wants.

I'm prepared now and accepting. If he can deal with it, I certainly should be able to. I love the stories he tells, and it's given me a real insight to soldier life—a much more intimate side than most see. It's fun in that respect. I'm glad I'm living it vicariously, instead of actually. I'm not getting the attraction. It wouldn't even be a nice place to visit. I've read enough about it. I'll stay here, thanks.

That should do it. Back to bed.

Or maybe switch to the porn screen...

25

STEALING CAKE

~Adam~

"You jizzed on my pillow."

"That's not a very original idea."

* * *

The fun never stops. Bruises line my arms in an inch-and-a-half ring all around, showing where tourniquets demonstrated proper and improper perfusion in my hands. Mac was the same, and the screams that filled the air around us as we trained were a combination of hilarity, and in a strange way, competency. The serious nature of the training and its designated purpose is masked by laughter. It makes us enjoy the training a bit and relax before we really have to do the deed.

* * *

"I'm not writing it," I told Lance on the phone.

"You better write it, or I will..."

"No, how about that. It is a pointless story."

Silence.

"Fuck," I said defeated.

* * *

There I lay on a green wool blanket that, like every blanket I have ever seen issued, is cut in a shape that is rarely square—and even more rarely—the right size. (Something that everyone notices when making his bed, because apparently there is not a single properly fitted wool blanket in the United States military. Size is not important in this instance.) I am the patient, lying supine in my uniform, and my "medic" is proceeding through his assessment. I am prepared to accurately represent a casualty for testing purposes. It isn't a fun process, but it signals to us that we are almost done with this training.

Priapism check comes, and he is professional, nothing rough or abnormal. The back of his hand slides over my genitals to check this common symptom of a spinal injury: an uncontrollable and painful erection, priapism.

"I'm checking priapism," he says aloud. Then, in a whisper, while looking into my eyes, "Like three times, because I love you."

The assessment continues.

My gaydar had beeped when he walked into the room, something about the gentle way he carried himself, his soft features, and his voice with a hint of femininity.

But it was at that moment it exploded.

I allow the incident to slide past due to a combination of shock and disbelief.

Throughout the next few days, I notice his behavior more and more as he attempts to probe me verbally to see what he can get away with. I ignore him or am downright unpleasant. That shit is ridiculous. A fucking Staff Sergeant in the U.S. Army hitting on a Specialist. It turns out guys are chasing tail no matter where they go—gay or not.

Also, when I mentioned this to Lance, he got jealous. Ha. [Lance: I knew this sort of thing happened. Now I get to hear about it firsthand... so to speak. Don't ask, do tell.]

* * *

"Don't touch my cake. I will stab you. I'm going to get my milk, don't touch my cake." Wielding a butter knife, Joey threatens Mac in a joking manner that one might almost take seriously.

Before Joey is to the cups, half of the cake is in Mac's mouth. Hunt takes two bites. Joey realizes what is going on when the laughter in the entire cafeteria alerts him before he arrives at the milk machine. Mac is now fighting to avoid choking on the cake while laughing.

Before Joey returns, all that remains of his cake fills Mac's still open mouth surrounded by white frosting.

More empty threats.

Joey goes to get another piece of cake.

Mac washes the cake down with Joey's milk.

Our bellies ache enjoying the show.

* * *

Mac sat at the foot of the bed. "How are things coming along?"

Then another medic approached in his slow, methodical manner that he always employs when he attempts to grapple anyone. His target was Mac.

Then, the tables turned. They tackled me, not uncommon. We have been doing a lot of grappling as of late.

This time Mac jumped in.

Then another medic.

Then Hunt.

Then Joey.

Then another medic.

It starts with my feet. They wrap my ankles with medical tape. With a guy on each arm, they bind my legs, working from the bottom and wrapping with two-inch tape up to my knees. Mac tapes my hands into a formed fist, one by one.

One of my captors makes a vain attempt at holding my feet. Still, he has trouble.

After a great deal of struggling, I end up on my back with my hands bound together. My legs above the knees are now bound. I squirm around on the floor as they all enjoy the show. I bite and claw and squirm until my hands are almost free.

As I chew myself free, Hunt chimes in, as he always does, with a quick witty comment. He is the almost sleeper, his pleasant, California surfer-blond, beach-bum features match his general demeanor. Most people don't expect trouble from him, and often we forget to include him as well, although, he is often standing right there instigating. "On the bright side, we know that if we see him on a video about to get his head cut off, he'd take, like, four of those fuckers with him. It took six of us to get him like that," he says.

Everyone laughs.

Dicks.

In the end someone gets a scissors and cuts the tape.

There is a significant amount of laughter as I rip the hair off my legs from the tape and lay on the ground fighting the excruciating pain that is now visiting itself upon my calves and wrists.

26

BABYLON

~Adam~

"What do you think is harder, being a medic or being an infantryman?" one of the less experienced medics asked me.

"I haven't really thought about it."

"I was just thinking that the job of medic seems to bear a greater amount of personal responsibility by nature compared to a rifleman."

"How so?"

"An infantryman's job is to kill the enemy."

I understand. "But the medic has the responsibility to save the lives of his friends, comrades, and the enemy, in addition to deciding who he can't save."

"Exactly." He smiled, knowing we are on the same page.

"I can see that. As a grunt, the blood on my hands belonged to someone who was trying to kill me. As a medic, that blood belongs to people I care about." The lump crawls up my throat, remembering Sadaam's castle in Babylon, Iraq—and Cory. "Grunts just have to pull the trigger. Death is an acceptable risk. Not much we can do about it once the hammer falls."

Turns out, killing people is easy. It's saving them that is hard.

27

SMILING BABIES

~Adam~

Our training is complete in Wisconsin. After a long drive to Texas, I met up with a beautiful single mother who was quite welcoming, I made the grueling drive through New Mexico and into Arizona. And there I found myself sitting in my brother's home enjoying the verbal jousting match between him and his wife, while my niece crawled around on the floor. She was wearing the most beautiful smile in the world and a red onesie that read: "If you think I'm cute you should see my uncle." [Lance: And he thinks I'm bad.]

I am here, in a small Arizona town, watching my brother shove chips into his mouth, while Max—his male Boxer—lies at his feet. My niece is trying to use his butt to stand up, to no avail. I laugh from over my laptop, writing along about the last week of travel and adventure.

* * *

My time at home was bittersweet, as it always was. I spent a couple of more days with my family. I attempted to be a kind, considerate son and assist with yard work and other household chores that my father was unable to do and my youngest brother was unwilling to attempt. I left: the yard raked of pine needles; Mom's new sink, almost installed; a new linoleum floor, almost all laid; a treacherous hole in the floor leading into the basement, all jobs for Mom to finish because we ran out of time and supplies.

28

THE DRIVE HOME

~Adam~

Not long after I returned, Las Vegas highways proved themselves to be as deadly as any other, claiming the life of one of the Cavalry's finest soldiers. Not one of those no-name types of situations, a rank and a name that we may have heard in passing. This guy we all actually knew and liked.

SSG Matthew Sneck was standing in my Angela's office an hour before the accident, called his mom, told her he was headed home.

Fucking Christ.

29

A FLAG FOR HIS MOTHER

~Adam~

I went to his service.

30

INDULGING IN EXCESS AND GOOD-BYES

~Adam~

I am exhausted from the lack of a solid night's sleep. I shall not complain about the reasoning for the inconsistencies in my sleep patterns, but the fact remains, I'm beat.

Every day, as well as every evening, I fill or have filled for me. I'm trying desperately to put my affairs in order before I leave.

One week.

In one week from this very moment I will be breathing Indiana air. More than likely it will be like the rest of the Midwest air, clean with the subtle hint of manure.

Crockett is excited in some ways. His wife is moving out there only a few hours from where we will be stationed. I am excited because that means I will have a place to go kick back some drinks and act a fool.

~Lance~

The party.

After having an awkward, slightly tense discussion with Adam on who was going to be there a couple of days ago:

"Can I invite Kayla?" he asked.

Uh oh. "Why?"

"I thought she might like to come."

Think. Think. Think. This was so not going to happen. "She doesn't know anyone who will be there. She's eleven and there won't be anyone there her age to talk to, so you'll spend the entire evening talking to her, and everyone there will want to talk to you. Of course, I could invite Joey and Annabelle, (My nine-year-old godson and his younger sister), then she wouldn't feel so out of place."

That might have been going too far. Oh well.

"She's nineteen. It is my party, isn't it?"

Shit. "Yes, but she's not even old enough to drink, and I could get into trouble if she's been drinking and something happens to her."

"I'll drive her."

"But you'll be drinking too, and I thought maybe you'd stay over so you could drink as much as you'd like."

"I just won't drink that much."

I needed to try something else. She was not going to be there and ruin this. Not happening. "I don't want her here." Brilliant. Not too jealous.

"We'll see," was all he'd said.

The next day he called. "I think Kayla might have to work."

"Oh. Okay." I tried to keep the ebullience out of my voice. "Thank you."

"Sure."

I knew she didn't have to work. [Adam: She did have to work.] He'd realized what this party meant to me. I'd rarely denied him anything, so for me to have been so adamant about it, (No pun intended) must have meant I really cared. True. Now everything would be fine. She didn't mean anything to him anyway, so why would he have wanted her there? Just to have a girl on his arm. Ridiculous. [Adam: Cock-block]

Thirty-five or so people showed up, including Crockett and his wife. It was a very hot evening, especially for mid-April. The drinks and food were plentiful. It's just too bad I didn't have any of the food before I started imbibing with Adam on the Jack Daniels Single Barrel I had bought just for him.

~Adam~

Crockett and I found ourselves cornered by a well-meaning Korean War vet who wanted to share his stories. We listened as he spilled his heart out, in a masculine way that only vets understand, and finished it with an apology.

As time goes on, and we get further and further from the literal conflicts in which we participated, the need to talk doesn't go away. Just the people we can talk to.

~Lance~

A couple hours into the party I was feeling no pain as I readily tended bar and chatted. Adam was mingling with everyone and would every once in a while mention, "This is my party." Or, "Crockett's going to Afghanistan, too."

After we all sang "Happy Birthday" to Adam while he stood under the "WE LOVE YOU ADAM" sign and next to the table of various dessert birthday cakes (that I'd made), things started to get hazy for me. I'd finally eaten a little, but it was too late. The Single Barrel had worked its magic. Another glass of that and a shot of some new Tequila liqueur did me in. The party was winding down and so was I. I remember saying good-bye to almost everyone. I don't remember some embarrassing conversation I had with Crockett about how to pick up girls—let alone the reason for it. And I do remember the toilet bowl.

Blackout.

* * *

New day.

Adam's there, relishing telling me about the things that are vague from the night before. "You didn't know the Single Barrel was 94 proof?"

"No. I didn't look. I only had three. They weren't very big."

"That's why I paced myself."

"You should have told me it was 94 proof."

That didn't work. He just gave me "the look." "You are an adult. You should know better."

Ouch. "Did you have fun?"

"Yeah. The sign and the cakes were a bit much. And it's not my birthday."

"But it is next month, and you'll be twenty-five. You shouldn't miss celebrating your twenty-fifth birthday."

That look again. "Okay."

Moving on.

[Adam: I did manage to acquire the "WE LOVE YOU ADAM" sign. I think I'll put it over my rack in Afghanistan. Kind of obnoxious. I like it. I guess Lance will be coming with me in his own way after all.]

31

KILLER BEES

~Lance~

Game night at the Crocketts'. Homemade chili and brownies. Very good.

The games... well...

I just missed the video game generation. Thank God. [Adam: This was not nearly as embarrassing as his trying to play "Halo."] Adam, Crockett, his wife, and even Adam's girl, have played these things for countless hours. To be really good would require a ridiculous amount of time. I'm not terrible... it's just that I haven't played. We went from game to game with Adam winning most of them resoundingly.

He must have said, "I'm awesome. I'm totally awesome," fifty times. Grrr.

By nature I am competitive, also. So, it is frustrating to play something you really don't know how to play and try to compete at it. Then, to have "Mr. Video Game" sitting next to me shouting, "I'm awesome," was salt in the wound. He did soften the blow a little bit by hand-feeding me brownies, which he did, again, because he knew it would catch me off-guard and I'd be embarrassed... or worse. I stayed seated for a while. It was still nice. [Adam: One for her, one for him, another for her...]

* * *

Easter dinner at Ed's parents. And Trivial Pursuit.

Yes!

My team: Adam, Grant, me. Opposing team: Ed, his parents, and Angela.

My competitive spirit was in high gear after the previous night's debacle.

"What country did the Killer Bees migrate from in the 1950's after escaping from a series of experiments?" Ed's father asked us.

Grant: "They're African bees."

"But that's not where they escaped from," I said, not knowing how I knew that.

Adam just said, "I don't know."

"I think it's Brazil."

Adam looked at me, wondering how I could know this. "Well, some of us weren't alive then."

"Asshole. I wasn't either, but I think it's Brazil."

"We say Brazil."

Right.

Game. Set. Match.

Vindication!

Take that Sonic and Wii.

Happy Easter.

32

BRICKS, BOXES, AND THE CAPTAIN

~Lance~

I met Adam at his place after work. I was here to help him pack up everything.

His girl was there also. This did not make me happy. This was my time with him. We only had a little while more together, and I had to share it with a twelve-year-old he would never see or think about again. Was sex with this bimbo really more important than time with his best friend? I know it sounds like I'm the jealous boyfriend. Well, tough. I am. And I really don't care who knows it. I was pissed. Actually, double-pissed, because now I was starting one of our last nights together mad at him, and I didn't want to be. I wanted everything to be perfect. (Well, as perfect as his going off to war could be.) I didn't want this memory to be occluded with thoughts of the trollop-of-the-month in it. I think he was using her as a buffer. Not Fair.

We had a drink while we packed and talked. Adam's girl didn't drink. She wasn't old enough and didn't really like liquor, even though Adam tried to get her to sip his rum and Coke.

I was folding his clothes and packing them. "Why don't you wear this?" I said, holding up a kelly-green T-shirt. [Adam: That he bought me. Ugh.]

"It's too bright."

"You look good in bright colors."

"Maybe. By the way, my request came through today... to move to another base. I'll be taking Crockett's place."

I stared at him. "Is this place more... active?" I struggled for the right word to let him know what I meant, without letting the girl know what I meant.

"Yeah. Some of the other guys agreed and are going, too. We want to do something, not just sit around. If we're going to be there we want..."

"Oh." I had to cut him off. I didn't want him to see my face. I needed to process this little bomb. So, I continued to fold clothes and didn't say much.

I began my inner monologue of what I really wanted to say:

"What, you didn't think I could handle this?

I could feel the stimulating angry wave begin. Good start.

"Is that why you brought her here?" I said. And the wave grew. "Because you were sure I wouldn't make a scene in front of her? It's unfair of you not to let me air my thoughts."

I savored the heated sensation as my thoughts reached near tsunami levels.

"I can deal with things, you know. Yes, I'll probably worry more, but I was going to find out anyway."

As I crested the top, I felt the final words shoot forth inside of me.

"This was pretty cowardly," I finished.

Really over the top. But it helped me. (And such fun to write later that night.)

Now, I let common sense prevail, and my fomenting anger changed its course. I started to realize what a jerk and bad friend I was being.

"I know this is what you want to do, so, I support your decision. Just be careful." That's what I'll say, and I know he'll appreciate it.

Still, I did enjoy my momentary perverse pleasure at being quiet for a while, hoping he was squirming inside and wondering what I would ultimately say. And he still shouldn't have had her there.

"Did you mean to throw out all these multi-colored condoms?" I raised my hand from a bag on the floor and displayed a bountiful fistful for all to see, letting the girl know that he wasn't exclusive— far from it. [Adam: You really never understood.] [Lance: So explain it.] [Adam: I don't like sleeping alone. But I appreciate your making her feel like a cheap object, as if she didn't already feel bad enough, because under different circumstances things with her and me might have been different.] [Lance: I doubt it. You're not in the same league.] [Adam: If I keep thinking I'm better than everyone, I'm going to end up alone.]

"Yeah, I don't need 'em." He gave me a look, showing his realization that my inner storms had dissipated and I had accepted his pronouncements.

I continued folding.

"Here, I think you should take this." He reached into a drawer, turned to me, and handed me a box.

It was the watch I had given to him two years ago for Christmas. I knew he really liked it.

"Why?"

"You gave it to me. I only wear it when we go out."

Tears sprung to my eyes. (As they do now writing this.)

He'd remembered that I had asked him months ago about having something to keep safe for him, something important to him.

"Thanks." I gulped and put it with a few other things he was giving away. [Adam: Like my Marine Dress Blue Hat, which I didn't agree to give up, but was unwilling to argue over.] [Lance: Thank you.] [Adam: Uh huh.]

The girl would stay with him that night.

We finished up packing, and I reluctantly said good-bye and soul-hugged him.

~Adam~

This isn't my last night. I have one left. However, she and I both know this is our last night together. This is a harsh reminder for Lance of what is to come. I hug Lance and close the door as he walks down the stairs out of my apartment.

The lights go out.

"You're leaving me," I heard her soft voice whisper.

Silence.

If she had shot me in the knee, it would have hurt less. [Lance: Boy, did you deserve this one. How could someone so seemingly intelligent, do something so not?] [Adam: Stupid penis.]

33

WALKING AWAY

~Adam~

The sun woke me. I couldn't see my books. My cherry-wood-paneled bedroom set was covered in a sheet and wrapped in plastic wrap. Boxes were all over. Kayla was still sleeping when I climbed out of my shower for the last time.

I won't be in this apartment when I get back. Grant, Ed, and Lance will store my stuff for me while I'm gone. My normal life will be in stasis until I return, taped up in those boxes and sitting in the backseat of my car, waiting at Ed's home for me to pick up where I left off, hoping I can catch up with everyone as they have continued to move along.

I kissed her. She smiled, until she saw I was in uniform.

I really am in the Army.

I really am leaving.

Her smile returned for me, and she got dressed as I continued to prepare for another Army work day.

I am an ass. [Lance: Really?]

I kissed her good-bye. Our lips released, as our hands did, next to her car. I made it a point to not turn around, but suddenly I became consciously aware of every step I took.

* * *

After the workday, I returned home. We were packing up things at the armory and handling last-minute administrative requirements. The work itself wasn't hard, but it was emotionally exhausting.

I slowly packed. Dirty sheets from the night before got packed as they were. No time.

Lance arrived; my bed was now disassembled and propped along the wall. The drinks flowed as fast as the conversation. It was the last face-to-face time we would have until I got back. We still had a few conversations that, as he put it, "Were better suited for the Tuscany."

I'm leaving.

We discussed friendship. He slammed me for how friendship comes across in my writing.

Friendship feels cheap when put into words, as does the other trio of words that I have been unable to say to anyone since my Susan. Words grab hold of something and attempt to quantify it. I make no allusions to the fact that I cannot quantify the things that drive me into the relationships I am in and the actions I take on the behalf of those relationships. There is no singular phrase or method to define friendship, or family for that matter. You just know. Or maybe you don't, until it is too late.

Grant tells me he hopes I jump on a grenade or end up a POW. He wants to use the story to get laid.

Ed tells me he will crash my car. He can't ride a bike; I know he can't drive a manual.

Lance doesn't cry because he knows I will get mad, but he doesn't hold back his soul hugs.

The guys are out there with their families, waiting just like I am, for this to start so it can be over.

In their own ways, they are mixed throughout this story, in the background of every story. I don't do anything alone. They won't let me.

Too drunk to drive, I did. I parked my car at Ed's, passed off the keys, said good-bye to his folks, told him on the phone good-bye and that I hate him, and left.

Lance drove me to my final destination of the evening. Crab Rangoon and one last chance to enjoy the female form awaited me.

No tears.

Crockett collected me the next morning. The moon was still high in the sky. My bags were packed and I was ready 'ish.

~Lance~

This is where I regret the writing and the tell-all part. But it was my idea and so I put fingers to keyboard.

* * *

The last night.

TEXT FROM ME: I'm on the way. Have the cocktails ready.

TEXT FROM ADAM: Sounds good.

I'd left work early to help him with his last-minute packing.

"Where's the drinks?" I looked around as I came in.

"I didn't know what time you'd be here. I didn't want the ice to melt."

"So, I get to make the drinks?" I wiggled my eyebrows at him.

"Not too strong. I have to fly out tomorrow. I don't want to be hurting."

Hurting? I'll show you hurting.

No tears. Just have fun.

It was surreal as we talked and laughed and made plans. These one-on-ones between us were the very best times. We could talk forever and still have things we'd forgotten to say. I made another drink. We talked some more. We made sure he had everything.

Time was up.

We had to go drop off his car at Ed's parent's house around the corner. It would stay there until I took it to my house.

"I'm not really sober, you know," he said. "And you still have to drop me off."

"I know. No problem." He was staying at his ex-girlfriend's (Angela) place and would be picked up by Crockett in the morning.

I dropped him off. "Come in for a minute," he said. "She wants to give you some liqueur she made, and you can see her place."

"Sure."

Draw it out some more. And I've been so good so far.

I got my liqueur, said, "Hi," then...

We hugged outside the door.

A soul hug. That I never wanted to end. Because letting go meant... Letting go.

"There are so many things I think I should say, but you already know them. Call me when you get there. Have a safe flight. I love you."

"I'll call you." Those weren't the three little words I wanted to hear. He just can't say them to me. It would have helped me so much.

I nodded and walked down the stairs. Talk about "The Last Mile," I think I would have rather.

I sat in my car for a couple of minutes. It was hard to drive with blurred vision. This was my first really bad time—and I had no one to share it with. The one I wanted to share it with was gone. Why couldn't he just have held me for a few minutes and let me get it out? He knew that's what I wanted. I know he did. It would have helped me so much—someone to share this awful moment with. I tried to stop myself from thinking: "I may never see him again." But how could I? The elephant in the room kept rearing its ugly trunk. I looked up and implored, "Dear God, please, please, please, please, please, keep him safe. Mom, watch out for him. I know you understand. Please let him come home to me all right." I pounded the steering wheel in frustration. "It's just not fair! Why him? Why? Mom, this hurts so much. Help me, please," I sobbed.

I cried some more and kept looking up at the window of the apartment, hoping against hope that he would appear and wave or smile... or something. But I knew it wouldn't happen. He knew I was there. I could almost telepathically feel it. I wanted one more look. But no.

It was time to go. I turned the key and put my car in gear. And slowly drove away. I didn't look back. I wanted to imagine and hope that he had come to the window to watch me drive away. That was the memory I wanted to have.

I turned the corner.

He was gone.

34

FUCKING ARMY

~Lance~

He's gone.

Off to Indiana and more training, before going directly to Afghanistan—not passing "Go" or collecting $200.

I sit here and stare at the computer.

These past two weeks were pretty great, I have to say. We saw each other every day but one. It might have been more, if the Army hadn't had him doing office and paperwork during some of his "off" days.

The first night he was home—and the last night, too—was just the two of us talking and hanging out at his place. It was a great bonding time. Natural and comforting. I think just what we both needed. [Adam: It wasn't as gay as it sounds.]

35

BACK IN THE MIDWEST

~Adam~

My new ACU-patterned sleeping bag is rolled behind me to provide padding for my back when I need a moment to think. Indiana air fills my lungs. The room is crammed full of lockers, bunk beds, and so much gear that we ran out of places to put it. Music plays in my ears, and I seem to be one of the few remaining soldiers awake, aside from those we have tasked to help at the various ranges. I type away on my laptop.

My phone blinks green in the corner of my bed. It changes to red whenever Lance or Kayla text messages me.

Kayla and I discuss what an ass I am. I let her get close. Now, three time zones away, she misses me. Four weeks ago she wouldn't have cared. Now she waits.

I fucked up.

Red light. A text from Lance. He is having trouble with his allergies.

Through my nose the Midwestern air flows, into my ears my headphones play. The volume is down, allowing the snores of the medics around me and the fan at the other end of the bay to fill the air. My eyelids begin to sag. I stow my laptop in my locker and climb back into bed.

There will be more tasks to redo, as the paperwork from our training in California was either incomplete, incorrect, or lost. Either way, there is plenty to do, and none of it I am thrilled about.

I hate how comfortable this feels.

36

DANGERS OF BELIEVING

~Adam~

I'm sitting here swatting bugs off my keyboard, three hours ahead of the world I was only four months ago accustomed to. I have adjusted. I almost forget I was a normal person at one point.

I was slowly building my life.

This will help, monetarily, finally erasing the financial burdens Susan saddled me with and able to be more comfortable in normal American society. I like the idea of casually dating the girls I find interesting.

I used to have regular meals out at the Tuscany or Emerald Isle with Lance and chances to argue about our sexual preferences, sipping various liquors and verbally sparring over random topics, generally driven by my school work. Lance always proofread my papers, after Angela stopped, following an argument over the possibility of excessive comma use.

I want to set my own schedule, be a little lazy, and not worry about what fun trouble my subordinate medics are getting themselves into.

I want to bury myself in the same sanitized commercial illusions that the rest of America has.

I lie.

Although everything I just said is true.

But...

Somewhere inside of me I want to be lulled to sleep by machine gun fire. I want to shave in a mirror shattered by mortar shrapnel. I don't want to shower. And I do want to spend all day feeling like I am at peace... in the middle of a war.

* * *

Joey: "The danger of believing in reincarnation is the idea that suicide isn't the end, just another chance at life."

* * *

My e-mail inbox is filled with updates from Mom and my aunts about Grandpa.

He likes his new home, lots of people to talk to and cute nurses. His walls are covered with pictures from home, which are constantly being rearranged. His plastic sheriff badge migrates around all the grandchildren's pictures. The nurses enjoy how helpful and mobile he is and his wonderful antics and stories.

37

THE G.I.B. (GUY IN BACK)

~Adam~

The lights have been off for about an hour now. Hunt is behind me enjoying a movie, while I listen to bands whose lead singers have had their hearts broken one too many times and vainly attempt to write.

Under my bunk, the mud on my boots dries. Above my head, my pants are draped over my wall locker door, airing out from a day in the rain. The PT (Physical Training) shirt airs out, still smells stale though. I debate the merits of washing the wet mud off now, or letting it dry and simply brushing it off later while thinking about the day's events.

* * *

I stare out my wood-framed window, a crude mock version of the Up-Armor that is on all HMMWV doors in theatre. Pleasantly green scenery speeds past outside, while a gentle breeze carrying the local odors blows onto my face. We are on a training lane, where a variety of potential and "realistic" scenarios will come up and we will need to act accordingly. I'm tasked to be a "nobody," another guy in back or GIB (Pronounced jib). I just do what I'm told. I think I can manage this.

"Halt. Possible IED," a voice alerts us over the radio.

"Roger," my TC (Troop commander) responds.

"We are attempting to confirm."

My TC calls everything he knows up to higher headquarters.

Again we dismount.

I take up my position in the brush.

The international signal that we are taking fire sounds—us shooting back.

The fire is to my right.

I can't see anything.

I look back.

Our turret gunner is unloading his weapon.

To my left, I see two soldiers attempting to figure out what is going on... like me.

I look toward the fire one more time. Still can't see.

Fuck.

Got to move.

Fight or flight response kicks in.

Epinephrine pleasantly flows into my bloodstream. My body doesn't know this fight isn't real.

I pick up and move back toward my vehicle.

I'm not breathing heavy. Suddenly, I am no longer aware of the weight of my body armor, or my weapon. I can't feel my wet pants, or how heavy my boots have become with mud and water. The feel of combat—real or not—lightens my feet and numbs my shoulders. The little infantry Marine takes over.

"Sir, I'm going to grab them." I point to the two dismounted soldiers to my left. "And attempt a flanking maneuver."

"Roger. Execute."

"Let's go," I scream to the soldiers and signal with my hands to follow me.

Whether they heard me is irrelevant; they come to me.

"Let's maneuver on them."

"All right." He is out of breath, maybe I am too.

As we push toward the fire, attempting to pick up one more soldier taking cover in a culvert, we hear the call. "It's friendlies."

We stop. Before we have the chance to get confused, fire starts from the other side of our line of vehicles.

The machine gunner has shifted fires and is pointing into the brush on that side.

Our little group takes cover around my vehicle and we begin to maneuver in the direction of the other dismount from my vehicle.

I am moving too far, too fast, to be considered safe.

I get to my partner. He rushes forward.

Someone bumps me from behind.

"I've got you. GO!"

I'm moving again. I pass my partner and find some cover.

"SET!"

Someone picks up and begins to move.

The fire keeps up as we begin to maneuver toward its flank and take out its source.

I'm getting deeper into the brush.

Every instinct screams fire.

Wait for a target.

Wait for a target.

"INDEX!" The call to stop pretending and return to the real world sounds.

We all stand up, as if there was no one just pretending to try to kill us, and us them. We saunter back toward the vehicles. It suddenly smells like wet leaves.

The hormones wash out less dramatically than they were pumped in.

Drowsiness sets in.

It is a blur as everyone talks about what happened.

I just want to get back to my bunk.

Soon, I find myself looking out the wood-framed window at the green scenery passing. My hand rests on the butt stock of my weapon; the wet sling I wrapped around it to keep it out of the way makes it cool to the touch. The air is blowing at my face, bringing with it the smell of wet plants and a hint of gunpowder.

38

HUMAN CONTACT

~Lance~

Sometimes, like now at 3:00 in the morning, I sit at the computer and try to organize my jumble of thoughts and feelings into something coherent. I read what he's written. I think about our conversations and try to make sense of it all. Shit. We've been talking most days now since he left. Texting too, but he finds times most evenings to call. The reception and privacy are minimal there, so he has to go outside his barracks and stand on some planks covering the muddied grounds outside.

We talk about what he's doing there and all the trivial things we always talk about.

I'm not exactly sure why the calls are so frequent now, whereas the previous pre-trainings were mostly text. I think he really wants the human contact with me more, until there is no more—which is all too soon.

Change.

Growth.

Adaptation.

[Adam: Really? Do we need to make it sound so gay?]

39

MAD?

~Adam~

Our white Escalade speeds down the main drag of an unknown town on twenty-five-inch chrome rims. Dad's driving has drawn the attention of the MPs, (Military Police) and they are beginning to follow us in their black SUV.

"Dad, switch with me. I'll take over."

"Sure." I dive forward, grabbing the wheel and diving into the driver's seat as he worms out into the backseat.

"The itsy bitsy spider..." Fingers make small steps, crawling up my legs and onto my back, ripping me out of my dream. I hope this isn't someone trying to be clever.

Then, my eyes open into the real world, bringing me to the sudden realization that I am not sitting on fine leather about to take part in a high speed chase, but am wrapped up tightly in my sleeping bag, on my top bunk. "Sergeant, what is up?" I look at the tall Staff Sergeant—affectionately known as Sam—smiling up at me.

"We have the green light. We are a go."

Fucking awesome.

He gives me my instructions. Who to meet. Where to meet them.

This is actually happening.

HKTs (Hunter Killer Teams) are a go.

~Lance~

TEXT FROM ADAM: You're going to be mad at me. 8:03 P.M.

What the hell kind of text is that to send? There are three things that come to mind that he thinks I would be mad at him for.

1) He's decided he doesn't want to write anymore. (Yes, I would be very mad.)

2) He led the girl on with more crap. (Not mad, just disgusted.)

3) He's volunteered for some new dangerous assignment. (Not mad. I said I would support him; I will. Afraid for him, though.)

TEXT FROM ME: Call me.

TEXT FROM HIM: In a couple of minutes.

Phone rings.

"I will not be mad unless—

"I haven't turned gay and I don't have a boyfriend."

Well, I hadn't thought of that one. (Mad? Maybe...)

"So, what is it? I thought of three things it could be. You having a boyfriend wasn't one. The only one I'd be mad at is if you wanted to stop writing."

"No. Of course not. I was asked today if I wanted to be part of a special assignment group."

"And you said... yes?"

"Yes. This is what I wanted to do. It's very exciting."

Inside, I sighed and my stomach clenched a little. "If this is what you want, I'm glad for you. I guess this means you'll be "outside?"

"Yes."

"And this means more training?"

"I know. It's exciting. I'll let you know what's going on."

"Okay. Goodnight."

40

How To Be Excited About Danger

~Adam~

One of the platoons watched as I found myself again in the mud, with my new group of compatriots, my sniper team. We had assembled our ghillie suits, or silly suits according to Kaitlyn—who was visiting Crockett today. I just think they make us look like the lion from "The Wizard of Oz."

We had been selected to be part of a special sniper-driven operational team to operate within the region. It was the kind of thing us lowly enlisted guys always dreamed about. A small team making a big impact. That was going to be us.

~Lance~

"I really am glad you're excited about your new job—as dangerous as it might be."

I meant it. Does this shit never end?

"Thanks."

His voice had a boyish excitement to it. It was infectious.

"You learning a lot of new things?"

"More medic stuff, and some things I learned before but didn't need. Now, I do."

"For when you're "outside.""

"Yeah."

Just breathe.

41

MAN OR GOD?

~Lance~

TEXT FROM LANCE: "Got your picture."

I set my phone down and stared at his picture on my computer.

Adam had just e-mailed me a picture that Crockett took of him after he had done some very muddy maneuvers. He is in his shower area, in front of the stalls, wearing his Army-issued tan T-shirt, pants, and dark sunglasses. The lower half of his shirt is still wet and darkened from the water. The rest is mud-covered with splotches and chunks of dried mud everywhere: shirt, bare arms (definitely buffer), and face. [Adam: Really?] His hands look like he had been making mud pies all afternoon. His sunglasses are spattered as well. His hair, which has grown out since I saw him last, is standing up all over in a not unbecoming, spiky fashion. The "mousse" holding his hairstyle in place, I realize, is U.S. Army-issue terra firma. (Maybe they should market it.) Pants: drenched and glued to his lower body. [Adam: Really?] I can't see his boots. He may be mud-covered, but he still looks pretty good. [Adam: Was any of this necessary?]

TEXT FROM LANCE: "I printed a copy of your pic. I put it up in my dressing room."

TEXT FROM ADAM: "Uh huh. So you didn't cut out the back and replace it with a light that appears to emanate from my body?"

TEXT FROM LANCE: "Now why didn't I think of that?"

~Adam~

The sun beats down on dried earth and reflects off the sheet-metal picnic table, through my Oakley shades, leaving raccoon-like tan lines on my face as I watch Odie assemble his ghillie suit. I pick his brain, learning more from casual conversation over pieces of jute, tied to the webbed ghillie suit than the PowerPoint classes that I received before I assembled my own.

The table is still dusted with a thick coat from where mine lay previously, now tucked into a bio-hazard bag in my locker. I am beginning to realize how little I know and how much I have to learn before it is the Afghani sun shining through my sunglasses.

I have been making a solid attempt at studying, picking through medical textbooks, trying to live up to the expectations that are held for me by my team and SSG Khan, who recommended me for this new job.

I am now watching out specifically for these three guys. This is easier and harder. I will be right there with them. When they get hurt, it won't be a big group to move them and protect them. It will be me.

In the gym, my priorities have changed. I'm not trying to be as aesthetically pleasing as I was before. [Lance: Read: Making myself look hotter.] It is about survival. I have to be able to pick, not only myself up and move, but also possibly one of them.

My medical considerations are not just for immediate life threats, but depending on mission, terrain, weather, and enemy combatant considerations, long-term sustainment of a patient is a new consideration. The other thing is how do I do this with only the equipment on my back?

* * *

There is a general malaise that exists, like a heavy cloud, in the medic's barracks. We all so desperately want to relax before this deployment, and unless the individuals pursue the training or it comes from on high, we just watch movies. This attitude is a hard one to shake.

* * *

Movies are constantly playing on everyone's laptops, distracting me from any constructive activity as the days seem to fly by with nothing accomplished. Those who make an effort to study are verbally battered, but are also pursued to get their brains picked. I keep my headphones on, ending most conversations before they start.

I can feel the split happening already. We are a part of the platoon, but splintered, an avulsed segment. A piece of me wants to stay, but the other part knows I'll be happier caked in mud, out of breath, and far away from the safety of an Aid Station. [Lance: Avulsed? That's it. No more commenting on my use of vocabulary.]

* * *

As I lay my head on the magical foam pillow I brought from home, my Sonar pings. A smile pulls up the corners of my mouth. Kayla is going to keep me company until I pass out, as she has so many nights since I have arrived, dancing around issues that neither of us are willing to talk about. [Lance: Still?]

Click here for link to photos and/or video

42

TALKING TO MOM

~Adam~

May 13, 2009

E-MAIL FROM MOM:

Adam,

We have to be at the hospital at 10:00 today. Surgery will begin one-and-a-half to two hours later. I will let you know when they take him as soon as I am able to get on my computer.

Pray for him, and me too. I am shaking and woke up with a headache. That is the inside. On the outside I appear cool, calm, and collected—as usual.

—Mom

E-MAIL FROM ADAM:

Mom,

Thanks. Keep me posted.

—Adam

May 14, 2009

E-MAIL FROM MOM:

Adam,

If you cannot reach me and you want information on Dad, call the ICU at... You three boys have permission to ask questions about him. They prefer that you call me first, and if you can't reach me, then call them.

Because of all his hook-ups and his neck brace, he will not be able to talk to anyone. I will keep you posted on his progress and when he is up to it put the phone to his ear so you can talk to him.

—Mom

E-MAIL FROM ADAM:

Mom,

Sounds good. Thank you.

—Adam

2130: TEXT FROM MOM: "Dad is having trouble breathing and is unconscious."

2134: TEXT FROM MOM: "Blood sugar is really high, which is probably why he is unconscious."

2135: TEXT FROM ADAM: "A nurse better be there right now."

2150: TEXT FROM MOM: "5 of them are working on him. They are transferring him back to the ICU."

2158: PLACED CALL: No answer.

2218: RECEIVED CALL: He is having some bad reactions following surgery, and they are working through it.

2333: TEXT FROM MOM: "Dad woke up and can wiggle his toes, fingers, etc. Breathing fine, on respirator. They believe it was caused by slight swelling in the throat. I will be heading home soon."

May 15, 2009

E-MAIL FROM MOM:

Adam,

Dad is awake and alert. He is still on the ventilator, but they have it set so that he is doing most of the work. He is currently getting dialysis in his room in the ICU. He had a good smile for me. He did not know why he was back in ICU and on the ventilator. When I explained it to him, he understood. He has really good color now that his is breathing correctly. His blood sugars are back under control.

—Mom

E-MAIL FROM ADAM:

Mom,

Thank you.

—Adam

43

TALKING AT DAD

~Adam~

There were no birds chirping when I woke up. The majority of my platoon was still fast asleep, aside from Demille, a good friend and soldier, whose flashlight reflected white light off the ceiling through my eyelids, waking me three minutes before my alarm. The longest three minutes of my day.

I hopped off the top bunk and attempted to remain silent. I didn't want to wake Hunt, but I am no ninja. I loaded up all my gear on my back and looked out the window. Rain poured off the roof, inviting me outside for what promised to be a long day.

I gathered myself, looked out across the mud-covered expanse leading out to where the HMMWVs were parked and my platoon was gathering. At the doorway, I stood next to SPC Konrad (Specialist)—the forward observer in my team—took a breath, and stepped into the open.

The mud didn't want to release my boot when I made that first heavy step into it. With a slopping noise, I broke free and began my short walk. The water ran off my Kevlar onto my vest. My vest kept my torso relatively dry, but what clothing was not covered by gear, soon became cold and wet. My blouse stuck to my arms. My pants stuck to the front of my thighs and the back of my calves.

Three minutes outside and I was already uncomfortable. This didn't bode well.

In formation, to my right, stood Sandy, classic, well-built white guy, the spotter from our team.

To his right was Finch, another ginger who appeared more weathered than most.

My sniper team stood in the back with the rest of the platoon we were attached to, waiting in the rain.

Together we are reminiscent of a really cheesy National Guard commercial.

It starts off with Konrad, who with his nose pulled up looks like the Mayor of Who-Ville, wearing a vest dealing poker in a casino as the camera circles him.

The next shot is of Sandy and me sitting in a class wearing blue jeans and T-shirts, swapping Marine Corps stories and giving our teacher hell. (That is until Julie slaps both of us on the backs of our heads.)

Then it leads into Finch, wearing a silly security uniform, doing stunts in a company vehicle while on duty, in Palm Springs. The camera would make fluid, but unnecessary, movements to create the illusion of action as it zooms in on his clean-shaven, weathered face and fades to a shot of him covered in camouflage face paint with his ghillie suit over his head.

The camera pulls back revealing Sandy next to him as they lay behind a sniper rifle. Close by, covering their backs, are Konrad and me. Konrad would have the radio to his ear, and I have my rifle resting on my small, trauma medical pouch.

Just as a bomber flies overhead and drops a bomb somewhere, the flash would fade away to the four of us standing on the top of a mountain in our fancy blue Army uniforms snapping to the position of attention as the sun sets. Then, whatever the Army catch phrase of the day is flashes across the screen, along with the National Guard symbol. And we would feign professionalism until a shampoo commercial comes on.

When we got the word, we mounted up and rolled out. I took a nap en route. Our team did a quick dismount and moved into a small, hasty-hide position to provide security for the rest of the unit as they marched out to the little FOB (Forward Operating Base) we were going to inhabit.

(Konrad is not very quiet, it turns out. We have some work to do, it seems.)

We met up with the vehicles and I fell asleep... again.

We arrive at the little FOB, dismount, and take a few naps. My first nap is interrupted by mock indirect fire. I woke up, treated and transported some imaginary casualties, and went back to my nap.

We get woken up again. More indirect fire.

A quick patrol.

More gunfire.

More casualties.

I dropped my gear at the foot of my cot and went to piss.

I lay down, trying again for that nap.

No time.

We suited up again.

Now, in the back of a HMMWV I tried to nap again.

BOOM!

We watched as directly in front of us, over a berm, pieces of artillery simulator flew into the sky, followed by a white van driven through the gate and headed our way.

"Fucking go!" Wills, the TC, yelled, a break from his generally silent demeanor. We were still in awe of what we were seeing.

The vehicle started, and we began driving.

Through the center of the base, we drove with another vehicle, at speeds just slightly exceeding safe levels. We followed them.

The M2 (.50 cal) kicked links and brass into the cab as we followed close behind. Racing through the different obstacles, we maneuvered toward the van we pursued. With the back doors open, they returned fire.

They stopped.

Someone got out.

We stopped.

I jumped out.

Overhead the M2 continued to fire.

Sighted in and fired.

My blank adaptor (not real ammo, just noise and mess makers) flashed with every round.

The bolt stuck to the rear.

My magazine fell as I pulled out a new one.

Magazine inserted, I released the bolt and listened to the familiar sound of a round chambering.

I fired a few more.

"MOUNT UP!"

I picked up and jumped back into the vehicle, and we continued to follow as the van drove away.

Just outside another gate, the van is demobilized, and our role-players were faking dead in the back of the vehicle.

We did our admin stuff and cleared out, spirits high.

"And one more thing, I saw every soldier in this unit running across this base chasing after that van. That shit made my dick hard, everyone marching to the sound of the guns. That is the attitude I want to take overseas," the Colonel told us, standing tall in front of a squadron formation. [Lance: When he texted me almost this entire story, I actually found it pretty exciting—if not dick hardening.]

I found myself in the chow hall, amped up from my little adventure.

"Joey."

"Hey, Fenner, what is up?"

"I was in a high speed chase."

Joey and I exchanged a brief conversation, and I continued through the chow line.

Later, I ran into Joey. Who was incredibly jealous. His weight was holding him back from something he wanted again. I could tell he regretted every time that he went to chow and bed, immediately after coming off convoy escorts on his last deployment, instead of going to the gym. (We all feel that way; Joey is one of the best medics, if not the best. But... he is fat.)

* * *

TEXT FROM MOM: "Dad is in good spirits this a.m. They are trying to get him to breathe on his own. He is in pain from where the tube is. I will be in school all day today but checking in on him all day."

TEXT FROM ADAM: "Thank you."

Later that night, I called. Sitting on a cot near the door of the tent, I talked at Dad. We don't really have much to talk about in general anyway. Him not being able to talk back was interesting, to say the least. Mom kept letting me know that he was smiling when I said certain things. I made sure to tell him about the weather, and I eagerly awaited the weather report from home that he loves to give me.

44

ZIPLOC REDUX

~Lance~

Just as I was falling asleep last night, I started to think of Adam. (Big surprise there.)

Which led me to start thinking about the imminent danger.

And Ziploc.

I made my way to the office and powered up.

Adam made a reference a while ago about how he would like to take all of his loved ones and just store us in a Ziploc bag while he's gone, to unfurl later with nothing changed, no passage of time.

I think this thinking is slightly skewed.

Better. How about he goes into the Ziploc bag, all snug and safe for a year, and we let him out at the end and continue on? He is the one who will actually be doing the adventuring into the unknown, into a foreign and exotic (I use that term loosely) land. Our lives will be pretty stable over that year, with some progression, hopefully, and some change. I'm sure he can catch up quickly. Either way, a year in Afghanistan, or a year in a Ziploc.

And because it is Afghanistan, (I'm sure it's not on anyone's "must see" list) he won't be missing anything.

Yes, he had a good idea with the Ziploc—it was just for the wrong person.

[Adam: These are the types of conversations that lead to comments like, "Good evening, Officer. What can I do for you?" Besides, I'm too awesome to be contained in a mere Ziploc bag.]

[Lance: Sigh. I should have known better.]

~Adam~

We only got shelled once before bed, and I slept well, aside from the erection.

Team bonding time consisted of swapping pictures of ex-girlfriends. Memories of previous conquests [Lance: Interesting choice of words.] had me sending dirty text messages out to the different women who have been moving around in my life. Not helping the problem at all. It is going to be a long year. One month, or so, down.

The morning came, and I still had not. We prepped for our movement out of the FOB and back to real bunks.

The kids of second platoon swept under the cots while we packed our bags into the vehicles. Easy day ahead, a short mile plus walk back, and we would be home.

* * *

TEXT FROM MOM: "The ventilator is out!!!"

TEXT FROM ADAM: "Yay. That is good."

* * *

We were jubilant when we stepped off, making jokes and laughing while we walked. The air was cool, and once we started walking, it felt perfect. The sun shone and the birds were out. It really did feel good.

"I feel like running. I feel so good right now," Konrad said while I fought with the trauma bag that was still rubbing my neck.

"I can't disagree. I do feel great this morning."

"INCOMING!"

We all ran off the road, diving into the morning dew-dampened grass.

"Really?" I asked, a smile still on my face.

The distance suddenly felt less like a complement to an easy day.

We were finally up and moving. My knees and elbows felt cool. The moisture darkened the dried mud stains from the previous day.

A quick jog and we moved again onto the side of the road and took our positions in the grass.

"MEDIC!"

I ran over and helped treat a casualty with a few other medics.

We loaded him up and we kept moving, while other platoons assaulted imaginary objectives.

"Can snipers split off and provide over watch?" was the question proposed to the Lieutenant.

"Yeah..." He gave us the go, and we coordinated the little details of our mission.

Before long, the four of us were hiking through the woods adjacent to our comrades while they moved along the road assaulting various objectives. Blank M4 and M2 fire filled the air. We pressed through the woods, firing on the few aggressors we saw.

Along the road, a large white pickup moved into the center of our troops.

Two soldiers got out. "Who is the commander here?" they yelled over the gun fire.

"Get down," Finch whispered. We lay down and attempted to blend into the vegetation.

"Where is the commander of this unit?" they yelled again.

"Unload and clear," we were directed in a whisper.

Finally, everything calmed down and we reattached to the unit.

A captain told the tale.

"I am all about training, but HOLY FUCKING SHIT! This is an active airfield," the Sergeant told our Captain. "I won't tell range control, but you guys need to head back."

We all laughed. I guessed we would rather get in trouble for training, than for not.

On the way back, we got hit by more incoming.

More casualties.

More tourniquets.

More soldiers to carry or drag.

Across the road.

Ha.

A long warm shower and dry socks welcomed me back into the bay.

45

STUPID TURTLE

~Adam~

The mosquitoes were beginning to come out. I lay next to a road, in a slightly dug in position.

Konrad, our radio operator/forward observer is behind me listening to the radio. We stay low and quiet as a HMMWV nears, coming along the road, hoping our ghillies will provide the camouflage they promise.

The vehicle gets closer and slows near our position, slowly creeping past.

I am five feet away. I sink even lower into the ground.

It stops.

Fuck.

The transmission audibly switches into reverse and crawls backward.

Fuck.

He moves about five feet back and stops.

I recognize him as one of the OCs when he gets out.

He is looking right at me.

Goddamnit.

"What are you doing there, buddy?"

Busted. "You caught me, Sergeant."

"Holy shit! You scared me. I didn't even see you there."

Liar.

"I just saw this turtle and was going to move it out of the road."

He bends down and retrieves a turtle from an area unseen. He sets it onto the side of the road near where I was lying. Like a soup bowl with legs, it begins to crawl into the brush.

Did that just happen?

Did I just get compromised by a turtle?

He leaves.

Finch and Sandy move up from the area where they were resting and start heckling me.

Sandy goes off to find a new position, where I again set in low, resting my elbows in the dirt and get myself ready to watch an empty road.

The turtle, against his will, comes with.

* * *

I spend the day alternating on and off watch. I pass the time spent off-post eating, swatting mosquitoes, and killing the ticks that I find crawling all over me. We also managed to settle down in an area with cell phone service.

I kill time, and my battery, text messaging with my Angela, and with the latest woman I've met, who has been stealing my time.

I made the conscious decision to slowly drift away from Kayla. (Not because of Lance.) [Lance: Thank you for waking up. I don't need the credit.] Golden-flecked eyes don't see text messages from me nearly as often as before. She really does need to forget about me and find a nice boy who won't leave her to fight wars that aren't his own.

Dark-brown eyes now catch my messages on the other end, and long ebony fingers type the reply. We play the question game: I ask her, she asks me, and we see where the conversations go.

I look forward to returning to cantonment area, (the normal part of base) and resuming my schedule of PT in the morning, study some medical stuff, and then meet up with Lyrik and a few other people. We may lounge around the pool or make runs out in town. The sun will set, and we sit closer together than a professional relationship would allow.

We find, create, and enjoy our little chances alone to act like teenagers, just enjoying little kisses. Or a long kiss in the fifteen-passenger van, kissing soft, freckled lips and teasing her about playing connect the dots with all the freckles she keeps finding on her dark skin. [Lance: Another girl of the moment? Snatch that opportunity. Hmm. Good choice of words.] [Adam: Surprisingly crude actually. You've been spending too much time with Grant.]

* * *

Mom called. Dad isn't out of the hospital yet. I swat flies as she tells me his blood sugar is out of control. Some tests say 700, some 900. (That is real bad.) He is out of the rehab part of the hospital and placed into a more intermediate level of care. They say they are running out of options and he needs to look into a nursing home.

I pace up and down the hillside swatting flies while she tells me the news.

* * *

With the moon high in the sky, I fall asleep in the back of a large truck, waiting to go to my bunk after completing our mission. I awake to raindrops landing on my face and hands, find safety under the canopy of another vehicle, and nap again. The battery on my phone long since dead, again I am woken to head back to another little base to spend the night. With only three hours to rest, I sleep soundly on the cot provided.

Joey is on the other side of the tent. Naked below the waist, he forcefully makes Dilay—a Filipino medic whose heart is always in the right place, he just needs to find it sometimes—check him for ticks. Dilay seems more startled than anything else and merely shields his eyes as Joey lifts his sac and props his leg on Dilay's cot.

The darkness puts me to sleep as solidly as the sun wakes me in the morning. We head back, and my life resumes its normal path.

46

MEMORIAL DAY IN THE TWILIGHT ZONE

~Lance~

I was asked to sing for a Memorial Day service at the Veteran's Memorial Park Cemetery in Boulder City. Cool. The Governor, Senators, State Assemblyman, the Media would all be there. I'd sung for them the previous Veteran's Day, and I enjoy doing my bit for the military—now more than ever.

Little did I realize just how immediate it would be for me. Each of the respective politicians had his own variation on a theme, thanking those that had served, as well as those who are serving.

Uh oh.

The Senator began speaking, "And I want to tell the story of one young, courageous soldier I talked to in Afghanistan, who, even though his leg was dangling and blood was gushing from the wound, managed to staunch the flow of blood and continue to fight."

Thank you, Senator. I really needed the graphic details.

That was the worst of it, description-wise. But all the subsequent speakers with their tributes made me think of Adam. His face loomed in front of me the entire time I was there, a constant reminder of what was to come. I guess everyone else there had "Adams" in their mind's eye, too. I'm not unique, I know. It was still unnerving.

The service, overall, was very moving and poignant, what with various veterans of the wars there, going back as far as WW II.

I tried to keep my thoughts generalized and free of emotions while I was singing, but I kept remembering all the times Adam had come to see me perform.

But here is what is unique... and freaky.

"You were really great," a male voice from behind me said as I bent over and gathered up my music to leave.

I turned and saw one of the many caretakers of the cemetery standing there.

"Thank you. You're ver—"

I choked as I stared at the tall young man's chest. The only person I'd encountered all day with a name badge on.

And what was his name? In big, bold embroidered letters...

Thanks for being there with me today—Adam.

47

DEFINE GAY?

~Adam~

"Dude, I smelled the most delightful odor today... and it was Kiethley's dick." Joey started what I was hoping would be a well-followed story. Kiethley is one of our younger medics. He is a solid reminder that sometimes training junior soldiers is like housebreaking a dog.

I am going to end up writing this. I shook my head. "Hmm. Okay," was all I could muster.

"Okay. So Kiethley had just gotten done with a shower and was standing over here twirling his dick around."

I paused for a moment. "Uh huh."

"Suddenly, I'm struck with the most delightful odor ever, and I realize that it was Kiethley's dick."

I still can't come up with an appropriate response.

"Just ask Crockett."

Crockett reluctantly agrees.

* * *

"Okay, dude, I have to ask." I find Kiethley sitting on his bunk watching a movie from his ridiculously large DVD collection. "What makes your balls smell so wonderful?"

He smiles his big toothy grin, gets up, and with a level of energy and excitement, unusual for someone his size, goes to his wall locker. He pulls out the source and tells me a little bit about it.

My question's answered. I leave him to his devices.

* * *

The water starts off uncomfortably hot as I take my second shower of the day. I'm ready for bed, but I have an early day tomorrow and need to shower and shave ahead of time.

I look myself over for the remaining remnants of the mosquito assault I endured only a few days prior. I seem to be healing nicely.

"Hey, Fenner, is that you?" Kiethley interrupts my Zen 'ish moment with his normal child-like tone of voice.

"Yeah, what is up?" Before I have a chance to complete my sentence I can feel him on the other side of the curtain.

He opens it and holds out the source of his wonderfully smelling dick.

"Here. Rub this on your nuts, bro."

I hold out my hand and he pours some into my open palm.

"Wow, this smells like an orange slushee," I tell him, only slightly alarmed.

I can hear Kiethley talking to Joey and offering him some deliciousness in the same fashion he did for me. Then, to a very startled sergeant from another platoon.

"Fucking Kiethley," I say to myself and continue my shower.

~Lance~

I squirm a little in my office chair as I think of what to write about this... definitely gay experience. Yep. This was gay. The only way it would have been gayer was if Kiethley had offered to apply the soap. I wonder if he actually did? [Adam: *Shaking head*]

48

FINALLY KILLING THE HORSE

~Adam~

It was chewing at me, lingering just below the surface. I still held on to all the hurt and lost opportunity of my divorce. It wasn't anything big, nothing anyone noticed, but a casual conversation reminded me of all the bad... all the hurt. I just needed to end it, to finally put it all to bed.

E-MAIL FROM ADAM:

Susan,

I remember asking you not to forget about me, and ultimately, not hearing from you in two months would indicate that you forgot. Turns out you thought enough about me to delete me from your friends list.

By the time you read this I probably won't be in country anymore—not to make you feel bad, just the way it is. I'm not expecting a call or to get a reaction out of you, but I was reminded of you today, in a negative way, which may surprise you, but normally I don't think of you that way. But I need to get this off my chest.

I am trying really badly to grow up, close off stuff that is in the past, and move on. One of those chapters to close is you. Even after everything, for a long time I thought there was a chance. And even after seeing you and knowing you were with this new guy, I still held on.

And it wasn't until I was talking to this girl, and I asked her how she was able to stick with her ex-boyfriend through four deployments. She told me it is because she loves him, and when you love someone you can do anything.

You told me you wouldn't wait a year for me. You can guess what my conclusion was.

After everything that happened, that was it. I'm done. No more hope. Just like you made an effort to cut me off from your life, I'm doing the same. I'm deleting all your family's numbers and doing the MySpace friend thing, too. That way I can't even bug you if I want to. Ryah, as you could already have guessed, is all yours.

I wish you the best in all your endeavors and nothing but happiness.

—Adam

49

THE COLOR GREEN

~Adam~

The phone rings enough times for me to give up. He'll call back. Lance always does.

The weather is nice out tonight. The bugs aren't too bad. I would rather be avoiding them inside, if my cell only had enough service to have a phone conversation in there. I leave my fold-out camping chair and water bottle on the corner of the building and take my phone back to the picnic table where Joey is making conversation with various soldiers he knows from his last deployment.

Some head out just as I come to say hi and join the conversation. The sun has long since set, and some of the mosquitoes have already found a spot to sleep, with their tail ends full of blood.

Sam sits across from me, a beautiful man, or as Joey puts it, "The most beautiful man." He is Odie's sniper. On the other end of the bench where I take my seat, Sergeant O sits—the traditional, former Marine, Hispanic-father figure. Joey paces near me and participates in the conversation, as he often does.

"So what is up with your girl, man?" Sergeant O asks.

"She is in Vegas now, on leave."

"How are things going with that?" He has been curious since he saw the two of us sitting together on this same table a week prior.

"It's hard. They are trying to charge her for hanging out with me."

"How the fuck?" Sam and Sergeant O both ask. Joey has already heard this story enough times to be sick of it.

"All right," I begin my tale. "A couple days ago she tells a squad leader in her platoon she is going to Walmart. She gets the green light. We meet up, and with a few other people, go. We decide to get some food but don't want to get into trouble by going anyplace out of the way. So, we hit up the restaurant right across the street. We aren't the only ones with this idea. When we walked in, there were a lot of soldiers already there.

While we are ordering our food, I see her First Sergeant and that squad leader she told walk in. Before long, she is asked to step outside by her First Sergeant and then scolded for being with me and not having a female with her. She lies, saying the girls are still shopping. He believes the lie but is still mad.

We enjoy our meal and head back to base. I drop her off, and when her First Sergeant finally gets back, he informs her that she will be charged."

"Dude, this is all fucked up," Sergeant O interjects. "So what the hell is she being charged with?"

"Well, he is saying that her female buddies were not good enough because they weren't from her unit. Also, he is saying that she drove in a civilian vehicle."

"How the fuck? Dude, she needs to talk to somebody about this." Sam and Sergeant O come to similar conclusions, as I already have.

"Yeah, it gets worse. Because the vehicle was not from her unit it is considered a civilian, even though I have a log stating that I drew it from my unit. This all took place a few days ago. She went in, signed some papers, and was waiting to find out what her punishment would be."

"Dude..." Everyone begins to offer advice and express their distaste for the situation.

"Question. Is her chain of command black?" Sergeant O asks.

"Everyone I have met."

I receive more advice, information about equal opportunity complaints, and how JAG can help.

* * *

We have been discovering that this little interracial thing we have been participating in has been, well, normal for us. This hasn't, at least between the two of us, felt any different from anything else. And in my living area it isn't a big deal, aside from the kudos from a lot of guys I don't really know, and harassment from those I do. But in her area, where she lives, people that once made an active effort to come up, shake my hand, and say hello are now actively trying to ensure that we can't hang out.

Maybe they are just jealous that I carry a shotgun and I stole the attention of the most sought after female in their unit. [Lance: It seems like it's less of a deal to be gay than it is to be in an interracial relationship. Whodda thought it?]

* * *

We exchange ideas and I enjoy my chance to vent a little. Ultimately, we all understand that it is up to her. I can fight, but it won't help. So all I can do is pass along ideas and see what she does. My command is backing me up on this, even as hers tries to get me into trouble.

Conversation fades, and soon we all have to go our respective ways. I try to call Lance one more time before I'm done for the night.

"Hey, perfect timing. I was just looking at porn..." he answers the phone.

"Uh huh." I can't even pretend that is how I wanted him to answer the phone. [Lance: Is there nothing private between us? Do I have to edit my conversations before I voice them? I'm so glad I didn't say what I thought of saying.] [Adam: Something for you to think about.]

50

SMILING THROUGH A BAD FEELING

~Adam~

I stood at the threshold knowing what I was about to do and the consequences that would follow.

I took a breath and stepped across.

I entered Mac's little living area with a roll of medical tape and a crazy idea. I grabbed his shoe and taped it to his sandal. The other followed. Then I threw them under his bed into a pile of other things. Next his loofa. I removed it from its hanging location against the wall and taped that up as well.

My revenge was wrought.

The game was afoot.

* * *

I walked back into my area, relatively lost in my own thoughts. I looked up to where my lock hung from my locker. Now, it was about the size of a baseball—wrapped in duct tape, gauze, and medical tape, and as I discovered as I dug my way through the mess, to the amusement of a crowd that gathered, petroleum gauze. Within about fifteen minutes my lock was free, and I could carry on with my mission—whatever that might have been.

* * *

I again stood. The bay was empty, except for another medic who patiently sat across from Mac's area, eagerly awaiting whatever it was that I had planned. I walked in, armed with roll after roll of gauze, Ace wrap, medical tape, duct tape, petroleum gauze, and surgical lubricant. My audience instigated and offered ideas that I could incorporate into this little mixture, along with justifications for use of this equipment as equipment familiarization. Several socks, his shoe, someone's sandal, all got caught into the web that I spun. When I walked away from his lock, it appeared to be a football with a bit of Ace wrap stretched across to the other side of his area.

I did later return to find him wrestling with it, and my own lock blackened with fire. As he used surgical scissors to push his way through to his own lock, I pulled out a needle and began to pick out the blackened mess that he'd melted into the keyhole of my lock. Clever fuck.

Soon, we were both laughing. He managed to get his items free, at the expense of a sock that he didn't realize was there until it was too late. And I managed to pull all the little melted pieces of string out of my lock.

We were even.

* * *

I was busy studying from a book I stole, temporarily, from Dilay. "Hey, Fenner." Mac caught my attention, wagging Dilay's new carton of cigarettes.

I smiled.

When our powers combine...

We began wrapping. Soon, we realized that the removal of one pack had severely weakened the integrity of the carton and we needed to stabilize it. Mac grabbed one of our malleable splints and we braced the carton. Again, we began to wrap. Tape—gauze—tape—gauze. Somehow a small soda bottle got mixed into it. Tape—gauze—petroleum gauze. (It helps that Mac is our medical supply sergeant.) And with the help of some small BBs, that I thought were conveniently placed to make a mess, we were done. It looked like a pipe bomb.

We placed it above his rack. It looked like some insect had laid its eggs. It loomed ominously, until he found it. He made an active effort to ignore it.

"Hey, Dilay, can I get a smoke?" someone asked.

"No problem."

He began to root through his area, digging and complaining. His audience grew."You looking for a rectangular shaped object?" Irons asked with a shit-eating grin smeared across his weathered Hawaiian features.

"Goddamnit. Fuck my life," Dilay said looking at the cocoon hanging above his bed.

I got my camera and began to film as he removed the nest and started to dig through. The platoon as a whole surrounded his bunk to laugh and comment. The video stretched on for nine minutes as Dilay wrestled, made different humorous statements of surprise and the occasional accusation directed toward me.

"I know this was you, Fenner. I know it. That is okay. I've got something for you," Dilay threatened.

We all laughed and enjoyed the show and congratulated him when his mission was successful. "You want that smoke, man?"

"No. I don't smoke," he replied with a smile.

More laughter.

I put my camera away in my locker as everyone went their separate ways.

"Hey, Fenner, can I ask you a question?" a medic said, grabbing my attention.

"Yeah, what is up?" I took a seat next to his bed, where he was lying back.

"When you were in Iraq, did you ever get a premonition that someone was going to die?" he asked me, unable to look me in the eyes.

"No. I didn't have anything like that the other times. And we only lost one guy. We were close, too, but that was different," I said.

"Because, as you were filming and you brought the camera toward me, I suddenly felt like I was watching it—but later—and seeing people who didn't make it home." He distracted himself nervously as he shared his experience with me.

"I never had bad feelings about my last deployments, but this one is different. But then again, I have never felt this inadequately trained before either." I took a second. "Any idea who?"

"No idea, I don't know who it could be. This training, or lack thereof, has been ridiculous to send us off for what this mission might possibly be," he spoke, unable to hide the shaken look upon his face.

"I have never had this feeling before, but this time... I don't think I will be coming home," I told him, breaking the mood. [Lance: I won't even tell you how devastating this is to hear. God will not let anything happen to you, or me. You have too much to do yet with your life. I'm going to ignore it. I have to.]

"Really?" he asked. The conversation was almost jovial until that point. Now, for a moment, it was serious.

"Yeah. Everything about my life feels like it is leading to this. Like everything in my life has been wrapping up."

We continued talking. Soon, we were laughing and throwing more crazy ideas back and forth.

We talked a little bit longer; soon, it was well past the point of a late night. "You want to see that video again? See if the feeling comes back?" I asked him.

"Yeah. Would you want to know?" he asked me.

"No, but I wouldn't do anything different if I did," I told him handing over my camera.

I grabbed my hygiene supplies and headed toward the shower.

As I stood in the small stall, hoping the hot water would stay hot, I remembered sitting in the pits at the range, shooting the shit with Sandy and a few other people, waiting for the sun to go down to do our night shoot with the long-range rifles we had only recently gotten.

"Okay, Fenner, hypothetical situation," Sandy had started.

"Uh huh."

"We are in our position. Konrad and Finch are dead. I am critically wounded and can't move. There are 200 enemy troops, 100 meters away, charging our position. What do you do?"

"What are our air assets?"

"None."

"Arty?"

"None. QRF are ten minutes out."

"Grenades?"

"Two. You going to run or stay? This is a no-win situation. You run, you may live. You stay, you will die."

I thought about it for a bit. Two-hundred is a lot of mother fuckers. "Konrad handles air. He can take out a lot of people at a distance. You and Finch do the long range shit, but I carry an M4, a shotgun, and a pistol. A hundred meters is in my range. I'm not leaving, dude."

"You know, sometimes you say shit like, "I play D&D," or "I'm the Dungeon Master." Then sometimes, you say shit like that, and I'm like, 'That is my fucking Doc!'"

The water started to get cold. I had been done for several minutes anyway. I dried off and shaved before heading back into the bay.

My camera had been returned to my locker when I got back from my shower, but the evening's Nostradamus was asleep.

The next morning, when I finally made my way out of bed, I saw him. "Did you get that feeling again?"

"Yup." His cocky smile wasn't what it normally was.

Click here for link to photos and/or video

51

ANOTHER BOMB?

~Lance~

I mentioned the above anecdote to Richie, as he had just walked into the office to see if I was writing, and he said. "There was a "Twilight Zone" episode like that, wherein the people kept disappearing from a photograph, meaning they were going to die."

"I remember now," I said. A chill went up my spine.

Adam knows that I get into the paranormal things. I'm sure he knew how his story would affect me. There is so much unknown out there. Who am I to deny any possibility? I just pray that this incident never plays out. It definitely unnerved and upset me, though.

Also unnerving was our most recent conversation.

I said, "Do you feel you could use more training in the shooting and the medical department?"

"Definitely."

"Then, why aren't you training as much as possible?"

"Money. It's expensive."

"But isn't that what you're there for? To train for going over there? Shouldn't you be as knowledgeable as possible?"

"You'd think. They'd rather build another bomb."

"Another bomb that'll never be used, instead of training you guys?"

"Yup."

"It's just so wrong."

"Yup."

"Do the other guys feel the same way?"

"Pretty much."

"And they haven't told you what exactly you are getting into, where exactly you are going, or when you are leaving."

"Nope."

"How frustrating."

"Uh huh."

I feel another rant coming on. But I guess I don't need to. He pretty much summed it all up with his yups and uh huhs. I'm learning a lot. At least I'm getting the firsthand info I asked for.

Swell.

52

A BOOZEHOUND WITH A SECRET

~Adam~

The van is loaded up and we make our way to the airport. We laugh and make jokes along the way. After a little while I hide between my headphones and slip into my own thoughts.

* * *

TEXT FROM LYRIK: "I'm an E3." They demoted her.

TEXT FROM ADAM: "I'm sorry, are you fighting it?"

TEXT FROM LYRIK: "I signed an appeal."

TEXT FROM ADAM: "Good, is there anything I can do to help?"

TEXT FROM LYRIK: "No."

Ouch.

* * *

The wheels lift off the tarmac and we are now en route to our destination. I fall asleep for a bit.

I stop the stewardess and ask for another Jack and Coke. I'm on the up end of my second buzz of the day.

We had four days off, just enough to get a girl pregnant. Not a goal of mine, but it happens. My intent was to let off some steam and get back to work.

Wheels touch down at McCarran International Airport.

The air is dryer here than in the Midwest. I head over to the carousel and wait for my bags. When they arrive, I scoop them up and make my way up to the second floor where my ride is waiting for me. She doesn't like elevators or escalators, and the Las Vegas airport doesn't accommodate those few people left who are comfortable using stairs.

Angela insults me briefly in the same way that we always have. There is a comfort gained between two people when they dated as long as we did, and have been friends for as long as we have. I grab her by the back of her hair gently pull her head back by the roots and kiss her. Our lips and tongues get reacquainted.

Human. I get to pretend to be human for a few days. No uniform, no babysitter. My own schedule, booze, and sex.

On the way back to her place we swing by Ed's. He has been watching my car and I want it back. He isn't home to open the gate. So, I jump the fence and make my way down the street. There it is, at the end. Cherry-red under a thin coat of desert dust, with that same splotch of bird shit on the hood.

Just as I left it.

I use the garage code, walk in through the garage door I knew his lazy ass would leave unlocked. The keys are where I left them. Ed's overly friendly mini 'ish schnauzer greets me with confusion as I take what I want and leave. Like I was never there, the doors are shut behind me and I slip back into my seat. The stick shift is hot to the touch. I start the ignition, a familiar purr fills the area around me, and after some coaxing of fluids back into the engine that gravity was so kind to settle for me, I am off.

I set my bags down in the apartment.

Reset.

We spend the rest of the night enjoying a movie until jet lag and my third buzz of the day catch up with me.

I spend the next day running errands. Jose, my stylist (yeah, I have a stylist) cuts my hair.

The next day we spend on the lake. Lance is at work while I ride the wave runners on an exceptionally windy day. I piss some people off at the dock, break a piece off Sandy's wave runner, and head home to set up a tent in the living room and make s'mores on a propane stove on the porch. We were too lazy to do actual camping.

Sunday comes. Lance's Friday. I have gotten time to myself without him. Our time is always pleasant, but his demeanor often feels as if I am being smothered. This was my way of preventing any of that.

I text him. "What are your plans today?"

"Work till 6:15, then maybe dinner with Dan. You want to come?"

"I'll try."

"You are awesome," he replies, still unaware that I will be there.

53

THE BEST PRESENT EVER

~Lance~

"What? Nothing for me?" a voice asks me as I walk away from my final set of the day.

I turn to acknowledge the voice. "I'm..." I stop breathing. Impossible. "You... What? How? It can't be?" I stared into brown-green eyes—just like mine.

"I thought I'd surprise you."

The tears slam into my eyes. "Oh my God!" I barely squeeze out as I rush to hug him (Soul Hug), crushing him to me to never let him go—also verifying that he is flesh and blood and not some illusion.

He's real.

Adam.

"Didyougetyourleave?Howlong?Youlookgreat!Whendidyougeth ere?Ican'tbelieveit!Whydidn'tyoutellme?" I'd finally found my breath, but I was still numb. I had never been so shocked. I (and I hate to admit this) almost passed out and now understood how a person could do it.

"I knew two months ago, but I didn't want to tell you and get you all excited and worried, or take days off from work—which you would have."

Probably... Definitely.

"I thought this would be a great surprise. Only the ex knew and I'm staying with her."

"You could've stayed with me."

"I know. But you know why."

"Right. Reset."

"And reset and reset."

"When did you get here?"

"A couple of days ago."

I froze. At least inside. A couple of days ago? "What have you been doing?" I tried to keep the edge out of my voice.

"Stuff. I went to the lake with Sandy and Angela."

Yeah. I wouldn't have wanted to go anyway, spending the day on the lake and playing in the water with him. How boring. He's been here two days. I wanted to be hurt and get angry. I was hurt and angry. But instead, I said, "When do you leave?" It's not like I would pull a 180 and start berating him. That's not me. Besides I'll write/vent later tonight.

"Wednesday. So, I planned it so that we could do Tuscany tonight. Hang out tomorrow—maybe do book stuff. Grill Kobe steaks on Tuesday, and Wednesday I fly out."

"Sounds great. Except the flying out part."

"Yeah, I know."

Unbelievable. Really. He'd planned it all out, so he'd spend the bulk of his leave with me. I'm sure this was meant to assuage the guilt of his being here two days already. He can't possibly think I didn't realize it. He's crafty but... [Adam: I knew you would be pissed. Sometimes you need to realize you smother me. I would rather take the hit of your being initially pissed than to have to tell you repeatedly that I have plans with other people.] [Lance: I know you have plans with other people. I just like to know. And this time was big.] [Adam: I knew you would be hurt and mad. I also knew you won't leave, and neither will I.] [Lance: That was good.]

We didn't go to Tuscany. We stopped by next door and visited Richie, who invited us to dine at the steakhouse there at Harrah's.

Great meal. Better company. Back together again. We chatted and ate and drank—not too much—and just enjoyed being together. One side note: While we shared an Armangnac, we discussed Amontillado, a sherry, with the sommelier, and we decided we needed to have it Tuesday night with our Kobe steaks.

At home that night I stupidly told Richie about Adam being home for two days.

"You see, it's happening again. He doesn't care about you as much as you care about him. Two days he was here."

Why did I tell him? I knew I would get no sympathy. Sometimes I think I have masochistic tendencies. "But the surprise was so great," I semi-lamely eked out.

"Yeah, so great he waited two days to tell you."

I had nothing else to say. I did have a propensity for caring more for my friends than they did about me. I didn't believe Adam was one of them. I knew him a lot better than anyone.

But, come on! Adam! How could you? Do you really fear loving me too much? I know I'm your first friend who cares so much about you and sometimes you don't know how to react or feel, but it's okay to show affection. It's okay to love. Haven't I shown you that? Haven't my friends—now yours—shown you? You do such incredible things for me—like surprising me now—then you counter it. Why would you tell me you'd been here two days already, knowing I'd be hurt? Fuck. Open up. Stop protecting yourself and hiding behind the getting-laid excuse. Getting laid is not more important. It's evanescent. I'm not. You know this. All your relationships will prosper from this. Trust me. Trust your instinct.

[Adam: I believe we have different definitions of friendship. My buddies, although cold and callous, are my friends because we don't put any requirements on our relationships (I hate that word). Grant may never say anything nice, ever, but he has never said no when I needed help. And Ed is Ed. He is the friend we can't take in public. He is fun to hang out with, however. You believe that unless we are talking daily and sharing each other's feelings that our friendship is not as good. That stresses me out.] [Lance: Duly noted and I will remember this. I do like to keep in touch. But if we don't, I do not think that our friendship is not as good. I know better. Thanks for telling me though.]

I would get over this. I can't sustain anger for any length of time, and I wouldn't let this lessen his surprise or cast a pall over our short time together. I wanted to enjoy it to its fullest, for somewhere in the very back of mind was that looming insidious thought: It could be our last time together.

Monday, we got together at my house, and then met some friends for dinner at an Irish pub. We did discuss the book, worked around the house to get it ready for the next night, and hung out by the pool. Yep. Yep. Yep.

Adam had a nice paycheck he was just dying to blow all of on whatever he wanted. This included the steaks, the Amontillado, and instead of Armagnac—which he couldn't get—he got a bottle of eighteen-year-old Johnny Walker Gold Label.

The meal was great. Richie, Grant, and Angela joined us. Adam had a special marinade he used to prepare the steaks, and they were cooked perfectly.

[Adam: It isn't special, or very clever. Soy sauce, Worcestershire, and papaya.]

"How do you like the Amontillado?" I asked around the table.

"It's too sweet. You can have mine." Richie.

"The beer's better." Grant. He passed his glass over.

"It's all right." Angela. She slid her glass to Adam.

"It's good." Adam.

"I like it." Me.

We finished the bottle.

After dinner we sipped on the Gold Label... just all right. Mutual consensus.

[Adam: It did taste a bit like peat. Smooth. But like peat.]

We didn't get too toasted, just happy.

The night was what it should have been.

* * *

Now, here I sit at my desk the next evening, reminiscing over the whirlwind of the past three days. The hurt of his not telling me he was here has diminished almost completely. I recall that first shock of seeing him, and I still get that strange rush of feeling. Only Adam.

He's on a plane headed back to beautiful, rainy, windy, ugly Indiana. He'll only be there a few more days. Word is they ship out by the end of the month—that's five days from now.

Swell.

I've also realized now—I'm owning up to this and putting it into print—that you can be in love with two people at the same time. They're just different. Love is about understanding one another and the deep feelings that go with that. For me it comes down to: If that person died, would my life be irrevocably changed? I have to answer an undeniable "yes." A piece of my heart and soul would be gone. I feel it daily with my parents, and I know I would with either Richie or Adam. I think I'm pretty lucky in that aspect.

And I couldn't be happier for the greatest present Adam ever could have given me.

Thanks.

54

HEAVY BAGS

~Adam~

My time in Vegas was short. Debauchery and socializing that was less than rowdy passed the time quickly, and the good-byes were as quick as the greetings.

* * *

The space between our bunks is more open; the wall lockers are empty. Hunt, Crockett, and the platoon sergeant already left yesterday. A lot of other guys have been pushed to the other bay to await their flight in a couple days. Those who remain are either out tomorrow or just didn't want to move yet. All around the individual bunks that are still occupied lie packs that will push the limits of those who are set to carry them, burdened with the excess crap that either they or the Army has put on their backs.

My bags are as ready as anybody else's. Odie and I enjoy Chinese food for the last time as he flips his way through a men's magazine and complains about all the little whores inside and how he can't trust women because they are all sluts. I argue with him, the same argument we always have about the genuine human nature of women and their capacity for love and honesty.

We don't feel like we are going to war. We know we are. Our bags are packed, and we are ready to do the job. But something feels like it is missing, like this isn't it. Not a euphoric quiet before the storm... just nothing.

I haven't made my final calls yet. Aside from Lance's, I don't expect them to be dramatic. He doesn't know yet that I am leaving tomorrow. I kept it a secret. For personal reasons I withheld the date and played it off. "I don't know yet. As soon as I do, I'll call."

Like a band-aid, quick and easy. "I'm leaving tomorrow. I'll contact you when I can. I don't know much else." It changes so much anyway, no reason to worry anybody else about date changes and flights, just stick with what solid things I have and pass those along. It is easier on everybody.

My pack does look heavy.

* * *

The Squadron Commander gave his final speech before we all went out. It wasn't Mel Gibson in We Were Soldiers (mostly because Gibson is shorter), but that is a good way to envision the situation.

I'd heard a few of these, and in general they are a litmus test of who does and does not drink enough water throughout the day and an opportunity for Medics to drag exhausted Soldiers out of formation. But our Colonel is one of those few who never forgot how much fun he had as a lieutenant running around getting dirty.

He said two very important things. The first being, "Tell our story." This I can do. The second being, "I'd rather you ask forgiveness, not permission." It isn't his way of saying do whatever we want, but as Joey so aptly put it, "I think the Colonel just cut us a blank check to do whatever we want." I don't think that was particularly it. I think he simply doesn't want leaders afraid to make decisions.

* * *

Mac drives the van back to the barracks. We are wrapping up a quick trip to the movies and shopping. Our last trip.

"Dude, your knife is about as dangerous as a fork," I try to explain to Odie.

"Dude, this thing will fuck you up."

"Look how small it is."

"Hold out your hand."

I do, against my leg, and he begins to dance the tip of the blade along my protruding veins.

"Hold still," he tells me, the knife now folded at a right angle.

Before I realize the individual thoughts we share, me not believing he would do it, he believing I would not move, the tip cleanly enters the vein, and as smoothly as it enters he pulls it out. [Lance: !!! Is he an asshole?] [Adam: :)]

The blood pours out, like a leaky hose. Blood sprays over his pants in a long enough moment for us to exchange glances of surprise and excitement. And for me to realize that I am bleeding and need to do something. I jam my thumb into the point of origin as hard as I can.

"Really yo?" Joey looks over at us. I feel like we are five-year-old boys who just got caught by Dad. He reaches into his pocket and hands me his handkerchief. Occasionally Joey shows us that he is actually a father of two boys—not us. I place that where my own hand once held pressure and let it soak up the blood for a bit.

After some excited whispered conversation about the events, leading to the slight reduction in my total body volume, he finally uses the bandage to wrap my hand in a cleverer manner.

I would be lying if I said it still doesn't hurt. Or that it hasn't swollen up.

55

LAST WORDS

~Lance~

"Hi! You doin' okay?" I can't believe my throat is closing off as I say this.

"I'm fine. You?"

"Okay. As well as can be expected." I was sitting in my green room after a show waiting for him to call. He said he would after he was done with stuff. "It's late for you, like twelve-thirty. You all packed?"

"Yep."

"What time you going?"

"Early. How was your show?"

"Good. Did you call everybody and let them know?"

"Everybody that needs to, except my mom. I'll try her in the morning. I couldn't get hold of her."

"If you can't, let me know. I'll call her for you."

Won't that be fun.

"Okay. I will."

"We still have your bottle of syrah to drink that we didn't get to the other night."

"Right. We'll drink it when I get back."

Get back.

It's starting.

"I don't wanna hang up, you know. I wanna talk all night."

"I know, but I'll fall asleep on this picnic table."

Here we go.

"You keep yourself safe for me."

"That is the plan."

The tears are flowing. He knows. I'm glad.

"Remember, I'm always thinking about you, when you're over there, if you're feeling alone."

"I know you are."

"I love you."

Pause.

"I know you do."

Still can't say it.

"Let me know as soon as you can where you are and what's going on."

"I will."

"Have a good night."

This is it. "Bye."

"Bye."

Click.

I turn off the computer.

~Adam~

Sitting in the terminal in a little airport that only the Army seems to use, I said all my good-byes.

The last of them anyway.

I said good-bye to Lance last night. I made an effort to keep it short. I knew it would be hard on him.

I had to hang up the phone before he really lost control.

Angela, I also called last night. She had hinted that she might miss me, even if I am a pain in the ass.

I tried a few Marine buddies. Only a couple answered. It was good to talk to them. It wasn't really like a good-bye with them.

A lot of other people found missed call messages on their phones. A few found voicemails.

Kayla I talked to while I was on the bus ride to the airport. The conversation was short but friendly. I wish I didn't have to stay away from this one.

Mom was easy—not her first rodeo. She talked my ear off for a while before asking what I was up to. I told her I was calling to say good-bye, then turning off the phone. She said her piece and passed the phone off to Dad. Dad sounded indifferent. "You know what to do. Be safe, big guy." His health has always given me the idea that he may not be around much longer. The idea sends a wave of heat up my neck and into my cheeks, where I send it back down from where it came. It isn't for the loss of my father. It is because I wouldn't see a difference in my life. Because I never let him be a part of it. And also the feeling that my son someday might feel the same for me.

My brother Evan and his wife Kristin were about the same. "Keep your head down," Evan would say. He knows how this stuff goes. And, "I love you," Kristin would say. She has always been like my little sister. She just had to marry Evan to make it official.

"You take care of my niece," I would tell them.

My phone company was last.

And after 15 minutes navigating through the automated system to talk to an associate.

"Look, I just want to freeze my fucking account."

"We are sorry to inform you that our call center is currently closed. Our business hours are..."

"Ugh."

56

WAITING

~Lance~

He's on a plane to Afghanistan, or somewhere near there. And I sit here with my new best friend, Hewlett Packard, my lifeline to him.

He said they would probably go somewhere else first. I'm sure it's another tourist destination. I'm at work, on break, writing about him. Now the fun starts.

I get to sit here and wait until he e-mails me to let me know what's going on.

Relying on a computer. Ugh.

It was never a curiosity of mine to know what it felt like to have someone you love go off to war. Really. I would have passed on this life experience.

And if Grant mentions one more time about him getting shot or not coming back, there will be one less cop in Las Vegas.

57

LETTERS NEVER SENT

~Adam~

Dear Mom,

This is a long time coming, both the epiphany and putting pen to paper, so to speak. I realized, through a variety of circumstances, something about the course I have taken in my life and its effect on those around me.

I remember my original reasoning behind signing on the dotted line the first time and later putting that little eagle, globe, and anchor on my Class A cover, thereby branding it into every facet of my life. I wanted to be something. I wanted to protect my family. And I wanted to be the best I could to do that. I followed the course and stayed true to that reasoning; I survived, I grew, and I learned from every mistake that I made (for the most part).

Two major things I have learned recently weigh heavily on my heart. The first is that, I realize now, the more time I spent learning and growing in order to protect my loved ones, the more I distanced myself from them. I have felt it for a long time, but have not been specifically able to describe the feeling. I can't identify with those who say they love me. I believe they do love me, some part of me or what I physically embody. But I left home in a Dodge Caravan in August of 2002. And I never came back.

Every time I visited family, it became more and more obvious—I don't fit in. In leaving to protect my family I lost them.

Second was the realization that, although I follow through with the actions that stay true to the ideology that everything I do now is to someday provide and protect a family of my own, ultimately it is a selfish endeavor.

I am constantly seeking validation in myself, engaging in the competition in every way to prove myself to others so they can convince me of my worth. Because I do not believe in it. My chosen path is selfish, and like so many selfish paths, it is lonely.

It has cost me a marriage, and with that my second chance at a family. The result of that cost me a chance at a second honest relationship. I hope desperately that the realization of this will prevent tears from rolling down the cheeks of future loved ones.

I do not know where to go from this point. I feel as if I have gone too far. I don't know any other way; I have no other goals.

I am sorry I am far from the son you drove to the recruiter's office, or the one you kissed good-bye before he invaded foreign lands. I know he won't come back.

This is me. I have left pieces of my heart among the seashells scattered in the sand of MCRD (Marine Corps Recruit Depot) San Diego, across the sands of Iraq, and in the beds of children whom I woke before I stole their father in the dead of night.

Your son now fights himself, realizing that the monster he has become, the monster he intended to keep away—all the while just wanting to be human again, to be somebody's son, somebody's lover, somebody's friend. Most importantly, I want to feel for them as they feel for me.

I'm sorry, Mom. The pieces of my heart that do remain hold strong to the last vestige of hope that there remains in me the boy that is your son. "Little fucker" is strong and battles daily with the monster. I can only hope his resolve is strong and that someday I will have the strength to be the good son you deserve.

—Your son

58

R.S.V.P.

~Lance~

Dear Mom,

I don't know your address now. But I know you'll find your own way to read this.

It's at a time like this that you're with me more than ever. I want to tell you that I'm so glad I didn't have to put you through the same things that Adam's mom has had to go through, although I'm sure I gave you your own fair share of sleepless nights. But you never showed it. You were always there for me: supporting me, guiding me, and raising me to be the man I am today. You were everything and more than a mom needs to be. So, it's only fair that I should try to be the best son I can be—which means I will still need you around.

You'll never be gone, because you're always in my thoughts and my heart.

Thanks Mom.

BOOK II

Finally...

1

MANAS?

E-MAIL FROM ADAM:

Hey,

I have arrived in the former Soviet Union, in a small country. There is a tale of a great hero named Manas who may be able to help you figure out about where I am. I can't do anything with a USB here so if you send me stuff, it may be a bit before I can do anything with it and vice-versa. Here safe and sound, just tired. It was a long flight.

Things I learned on an airplane:

Those little U-shaped pillows are awesome.

When standing to pee—as in shooting—a solid base is essential.

The flight attendant schedules all scheduled meals around when I want to sleep.

—Adam

E-MAIL FROM LANCE:

A,

So glad you made it safely. You are in Kyrgystan, Bishkek, the capital, at the Manas Air Force base. It is a transitional place for guys going to Afghanistan. You are at the northernmost part of the country on the Kazakhstan border. You are north and a little east of Afghanistan, with Tajikhstan in between. East of you a ways is China.

You also said you would call and explain some things. Guess that won't happen. Or will it? That would be good.

Let me know all about where you are. According to Wiki, it's pretty beautiful. Things here are fine. Richie's contract with Harrah's is renewed. I'll check my e-mails every day now so that I can respond to you as quickly as possible. Of course, the ulterior motive is just to hear from you. Tell me everything—food, weather, living space, what you're doing, etc.

Hope to hear from you soon.

—L

E-MAIL FROM ADAM:

Hey,

I figured that would be a fun way for you to figure things out rather than me just telling you.

Good luck to Richie with his contract. Hopefully, Harrah's does what is best for everybody. Not much interesting here as far as living quarters.

—Adam

E-MAIL FROM LANCE:

A,

Nice quick response. Yeah, it was fun finding out where you are. The couple of pictures I saw of Kyrgyzstan made it look pretty scenic. Probably not your base though. If communication is like this at your next base, this isn't so bad. You feeling good? Is your next stop Afgh? And is it your final stop or will you have some trainings and/or debriefings? I think we are 12 hours different in time. So when you call! you'll know. I wish. It's 1:00 P.M. here now, so sweet dreams for you.

    —L

2

THE LAND OF MILK AND HONEY

~Adam~

"Are you fucking kidding me?" I sit on my cot, my laptop warming my knees, and look across the way to see SSG Davis (Staff Sergeant), the senior scout for the Death Dealer platoon to which our sniper team has been attached, standing in blue Jockey underwear. "You look like a gay wrestler. Why would you think that is okay to wear?"

"These are very comfortable and a chick bought them for me."

"Really, dude?" Davis makes his way over to me. Before I realize it, his bulk is leaning over me. Before he realizes it, my sandal is poised to attack those sensitive, poorly covered areas.

"You'll regret it," he says. I slap it gently to let him know I'm serious.

"If you do it again, you'll have a mouth full of dick." His legs close together slightly and he pulls away.

"You think so? You already flinched." We are both grinning at each other. We have a friendly stare-down, and he eventually takes his Jockey-covered ass away from me.

* * *

"Seriously, you are ugly as fuck," Sandy starts in on Finch.

"I am one sexy dude," he responds. "Lots of women find me attractive."

"They only say that to make you feel better. Or, it's like, a comfort factor. They know you are so ugly you won't be able to find another girl." I dive into our favorite team game.

"That doesn't make any sense," he tries to fight back.

"Really. Your face is fucked up. Your teeth are pointed inward and remind me of something I saw at the Shark Reef." Inside, I'm laughing as I tear into him. "Your head is shaped like a block, and your ears are disgusting."

"Hey. These ears were a rite of passage. It shows I'm a warrior." He inserts a legitimate argument about his wrestling experience and the resulting cauliflower ears.

"They are nasty, and your head is shaped like a block. Not to mention you're a nasty ginger."

"Hey, I look good, and these scars are from battle."

"I'm not concerned about the scars. But you can't blame your scars for not being able to turn your head." Sandy laughs. He loves it when we rip on Finch.

"You..." He tries to argue and makes an attempt to turn his head, but fails to reach any normal range of motion.

"Your head looks like a fucking pug."

He is starting to turn bright red.

"Seriously dude, you look like a dog." Sandy dives back into the little game. We are both laughing. Finch is trying to keep his sense of humor.

"Dogs can't look up," I say. We are starting to lose it.

"The back of your head looks like hot dogs stacked," Sandy throws in a zinger.

"That's fucked up. It does not."

Finch is not enjoying this.

We start really laughing.

"No, it does dude." Sandy tries to be serious. I nod my head in agreement.

"You know what?" He always does this. "I am a Staff Sergeant and I'm not going to put up with this shit."

"Really, Finch?" Sandy plays into him even more.

"HEY! That is Staff Sergeant." I'm trying to hold it together, so is Konrad behind me. He is just trying not to get wrapped into any of this, but knows it is funny.

"Really? Dude, I think we broke him," Sandy says, looking over at me, a big toothy grin.

Finch jumps up from his cot.

Dives over Sandy's.

Now he is positioned between us.

He begins to punch our legs.

Now we are laughing hysterically.

"Dude, seven and a half hours. It only took us seven and a half hours to break him." Sandy is curled up in his sleeping bag, laughing and dodging blows.

"I'm just going to have to come up with clever working parties for the two of you," Finch says quietly.

We really hurt his feelings.

The laughter continues.

* * *

"Konrad, bring me your M4," Finch yells across Sandy, who is trying to sleep along with me.

"Okay." He grabs his weapon and brings it over to Finch, who begins his inspection.

"So. Why is this covered in 'Hello Kitty' stickers?"

"It's funny. But if you want me to take them off, Sergeant, I will." The two of them have a brief quiet moment.

"I'll pick which ones stay."

I smile to myself as Finch critiques the placement and choice of each sticker in relation to function and form, as well as the idea of locations that will heat up and those that are in the way of proper maintenance.

It really is too late. The pictures are already on his Facebook.

* * *

The morning comes.

0430.

Why is the sun out?

I already hate this place.

We begin the day an hour before even reasonable. The day is filled with briefs and some quick in-country training as we watch the sun move across the sky. We wait for it to dip behind the mountains surrounding the base, reminding many of us of the Vegas valley.

Lunchtime brings us into the local dining facility. Odie and I find seats next to some Airmen in PTs, who are mildly annoyed at me getting in and out of my seat and banging my weapons against theirs whenever I pass.

As I shove ravioli, chicken wings, French fries, a mini pizza, and a chicken breast into my mouth, I notice my compatriot across from me. Lost in thought, Odie stares blankly into the packed dining facility. His lips are moving, but nothing is audible—not surprising over the noise of people talking. His right hand is clenching and unclenching. I stare until he snaps out of it.

"You ready?" I ask.

"Yes."

I start to grab my things. "Excuse me, folks. I'm not banging my weapons into you on purpose." I make my way through the rows of Airmen, who do look pissed both at my comment and because I am actually hitting them as I pass.

Outside the chow hall Odie starts, "I would kill myself if I lived here."

"Because it is so awesome?"

"Yes. There is no way I could come back from a mission and sit in there."

"It is like a high school cafeteria," I say as a pretty little thing in an Air Force uniform passes the two of us. She catches Odie's eye as well.

"This is ridiculous. This doesn't feel like a war. I couldn't deal with the changes in mindset." His head follows another very pretty girl across the street.

We continue to make our way to some classroom for afternoon briefings.

"I want to stay here. This is the land of milk and honey," I tell him, but my attention is following a sexy little captain as she passes.

Thank you, dark sunglasses.

* * *

Davis just showed me a picture he took of a pocket pussy lying against Sandy's sleeping head. Turns out his lips and the lips around his little sex toy look very similar.

3

I SMASHED THE HOUR GLASS AND ALL I GOT WAS MORE SAND

~Adam~

We have been billeted in giant tents far away from the main part of base. So, we have to catch a bus to get to the main part of base. It isn't a very long walk, if we were to walk straight there. However, the uncleared minefield that lies in the center of base makes us second think taking that shortcut. [Lance: Minefield? Nice.] We walk to the bus stop. And, apparently, so does everybody else. The bus is a little late, and the crowd trying to fit onto the thirty-man bus is about a hundred strong.

We decide to catch it at another stop, maybe earlier along the route. So, we walk. In the morning we stroll through the unnecessary desert heat along a fence with poppy plants growing through it. We finally find another stop, catch an empty bus to the stop we were supposed to use, let the bus fill up, and head to mainside.

The kids run to the edge of the fence. They come out of all the ruined buildings and cross the field. They scream at our bus as we pass, trying to stick their little hands through the fence that separates the base from the real part of Afghanistan.

Finally, we arrive.

* * *

E-MAIL FROM LANCE:

Hey A

It's 10 p.m. here. I got laid off today. They had cut backs at The Venetian and I'm gone. I'm going to go talk to Lisa, my boss, tomorrow. Maybe there's something else. FUCK!

I'll keep you posted on my job. I'll know more tomorrow. But hey, things work out for the best.

I'll get unemployment at least. I think it's $374 a week. Better than nothing. I have a "Three Waiters" gig on the 14th, too, here in Vegas.

Clint and Ed say hi. I have your car now. Ed told me Grant said if I didn't take it he would leave it in a parking lot somewhere. It is here safe and sound. I did not stall it once! You could have at least left a full tank. Just kidding. But it will be fine here. I'll periodically start it so it doesn't rot or whatever.

Is it a 12 hour difference between us?

Sounds like you're fine. I'm glad.

I will ttyl.

—L

E-MAIL FROM ADAM:

Hey

Wow, that sucks. I'm sorry.

Sounds like a lot of people are hurting on jobs. I am in an area that gets a lot of news, so I have been following all that. Keep me posted on what is up. I'm in Afghanistan now. Nothing crazy here.

—Adam

* * *

Bagram Air Force base is blessed with a massive shopping center, more amenities than are necessary. I try to make my way out as quickly as possible, but generally the people I'm with have different ideas. It doesn't really matter. If I'm not shopping, I'm sitting in my tent watching movies or reading.

Just waiting for the bird out.

Just waiting.

No bird in sight.

I upload my latest updates onto my external hard drive and take it down to the Internet center.

* * *

E-MAIL FROM ADAM:

Hey

Good luck on the job search. Still in Bagram right now. Nothing crazy. I will be here for a few days. I'll check out your bro's book. Internet time is sparse.

—Adam

E-MAIL FROM LANCE:

A

Just felt like sending you a pic. Speaking of that, when my boss packed up my things for me she said that she even packed the picture of me all mud-covered. It was you of course, but I appreciated the compliment. Thought you would like to know that. (It must have been the sunglasses.) I have a job interview Monday at Citicenter. It could be cool. I've applied also at The Venetian, Rio, and M... so far. Hope you are well.

—L

E-MAIL FROM ADAM:

Hey

Moving out again tomorrow, new place, not sure the details. Let me know how things go. Good luck on the job search.

—Adam

* * *

Jalalabad is no different.

Eat.

Read.

Watch a movie.

Eat.

Read—maybe another movie.

Eat.

Jump on the Internet.

Read.

Sleep.

Repeat.

4

FUN WITH VEHICLE ROLL-OVERS AND ENERGY DRINKS

~Adam~

The morning was a flurry of motion. Moving packs and bodies onto birds to make our way to Najil, far from the Land of Milk and Honey. COP Najil is one of the most remote Combat Outposts in eastern Afghanistan and quite different from Jalalabad or Bagram. The move happened too fast to send out one last e-mail.

Fuck it.

I was just glad to get out of there.

We watched out the window of the small contractor-run helicopters. My window seat granted me an aerial view of the base, then the outlying village. Beautiful green farms spread out from the large river that flowed through the center, suddenly turning brown at the base of the mountains. We flew over the dry mountains and wound around until we touched down on the gravel landing pad.

Sandy greeted us and directed me to my temporary bed.

Before I knew it, I was helping out at the Death Star, a remote location within the confines of the base, set high above on a hilltop that is able to overlook the entire valley and with the weapons to cover it. Konrad and I found a spot to guard and watched over our new home. Before the moon was at the top of the sky, we were welcomed by the local Taliban with a quick rocket attack. We thanked them with mortars, a hellfire attack, and a small artillery barrage.

We barely slept that night.

We were both excited to be finally in the middle of it. Not waiting. Not training. But fighting.

* * *

The sniper mission for now has been canceled. Not for lack of purpose. We could cause some significant damage/good in this region—butBrigade has put out guidance that requires us to have a certain amount of people, minimum, every time we leave The Wire. And four is not enough.

Finch is unhappy that he has become a squad leader— something he still refuses to accept. I am with Davis now as his medic. I can do Line Medic. I just want to work.

* * *

"We are on mission tonight," Finch told me.

"Really?"

"Yeah. Somebody rolled an MRAP into a valley and we need to stand security until it is recovered."

"Really? How do they plan to do that?"

"Well, they plan to blow it up. The crane they tried to pull it out with fell on top of it."

"All right. What time?"

Before I had a chance to sleep, I was on a HMMWV. Soon, I was posted on a single-lane dirt road, with farms stretching up the mountain on one side and a drop-off to more farms leading down to a dry riverbed. In a valley to my left lay this MRAP, the solution to the IED problem in the War On Terror that I am more afraid of than the IEDs they are supposed to protect me from.

Every time one of them rolls over, someone gets hurt, I was told.

They are giant, heavy, and difficult to drive. They roll over a lot, and these roads are not forgiving.

Most of the locals drive motorcycles or walk.

The sun rose in the valley with no incident, despite all our predictions. Six firefights in thirty-six hours before we got here—now, nothing.

We are relieved in mid-morning.

Refit.

Take a quick nap.

Get the quick brief.

Head out again.

Lather.

Rinse.

Repeat.

For four days.

I haven't had that little sleep in a long time. Finally, they got it out—in pieces, some on the back of a truck, some blown all over the valley by our explosives gurus.

Then, they got another truck stuck. At last, we were done and I could relax a bit. I sent out some e-mails, went to the Aid Station to say hi to everybody, and ended up falling asleep on one of the litters.

* * *

"Dude, did you hear about the naked kid?" I asked Joey.

"No." He was laughing. "What naked kid?"

"Okay, this is how I know we can't beat these people. I'm sitting by this house and the guy manning the gun yells to me, "Look at that naked kid.""

Sure enough, there is a kid, who has probably been walking only for a few months, completely naked walking up a very steep hill. No shoes. Butt-ass-fucking naked, this kid is out. He then walks past us. I even said, "Hi" to him, and he seemed excited to see me. Then he went inside and came out still naked.

The next day he is spotted by Odie and Sam as they are helping a different kid with his fucked up feet. They saw naked kid—still naked—sitting on the ground outside. Gravel and sand everywhere, this kid was dragging his ass on the ground—like a dog wiping its ass."

"So, this kid is scraping his nuts on the ground?"

"Yeah. How are we supposed to fight these people? They are born bad-asses."

"I'm going to call my wife and have her start having my son do that."

"Davis came up and started asking the interpreter I was hanging out with and talking to the locals. He was bugging out because he wanted to know about this guy we may or may not have talked to. Apparently, this dude gave him the look of a warrior as he passed."

"Okay. What does that have to do with anything?" Joey asked.

"Dude, in sixteen years some American is going to get the "Eye of the Tiger" from this kid as he walks past, and he is going to think he can kick his ass. And he will be wrong. How do you fight someone who at two-years old was dragging his fucking nuts on the ground?"

"What the fuck?"

"I need to find a local girl to marry and bear me superhuman children. Plus, I have heard they aren't allowed to leave their husbands. So once she marries me, she has to put up with my bullshit," I said.

"You sure have an affinity for a variety of women, for a guy with an Iron Cross tatted on his chest."

,

Click here for links to photos and/or videos

5

BOOTS ON GROUND

~Adam~

We awoke with the sun—much to my chagrin. And in proper Army fashion, I was dragged out of bed about thirty minutes before it was necessary. I made the best of it. I enjoyed a quick breakfast, consisting of what we could find in boxes left in the chow hall by the still sleeping cooks. Sandy and Finch kept me company as we complained about the coming mission.

Our first foot patrol.

With minimum drama, we exited the gate. My platoon spread itself along the road. I fell in with Davis' team/squad in the front as we made our way toward the first hill of the day. Harris and Coach, two local dogs, circled the formation with the kind of enthusiasm that only dogs have when they are allowed to do what they feel is their job. Harris was adopted by the unit we just relieved. He is a medium-sized, golden retriever-looking dog. Coach is about the same size, but she is such a mixed breed that mutt is the only word that seems acceptable. Her dark body and lighter gray ears followed Harris as they circled the patrol and ran ahead as scouts.

We made our way up and down the hills. Mostly up. But it does hurt more to go down. We traveled along the river, along small, dirt walls designed to hold water for the fields that we skirted as we moved from rally point to rally point.

I greeted the locals as I passed, receiving responses that mostly were confusion, but there were enough people who seemed genuinely happy to be exchanging something as simple as a greeting with me. The children were my favorite.

* * *

"Fenner, take the eleven o'clock," Davis shouted to me as we moved into the latest rally point.

"Roger," I responded, trudging my way through the newly planted corn and making my way around the strategically placed boulders.

I found a high wall to lean on with corn directly in front of me to distort the view of me up to my chest. I took off my pack, threw it on the wall, and leaned on it.

After a piss, enough time passed for me to catch my breath. A pair of brothers made their way to a watering hole about ten feet in front of me. The oldest of the two was no more than eight or nine. The younger was about four and wore the traditional pants and shirt that are loose fitting and never seem to fit. The fabric was a dark green that didn't appear to have been washed any time recently. And he wouldn't stop staring at me.

"Salaam," I said to him. My right hand lifted off the pistol grip and held it up to him. I then, in the formal greeting fashion, attempted to place it over my heart. My rifle was in the way.

The kid smiled and went back to watching his brother, while frequently staring at me.

Before long, the oldest was done and needed to move on.

As the two of them walked away, the younger one left his brother's side and wound his way through the crops until he was standing on the wall in front of me.

I held out my hand.

He shook it and smiled.

"Wa asalaama a laykum," I said to him.

"Laykum asalaam," he responded quietly and released my hand. He was unsure where to go from there. He slowly made his way back to his brother.

"Da Khoday pa aman," I said after him.

He smiled and ran to his brother.

"Take that Hamas," I said to Baltasar next to me. Baltasar's round Mexican features brightened. He wasn't originally part of our unit, but pulled in from the IRR after his active duty time was up. He has proven to be a constant source of motivation, despite not volunteering for this mission.

* * *

The patrol continued without any major incident. Harris defended the patrol from a pack of stray dogs, then found a chicken in the market and killed it, while both the patrol and the owner screamed.

We made it back, beat after enough hours to get a feel for the local area. Joey welcomed us at the gate with cold water. He checked on our possible heat injuries, and we headed up the hill into base, the last hill of the patrol.

Click here for link to photos and/or video

6

HOT ON THE TRAIL

~Lance~

E-MAIL FROM LANCE:

Hey A,

My bloodhound, dogged determination, and a little luck paid off. I know a lot about you now, where you are exactly, and have seen video and pictures of your outpost—the most remote in Afghanistan. What were you thinking? I found a website showing the guys from Illinois that you replaced. I've seen a video of the base and even pix of the doggies. So, you can't keep anything hidden from me. It certainly seems non-four-star. I know that you have outhouses and no running water. [Adam: So much for operational security. Do you know what my next mission is? Or where the IEDs are hiding?] You clean your hands with Purell. You have a new kitchen-type facility, one air-conditioned building, and you get mortared and rocketed! Often. You deter the Taliban insurgents, drugs, weapons, and timber smugglers, by being there, so they have to seek alternate routes. It's a half-hour walk to Little Round Top, a strategic viewing site. You have some Afghani soldiers on your base, one especial man is a valuable, former, aging mujahidin. (Do you use your Pashto now at camp?) Three soldiers were killed recently from a roadside bomb there, when they ran over it in jeep. It's three hours to the nearest reinforcements. (Nice.) You can't wash your clothes. How do you wash you? You must be starting to smell nice.

And I believe you practiced mortar firing with the outgoing soldiers when you first got there.

What's the temperature like? [Adam: It is hot, but not bad.] Is it humid? [Adam: We are right by a river, but it isn't bad.]

Do I have all this right? [Adam: For the most part. I haven't practiced mortar fire, just got to hear and watch it. I wash my clothes in a bucket and hang them out to dry. The two bucket method is the best, one to wash, one to rinse. I talk a little Pashto, but I am focusing on my medical studies. There are showers, but only two for the whole base, so we just don't use them very often.] Talk about wanting to know what you're doing. Now I know. Let me know any other camp details. It's really kind of fascinating.

I read your new stuff. The interaction with the kids was good. It made me a little wary as I was reading it, thinking the kids might do something. Thank God they didn't. But it was interesting.

Exactly how much mortar fire have you had so far? [Adam: Nothing crazy, incoming fire, a lot of outgoing though.] Any rockets? [Adam: Some rockets, nothing effective.]

Are you feeling okay? [Adam: I'm good. I wouldn't want to be anywhere else doing anything different.] Sleeping okay? [Adam: I sleep, sometimes a lot, sometimes not at all.] Eating okay? [Adam: Eating is a sore subject. The base is about a day or two from running out of hot chow and about three days from re-supply—so I will be getting cranky soon. Otherwise, chow is good.] You sound fine, so I'm not worried. At least you have Internet! I am assuming this is your permanent spot, as lush and inviting as it is.

Watched Pineapple Express. One of the worst movies I've seen for awhile. Pretty boring and not funny at all—even with James Franco! (Who looked like shit, probably how he looks all the time without make-up.) His acting was good though.

I guess I'll sign off for now. Let me know if I got everything right. TTYL

—L

7

THE NAJ

~Adam~

Every morning the sun rises behind the Death Star, a massive, poorly constructed, concrete square structure with four towers and eight gun mounts facing in every direction, forming a veritable star of death with its firepower.

Death Star sits about 800 feet above the rest of COP Najil (Combat Outpost). The drive down is treacherous and poor driving has cost lives.

The run up is worse.

The road runs back and forth down the hillside past the ANA outpost and the Mortar pit before arriving in the main area that is COP Najil.

From the mortar pit, the road continues to wind down. Roads begin to diverge, a small path leads just below the mortar pit toward the water tanks supplying our four-shower-head bathroom with over-bleached water. Further down, and directly in front of the small mosque that looks more like a wooden rail car with a speaker on top, the road splits. It is the only Afghan building with a clean floor. Turning south leads directly under the water tank past the urinoil, a clever contraption made of a fifty-gallon tank filled with oil and urine that drains into the ground. Utilizing the chemical properties of oil being lighter than urine, the urine settles to the bottom where it drains into the ground while the oil stays on top reducing the odor and spread of disease.

[Lance: I love travelogues. So interesting and informative. Make your reservations early!]

The path continues past third platoon—Hustler's area. Hesco barriers, the foundation of almost all base security, line the west side facing the valley. Hesco barriers are a simple fold-out wall made of metal netting and a cloth liner to trap dirt within. They come in a variety of sizes and are an easy way to build a solid wall to protect against whatever the enemy may throw at us. They are easy to use, just unfold them and fill them up. And in a variety of sizes they are a great asset to base defense. [Lance: Sounds great. I should get a few for the house. Is there a discount for buying in bulk? Does IKEA sell them?]

The cliff is to the east. These wooden huts lead directly toward the showers and another urinoil that I have had attempted to close off due to excessive use, poor drainage, and the obvious consequences thereof.

Again the road forks. Down the hill, to the west, is the chow hall. To the east, and back uphill are the shitters—hiding behind Hesco barriers and where we sit in the agony caused by chow hall, hoping for a single day reprieve from mud-butt. Past the shitters on the left, behind more Hescos, is second platoon—Death Dealer's hooches—two buildings built into the incline, each building propped up on supports to maintain an even floor level.

Inside the first building, the NCOs (Noncommissioned Officers) live. I have a bunk near the back. Make-shift shelves and desks line the walls. Everyone has figured out different ways to organize all of our shit into our little areas, using ammo boxes and random pieces of salvaged wood, which we have used to build shelves and personalize our living areas the best we can. The floors are dirty plywood, with some spots covered with rugs that we purchased in the bazaar. Atop the mattresses, we have found different ways to stay warm at night. I stay in my sleeping bag. The rest of the guys have sheets or the classic poncho-liners to keep warm. And to help them to feel more at home.

This is where we cool off and relax. Sandy and Finch are generally in their bunks. We joke around, calling them, "The laziest sniper team in the Army." When Davis isn't running around, he can be found in his bunk reading, wearing only his Jockeys. Wills quietly sits at his bunk next to the door, watching movies. SSG Deutch, our resident giant—the pinnacle of German engineering as he would put it; Gossamer as Sandy calls him—referencing the red-headed monster in "Chucks," enjoys watching his Discovery channel complete-box-set or "Reno 911," which he got from one of the Haji shops. SGT Clemente, another former Marine, sits by the door generally to be found playing one of his handheld video games. Our barracks are comfortable and pleasant. Being older and of more established ranks, things remain civil compared to the kids' barracks.

Cheap Times, a small building on stilts to avoid the water rushing underneath it during heavy rainfall, sits to the south of the barracks, where SFC Mendoza likes to sit and watch his movies and do film edits, a hobby of his and also his major in college. Otherwise, we use it as our platoon CP (Command Post). We have filled every corner with ammo, crew-served weapons, and comm gear. The walls are covered with platoon manning, vehicle distribution charts, and maps of the local area.

Outside, we have filled every possible nook available. As to our vehicles, the hillside doesn't offer much in the way of good parking, so we create and finagle.

Back to the Mosque.

The north leads through the ANA's living area. Randomly placed Hesco buildings, Hesco walls with a roof covered in sandbags, are scattered all along the hillside, affording them their individual areas to sleep and drink tea. The hill winds down toward the main 'ish road. To the west is the ECP. To the south, the rest of the base. South, toward the Chow hall is a large concrete building with a few moderately sized rooms—one would find the graveyard on the right, just in front of Taj's shop, the local Godfather. (A remnant of the Russian presence. A mass grave, as the story goes. The Russians lost one soldier while performing some sort of operations. They then went into the villages and killed six hundred locals. According to the local who told us the story, his father was buried here—alive.)

To the east is where the Marines live, who supervise and train ANA. Past the Graveyard is the flight line—an open, gravel area for the helicopters to land and drop off the supplies that convoys have found too difficult to drive to us. Still on the main drag, above the flight line, in what looks like a shanty town, is where the LNs (Local Nationals) who live on base, live along with some of the interpreters. I like to jog through. Mohammed (and the other Mohammeds) used to wave and say, "How are you doing, sir?" before his employer lowered his pay and he went back to his wife in Pakistan. They all are friendly and love to hang out under the wooden overhang on the wooden platform, where they lay their sleeping mats, drink tea, and pick on the painter for having three wives. (Two he left in Pakistan; one he acquired while here.)

Tucked into a small almost imperceptible hole is the Aid Station: built into the cliff, surrounded by Hescos, and covered in cami netting—designed to break up the outline of a structure or vehicle and offer shade—and sand bags. The Aid Station is just south of the flight line. This is the lowest point of the base, where soldiers actually sleep. This means they have some flooding issues and attract the most interesting wildlife. The rodents we expect. The cobra that feeds on them, they should have.

Following the uneven stone steps east up from the Aid Station is the MWR (Military Welfare and Readiness) where the computers and phones are. It is also where Coach likes to sleep. Several barracks are lined up to the south of the MWR, where different random units reside.

Between the MWR and the medic station, again on the main drag, is where the chow hall likes to store extra supplies, in a small open area in front of the building that is the chow hall. It is the only non-wooden, non-Hesco structure on the base and is separated into several rooms: the storage area for chow, the chow hall itself, the gym, and a small room for different visitors to sleep (north to south, respectively). The doors face west, toward the town of Dumlam on the other side of the valley. The west side of the building is a small alley created by the cliff and the building's back wall. A five-foot drop from the chow hall is ground level and the Mobile Kitchen Thing, where our one or two meals a day are prepared. The rest of our food is gathered through foraging. (Because MREs—Meal Ready to Eat—are not what they used to be.)

On the other side of the building is more billeting, made from Hescos and sand bags.

When I start on the flight line and jog south, I pass the Aid Station on the left, another shitter, and a urinoil. I pass through a small area cliff on the left and drop-off on the right. Just underneath Punisher Tower—a fortified position for observing the valley—the road curves eastward. After a good rain, the sand is thick and pleasant for running. If the rain has been absent for a while, it becomes soft and billowy. We call it moon dust. It doesn't take long before, once again, the road splits—left up the hill toward the Dealer barracks or south toward the Range.

I head south. The mechanics are on the left side. The right side is the motor pool/vehicle graveyard, where vehicles sit in various stages of maintenance. (This is about where Davis and I were jogging with our kits to test their durability and decided to stop, adjust, and fart. It is the only time I have had to walk away from someone in the open air. The chow out here does special things to our guts.) [Lance: Sign up now!] To the south of the motor pool is more ANA billeting; their Hesco buildings surround their volleyball court. On the other side of the road and east up another switchback uphill is another area for the ANA to stay.

The road ends at the range. The range is nothing more than an open space with some boards staked in front of a berm. But it serves its purpose well. We like to come out here regularly and shoot, ensuring that our skills stay sharp. The ANA always watch, waiting for us to leave our brass behind. This they gather and sell off out in town.

The range is the turnaround point. Again, heading north, the trail leads past the mechanics and toward the barracks. Before turning right, heading up back toward the barracks, is the parking area/shit burning pit: where the kids who burn the remnants of our evacuated bowels take the buckets, consolidate it all into one bucket, douse it with diesel, and leave it to burn. And where Davis and Deutch park their MRAPs.

Turning right again, there are more options: straight up to the east and the Dealer barracks, right and north to the Hustler area, or staying almost straight and run above the MWR back through the LNs area and then back to the north side of the flight line, just before the graveyard.

Make a left and start the track again. It takes about six minutes to complete the whole route. It isn't a very long route, but ultimately the COP is very small.

Assigned to COP Najil are a variety of different units. The active-duty brigade that we have been attached to has provided us with our mechanics and chow hall personnel. The Cav makes up the two maneuver platoons—Death Dealers and Hustlers—named in homage to our Vegas roots. The mortars are all Cav, as well as the staff and comm guys. There is a small contingent of Marines with the ANA. There are about an equal number of ANA as there are soldiers on the Cop. We also have some CA (Civil Affairs) elements of the PRT (Provincial Reconstruction Team) up with our ADT guys.

The concertina wire, a slinky-like barbed wire designed to snag clothing and slow movement through it, is relatively effective at keeping the local human population out, but the non-bipedal residents of Afghanistan are significantly less impressed by the wire—which many ASG have demonstrated to us to be nothing more than a minor obstacle. The giant porcupine roams in the back of the Death Star and has only been seen through thermal optics. The bobcat/cougar/puma, or whatever the fuck, has made several appearances also at the Death Star. At one point it was only a foot away from Davis' head while he slept, that was, until Baltasar scared the cat away, but not before it scared Davis awake, of course. [Lance: I'm thinking that maybe you should teach a course on how to make perilous, life-threatening situations fun and amusing for everyone.]

The kids have been known to capture the smaller wildlife and bring them to us in various containers. Like: The hedgehog in an ammo can. The spiked lizard on a string. A camel spider in a sliced-open protein powder container. And the viper, that they, thankfully, only contained and left outside. These have all been little attention grabbers for us. The mice have been a problem, but really only bother us in waves. The traps helped out a lot. There is a feral cat that has been found wandering, but more frequently we have found what he leaves behind after he is done thrashing around in the chow that the cooks leave out for those of us who eat late.

The dogs are a completely different element. There are the COP dogs that seem to be shrinking in numbers, and the wild dogs. We took a pretty good chunk out of the wild dog population when the "girls" were in heat—attracting every male for miles around in packs, causing a great number of problems. Santana, the small, dark brindle puppy, is growing every day and shows how spoiled she is more and more. One hundred "daddies," who only want to play, don't promote good discipline. Coach and Skitz spend their days either resting or trying to keep Harris out of trouble. This is a full time job for the girls.

The COP has an unusual life of its own. During the day, there is always entertainment: with the birds coming and going, mortars firing, the range being active, the children and locals so close that we can hear them laughing and talking, and everybody going about their business. At night, there is no visible light, except: the slivers coming from under the doors, the red lens headlamps walking all around, and the moon, which can easily light one's path, as well as the sun, with a pale blue light. The only sounds that can be heard is the hum of the generators and the new people falling, because they haven't learned all the subtle nuances of the individual footpaths snaking around COP Najil.

This is home, until the Cav decides to put our boots back on ground in Sin City.

Or I get hurt.

Whichever comes first. [Lance: Must you?] [Adam: In for a penny.] [Lance: Do you have to throw my own phrases back at me?]

Click here for link to photos and/or video

8

THE VALLEY

~Adam~

The outside world is relatively simple. Down the hill and out the gate is the main road, which the local government is making great improvements to widen and flatten out. On the road facing west is Dumlam. Behind it is the cell tower and a valley that leads into areas like Dowlat Sha, and other places I want to go visit like, Bumbi (because I like the name). To the north east is Parmawan, an hour's walk along the road, with the cliff to the right and the farms to the left. On the opposite side of the valley, to the northwest, is Gomrai. I found the woman of my dreams in a large home with green windows on the southwest side of town. She always wears bright colors, and I got to see her face. She looked pretty good through twelve-power self-stabilizing binos, too. [Lance: I'm guessing any woman would look good at this point.]

Behind Gomrai, starting from Dumlam and running west to east, is the North Ridge. Behind the ridge are some serious mountains that we have not had the pleasure of walking all the way into... yet. The locals like to take picnics and graze their cattle up on the ridge and in various areas of green along the mountain face. We like to test fire our crew-served weapons and mortars there as well. (We make sure there is nobody there at the time.) [Lance: How considerate.]

The valley is in the shape of a Y. The northern branch heads toward Dowlat Sha. The eastern branch heads past Parmawan, Khanday, and further toward Tili (where they decided to kick the Taliban out on their own. Rule one in Afghanistan: Don't piss off the locals.). The southern branch leads through the Najil bazaar, with the Jesus tree stands defiantly on the opposite side of the valley on the side of the cliff just west of Dumlam.

Past the Bazaar is the town of Najil. Past that is the Jaboom checkpoint, where the ANA and ANP have a small fortress made of Hescos. Further south is Watangatu. Watangatu is unremarkable, aside from the repeated missions out there, where I don't get to do anything but walk around the trucks. However, across the valley to the west, through a crack in the mountains, Clemente and I spotted a village way up there. The map says its name is Sigit. We want to go there, but have so far been repeatedly denied. From what we have been reading about how the Taliban operates, that is the type of area where they would like to live—and with the attacks that happen around Watangatu, it seems completely possible that Sigit is the place to go.

The valleys themselves are filled with farm fields—almost all corn, but there are the occasional marijuana plants (that haven't budded yet). The corn itself is meager, giant stalks with very small cobs of corn, in contrast to the massive ones found in America and more developed countries. They don't plant in rows, but instead by covering the ground area with seeds. The result is plants that don't get the required nutrients. Everything is harvested by hand, and everything is used: the stalks and leaves for their livestock, and the cobs for their own consumption. All around the valley, on the roofs of houses, can be seen cobs of corn lying out on rooftops, drying in the sun, while birds sneak bites before someone notices and scares them away. The locals don't seem to understand this, but they are being educated on more advanced farming methods by the ADT (Agricultural Development Team) that works with us.

Farms feed off the river that had long ago cut these valleys into the thick mountains that surround us in all directions. The locals have made excellent use of any area they can. Where the ground is not flat, they make it so, forming relatively disorganized steps of crops all over the area that have made patrolling through the valley interesting at the very least.

The fields themselves are not owned by those who work them, but by wealthy land owners in Kabul and other major cities. They have created a business relationship with those laborers, offering portions of the crop to the workers, while taking the majority for themselves.

The river, depending on the rain, varies in level. We all agree that it is still not to be messed with, making movement across difficult. The water is cold and runs fast. There is, however, a bridge/giant log just past Dumlam and further to the north that is an actual, finished concrete bridge.

When the rains come, the swell in the water level and the wash brought down from the mountains always brings the locals out the morning after. They run around the rocks and fight each other for driftwood that has washed ashore. There are not a lot of trees in the region, so wood is a valuable commodity.

The locals here are an unusually hardy people. It starts from when the children are playing in the mountains, running barefoot from rock to rock and in the scattered stones above and around the villages. The girls start working hard at a young age, tending the fields and livestock. The men out here, I have been told, are uneducated and lazy. The women do all the manual labor. They perform almost inhuman feats of strength and endurance, climbing to the tops of ridges to gather grasses or husks of corn to bring home to feed their livestock.

The men pick up a trade: selling their various goods in the bazaar, making or shining shoes, fixing cars, and also tailoring clothes.

I have found it funny that the cell phone salesmen are still young males who dress unusually well and have an air of superiority about them as they sit, feet propped up on their glass display cases, while they stare at their own phones, texting with whomever. It reminds me of the malls in America.

The girls are still shy out here. Many like to watch until they are noticed, or the camera, which I always have out, moves toward them. I can tell they are as curious as the boys are about us, but tradition doesn't allow them to pursue that interest as the males are allowed. They resolve to watch from a distance, peeking through windows, around corners, or through their face wraps.

The adult females won't even look at us. They turn their heads or just walk away. If they happen to be walking in the opposite direction to us, they will actually get off the road to avoid us. Their faces are almost always hidden under burqas or wrapped up in scarves. Those women who are not afraid to reveal their faces are well past the point of unattractive. Time does not treat these women well. The women of marrying age, who are attractive, we assume, are hoarded away for fear that we will steal them.

The males are not shy—the boys walking up, demanding pens and getting mad when they are denied. They need them for school, but I don't like their attitudes. The men are all different. Some come up and shake our hands. One old man who was eye level with my chest, (I am below average height, something Angela thought was very funny.) his beard thick and white and his teeth rotted through, took my hand and wouldn't let it go while he cheerfully talked my ear off and shook my hand. It felt like he was thanking me for deeds I had not done.

Others are stand-off 'ish, barely casting a look our way. The majority simply smile and wave. Something very important that we have learned is that they are always watching us. In every way, they see how we deal with each other and them. They act accordingly toward us. It makes life interesting and keeps us on our toes.

They like to ask us questions about every piece of our gear. My scissors and tape are of particular curiosity. I don't know if it is because the school-age children have learned that word in English and they are excited to use it, or because it alludes to my profession. But it does start conversations, at the very least. They are always interested when I tell them that I am a doctor. They don't have a word for medic or an understanding that I am not as well trained as they think. So, doctor is what I have to call myself.

The camera is another piece of curiosity. Some are very against the idea of it. Others think it is a very good time. I take pictures of the people and show them. The kids like to strike poses for me, leaning up against poles looking tough. And the moment the picture is taken and I am showing them, they are smiling from ear to ear.

It isn't specifically children, however.

Some of the older gentlemen enjoy the camera as well. They smile and joke while I photograph them and their friends. It is my way in the town of breaking the ice and hanging out with the locals. I can't speak to them very well, aside from the basic kindergarten conversations, partly because my Pashto is not as good as it should be, and because, in this valley alone, the locals speak Dari, Pashto, and Pashaye. I can't keep up with that. So, I just enjoy some non-verbal communication.

This is beautiful country, and by one patrol at a time, we get to see it. Every time Wills, Clemente, or Davis, and I go out in our little Ops, we push the limit, [Lance: Of course you do. Thank God, I can't grow gray hair.] [Adam: No comment.] daring each other further than we should go, deeper and higher into the mountains than it feels like soldiers have gone before. But it is this attitude that stretches out our influence and sends a powerful message to the Taliban. "We aren't afraid of your mountains; we won't let you own the high ground."

I don't dislike anything about the area. The people are generally friendly, and even more important, life is simple out here.

9

ICE CREAM PARTIES, POOP PATROLS, AND EVERYTHING IN BETWEEN

~Adam~

"I don't know what they are stacking. The fucking things are cold," Davis screams into the radio, obviously having passed the point of frustration about three minutes before I climbed the stairs into Little Round Top. I had been keeping busy with the move from the old fortified position from the previous unit to the Death Star and seemed to have missed some of the excitement.

"Roger. Stand by. We need Authorization from Battalion," the voice over the radio responded.

"So, what is up?" I ask.

"Fucking, I see thirty guys who are unloading vehicles and stacking shit into caves and other places. I want to shoot one Illum round over their heads to let them know we are watching and to see them scatter like fucking roaches. Make them think for a change. You know?" he tells me.

"Sounds reasonable enough," I respond.

We talk about the situation for a bit, every once in a while marveling at the massive optic we are using to see the enemy's activities from so far away.

About five or ten minutes pass before the radio squawks back to life. Jessie's voice on the other end says, "They want to know how many are there and what they are stacking."

"Alameda," Davis calls to Alameda, the young Hawaiian who is manning the Eye in the Sky.

"Yes, Sergeant?" His voice is soft to begin with, but it is barely audible over the roar of the generator.

"How many are there?"

"Umm." He sticks his face into the massive box and soon comes out with an answer. "Thirty."

"Can you tell what they are moving?"

"No, Sergeant. Just cold cylindrical objects."

Davis gets back on the radio and reports everything back up. About fifteen minutes have passed.

"Sergeant?" Sam asks.

"What?"

"Ten left, and about ten are having a meeting. It looks like they are done stacking stuff."

"So, how many are left?"

"Twenty are left." The sound of the generator fills the air.

Davis reports the changes to Punisher Base, the call sign for Najil's command post: twenty left and ten having a meeting.

In my head something sounds wrong. I attempt to clarify the information between the two of them.

After a lot of discussion and some semantics, we come to the conclusion that there are twenty people left on that hill.

"But how do we fix this?" Davis asks me as we brainstorm different ideas on how to correct the mistake without sounding stupid.

"How about you say ten came back?" I offer.

He makes the call on the radio.

Twenty minutes have passed.

"Base. What is the status on that authorization? Over," Davis calls out on the radio.

"We are still waiting. Over," Punisher Base responds.

Davis finally loses his temper, screaming across the radio waves. "Listen. Tell them it is just a fucking Illum round. One fucking Illum round. I don't know what they are stacking. It could be ice cream for a fucking birthday party. But if they are doing something fucking wrong, I want them to know that we are fucking watching them. And they are taking so goddamned long that by the fucking time they authorize it, the party will be fucking over."

"You aren't the only one who is frustrated here." Punisher Base, audibly disturbed, manages to keep their composure.

The final time is twenty-eight minutes, twenty-eight minutes before they allow us to shoot one round to light up the sky above them.

"If they don't trust us on the ground, then why the fuck did they put us here?" I ask aloud.

"No fucking shit," Davis says, looking defeated. [Lance: No wonder SNAFU and FUBAR are military terms.]

* * *

"You want to go around the Haystacks?" Davis asks me.

"Sure," I answer, excited to break the monotony of sleep deprivation brought on by post and my unwillingness to take naps during the day, instead dedicating my time to this move.

Before I know it, I am walking toward the first of many strands of concertina wire laid out to prevent the enemy from getting in. And, apparently, us from getting out.

"Alvanez. Take that pole and lay it across the wire so we can breach," Davis orders Alvanez, an eighteen-year old from El

Salvador whose accent not only interferes with his ability to speak clearly, but also with his ability to hear properly.

He responds with a series of questions that leave Baltasar and I laughing and cracking jokes as Davis does his best to properly communicate with him.

"Do it like in Vietnam. Just lay on that mother fucker," Baltasar offers, both of us cracking up.

We watch as Alvanez takes the bar and slowly lowers it over the wire.

And then follows it.

He is now stretched atop the thin picket pole, creating an opening for us to cross.

Movement stops, as does any attempt at a tactical movement.

We laugh, take pictures, and eventually cross over him.

After picking him up and getting to the next row of wire, we teach him the right way through demonstration. We cross with a minimal amount of excitement and head toward the small path leading up and around the mountain.

We slowly wind through, maintaining security as best we can with a four-man element, but keeping the mood light.

Davis stops the patrol. "Okay, guys, I have to shit."

"Really, dude?" I ask.

"Yeah, this can't wait. I'll do it in this cave that the shepherds probably sleep in. Does anyone have any baby wipes?" he asks.

Nobody seems to have any, and he is relegated to crumpled notebook paper. We set in a security position around him and wait, laughing and joking the whole time. Baltasar finally decides to pass me his camera. He wants some pictures with him in them. I oblige him and take a few of him.

Then the terrain.

Then Alvanez.

Then Davis in a variety of embarrassing positions.

Finally, after he is all ready to go and his uniform is back in order, we decide to head back.

* * *

At last I'm loading up into the HMMWV. Five days up top have been tiring, to say the least, and we have a patrol in the morning. I just want to catch up on the sleep that I have lost.

Davis jumps into the vehicle. We are finally ready to go. We spent a bit too much time doing our turnover to the next squad for the Death Star.

"Fenner," Sandy says, "you should stay up here. The team is staging out of Death Star for tomorrow's patrol."

"Yeah, right. I'd say 'no' anyway. What do they need a medic up here for? They have Dilay in the tower with his platoon," I respond.

"Whatever." He starts up the loaner HMMWV. Ours is broken again.

When we arrive at the base of the hill, in the hooch I bump into Sandy and Finch.

"What the fuck are you doing here, dude?" Sandy asks.

"I'm not going to do an OP in the Death Star."

"Yeah, you are. You are a part of this team," Finch dives in.

"It doesn't make any sense. They need me to go out on patrol, and you guys will be right there on the tower. I won't be doing anything."

"Dude, we are only staging there. We are leaving in the morning for our hide site," Finch says. He seems hurt.

"Wait. We are going to operate as a team?"

"Yeah, dude," Sandy says.

I look at my watch and the pile of stuff on my bed. "Thirty minutes?"

10

AN IDLE MIND—UH OH.

~Lance~

"Have you heard from Adam?" Clint, the newest, and only married member, of our D&D group says to me from across the table, where we decided the D&D guys would go for dinner.

"No, I haven't heard from him in a week. I had been hearing from him almost every day. Until he e-mails me, I'm in the dark."

"I heard this has been the bloodiest month yet for the American troops over there," Clint declares. He is normally sensitive to my plight. Then, seeing my face (I've never been accused of having a poker face) and my jaw dropped open, he instantly recants. "Well... it's... it's been all over the news. Don't you watch the news?" Talk about awkward.

"Yes, but—

Grant tries for the save. "That's only because of the Marines' assault in the Helmand Valley." Grant? Who knew?

"Yes. I know. And it's nowhere near where Adam's stationed. It's in the south, and he's in the northeast." I glance at Ed, who has been studying one piece of calamari like he's just discovered the origin of the universe in its tentacles, and then back to Clint, who looks like he wants to be the piece of calamari about to be eaten.

"Sometimes they get busy and can't communicate. There's no service in a lot of those places. I hardly made contact with anyone at all when I was over there." Grant again. Who is this stranger? Maybe my comments to him have sunk in, or maybe he's the afraid the gay guy will lose it and wind up shooting him with his own weapon. What a nice welcoming home for Adam that would be, to have to visit me in prison for killing his former roommate. Whatever the reason, I'm glad Grant's on my side... for now.

"I'm sure he's fine," I say to Clint to let him know everything's okay. He and I have become closer over the past few weeks, and I'm sure he doesn't want to jeopardize that. No worries. If I haven't killed Grant by now, he's safe. Actually, it would take an awful lot for me to get really upset or offended by these guys. I know they like to push buttons. They're good at heart. Besides, it's always fun to pick on the sensitive gay guy. The four of us seem to have gotten closer since Adam's been gone. It might be part my fault we weren't as close as when Adam was here; they felt that they were intruding some. I hope not. I like them all. Tension relieved, the rest of the evening goes great and the normal banter resumes.

Later that night, my mind strayed to thoughts of exactly what Adam might have been doing this past week. I mean, he's in beautiful, sunny Afghanistan after all. What could happen? Then I really started to think of things that could happen, but, being ever the optimist, I decided to dwell on the positive. And here's the result of my optimistic musings and what I think would make a great travel brochure. I know this is just so wrong, but, hey, I try to find the humor in everything.

THE NAJIL RESORT AND SPA

Welcome to the Najil Resort and Spa.

We are located in the vast Ali Shang valley, three hours from the nearest point of civilization. This is your perfect getaway, your chance to commune with nature. With mountain vistas in every direction, this is Big Sky country like you've never seen it and with a climate that is incomparable.

We have U.S. government-sanctioned accommodations and a 24-hour guard-patrolled security facility for your protection.

An eclectic, family-style restaurant serving a variety of cuisines is open from 0730 to 0830 for breakfast, from 1700 to 1800 hours for dinner and, occasionally, serves lunch.

We are pet friendly, and you will love getting to know our very own local (feral) pups.

Unlike other resorts, we have no noise restrictions (as you will discover daily).

Our very able, all-male, highly trained (mostly) staff, garbed in the latest couture for a natural, assimilating effect, fuses with the décor and terrain and heightens the overall ambiance. You may even wish to purchase some of our fine, unisex apparel. Ladies (and gay men) will appreciate the fit staff (eye candy). And for our rugged men, our staff will also be just the inspiration you need to become that rough and tough, manly man you've always wanted to be.

Our staff is on premises 24/7. They like it here so much, they live here. (Subject to availability)

We also have a medical staff on premises available 24 hours, should you need anything from triage to bullet removal. Just kidding (not really).

The accommodations are minimal but organic.

Our amenities include:

Pool (seasonal—monsoon season)

Internet Access (subject to availability and bribery)

Secured Resort Enclosure (razor-wire)

Communal Kitchen

Unisex Bathrooms

Laundry Facilities (buckets provided)

Our activities are endless, and you will find many that are not available at any other resort in the world. We want you in the best physical condition you can be. We start your day bright and early with our mandatory and invigorating calisthenics class. Here you will bond with the other resort visitors and our staff as you exercise your way to a new and healthier you. Our staff is always encouraging. They and will make sure you get the most from this essential experience.

Just added: our Ducking and Diving classes, behind a variety of structures and objects. A truly unique experience and one you can't (and won't want to) miss.

Some of our other activities include:

Hiking—various trails and skill levels available

Mountain Climbing

Rock Climbing

Rock Scaling

Rock Throwing (various sizes)

Hunting (insurgents)

Sharp Shooting (Actual sniper instructor)

Rifle Classes (including assembling and cleaning)

Knife Throwing—Multi-target

Jogging—various terrains and incline levels

Running

Survival Instructions—daily

Skeet Shooting (with real pigeons and assorted local wildlife)

We also have our local and unique entertainment including:

Air Shows (check for Times)

Fireworks/Rocket Displays (check for Times)

Local DJs—our staff is multi-talented and offer a variety of musical stylings.

Then, of course, for your indulgent relaxation we have the incomparable Najil Open-Air Spa. It is like no other spa you ever have—or ever will—experience. Open 24 hours. Never crowded. You won't have to wait in line or make an appointment, just show up.

Whatever you desire is right there and available at your fingertips. Here are some of the amazing treatments available to you. You may even want to create your own personal spa package.

Mud Baths (seasonal-monsoon seasonal)

Hot Rock (very) Massage—daytime

Cold Rock (very) Massage—nighttime

Natural Tanning Bed Facility—unlimited space available

All Natural Dry (very) Sauna

Weight Lifting-all natural

Be a part of the "In" group and the rapidly growing number of Americans who are discovering this unforgettable hideaway. Experience the new, ever-changing Southwest Asia. Once you get there, you may never leave. (Please note: The taking of photographs and video is prohibited and will be strictly enforced.)

What are you waiting for? This is a once-in-a-lifetime experience that you will never forget. Guaranteed.

Call now!

11

BABY STEPS

~Adam~

Halfway up the hill to the Death Star, we took our first break—well, what we believed to be the halfway mark. The .50 Cal was kicking Sandy's ass. Then Finch's. And again Sandy's. Finally, after about forty-five minutes to an hour, we arrived at the top.

I'd just left this place about an hour and a half prior. Now, I was a guest in the building that the guys and I helped move into, fortify, and wire-power into—with a great deal of lessons learned involving grounding and proper techniques for wiring up a building.

* * *

"Wow, dude, I didn't know you could do electrical work," Davis said to me, surprised, as I reported my progress after he returned with a working HMMWV while ours was being serviced.

"Yeah, I really can't. I opened stuff and stared at it until I figured it out," I told him.

He didn't have a response for that. It was a surprise coming from the platoon One Upper.

* * *

We crashed on the roof. The three of us fell asleep—sort of—listening to the sounds of radio traffic, all the while getting attacked by flies. I didn't bring a pillow and ended up using my sweat-soaked shirt. The litter I slept on was surprisingly comfortable. Around two in the morning, it was finally too cold, and I had to borrow the soldier-on-duty's jacket as a blanket. I was packing light and didn't think about the weather.

We beat the sun up. I snagged a Pop Tart and took it with me as the three of us walked to our hide position. We fell into our normal abusive banter, and finally, as the sun came up, we settled in. We had a good view of the entire valley and what was planned as the majority of the route.

I took rear security, which was a berm that didn't reveal anyone until they were right on top of us, but it seemed necessary for our protection to be in this position.

The sun crept into our hideaway, along with different locals moving around. A woman's shadow danced by us. She hiked the hill in sandals past us, carrying a big basket filled with the husks of corn she had more than likely pulled long before we woke up. She didn't so much as glance in our direction, passing just fifteen feet away.

A local boy pushed his flock by us in the same way. The bleating of the sheep made just enough noise to stifle the noise of Finch's fart and Sandy's need to chamber a round into his pistol. Eventually, a middle-aged gentleman did walk up on us. He seemed more surprised to see us than we were him. He waved and put his hand over his heart, and I reciprocated.

"Duh duh duh daa, duh duh duh daaaa," Finch said without warning.

"Finch, what the fuck was that?" Sandy asked.

"Do you guys remember the scene in that spy movie, where at the end the main guy is talking to this chick, on the phone, who is chasing him, and he says, "You should get some sleep." And at first she is confused, until he says, "You look tired." Then, that song comes on." He shows his big, toothy grin hoping for some acknowledgement.

"Yeah, I know the movie. Doesn't make you less of a moron," I joined in.

"Think about it. Sir, you should drink some water. Why is that? You look thirsty. Duh duh duh daa, duh duh duh daaaa." We laugh at him for a while.

"Roger, Dealer six. My element is all across the river and accounted for," Clemente reported to the LT over the radio.

"Except Alegria dropped his night vision. Duh duh duh daa, duh duh duh daaaa," I threw out to the group.

We all started laughing. It quickly became a game... until suddenly it wasn't.

"Be advised, SSG Demille is down," the voice over the radio reported. Demille—the other medic in my platoon, who is a little older, but not so old that this is too hard for him.

Through the optics, Sandy reported that Demille was throwing up.

"Dealer two. This is Dealer eye. Is that Demille's lunch coming up?" Finch asked Davis over the radio. "Duh duh duh daa, duh duh duh daaaa," he said, off radio.

The powers-that-be talked for a bit, and finally, it was decided that they needed to evacuate him with a small group on foot, and the rest continue on with the mission. The group split off and Sandy began to report back to us how badly Demille was hurting on the walk back. "Dude, he is lying down. He is really fucked up."

BOOM!

"What the fuck was that?" I'm not sure who said it first.

"Do we see anything?" I asked.

"Nothing. It is out of our view, like where I lost sight of that crew with Demille," Sandy told us.

"Fuck, dude. We couldn't do anything even if we could see what was going on," Finch said. A saddle was between us and our comrades, with a massive cell phone tower at its highest point.

We listened to the quick burst of PKM and small arms fire that lasted only a minute or so. Then Clemente came over the radio and briefed the situation. Without much time, they were reinforced by the rest of the patrol and heading back to base.

We broke down our position and headed out to make contact with them.

The walk up the hill was hard, but the walk down just flat out hurt. Baby steps seemed to be the key, small steps to keep control.

The walk back was quick, and as usual the walk through the gate was pleasant, except for the steep hill just inside, covered with moon-dust to fill the air as we stomped in.

No casualties, except for the one they already had.

The back-brief after the patrol was longer than necessary, and we soon returned back to our b-hut.

My bed was empty, aside from the trash Finch left for me while I was on the Death Star because he thought I took his porno. No thanks to Davis on that one.

I checked to make sure all the guys didn't have any medical issues. I sat at the edge of the bed breathing. I racked my brain.

Do I really get to chill out?

I should write.

Fuck it, tomorrow.

I dumped my excessive amount of gear and stripped down. For the first time in almost a week, my body was able to breathe. I took a shower that was long overdue, and shaved off over a week of facial hair. I lay down in bed after everything, and took a nap with headphones in my ears. A pretty girl singing about dancing and boys, lulled me to sleep. [Lance: Okay, then. You enjoy this? And I thought Cross-Fit was grueling—and that was only an hour. I sympathize with Demille, the throwing up guy. That probably would have been me. Show muscles—no stamina.] [Adam: He wasn't weak. He was throwing up before the patrol and still wanted to come out.] [Lance: Oh.]

Click here for link to photos and/or videos

12

TRANSFORMED

~Lance~

I just love revelations—not so much. I went to see the new "Transformers" movie the other day. Adam had seen it before he left [Adam: Twice] and said how good it was. I took my godson and his mom. (Richie doesn't like the science-fiction, comic book-type stuff.) It was really good and a lot of fun, except...

The movie opens and the bad Transformers are fighting the U.S. Army. (Here we go.) They are getting slaughtered and no match for the Decepticons, as they are called. Josh Duhamel, the actor in charge in the scene, is in his Army get-up giving futile orders and trying to save his men from massacre. The scene is pretty brutal. All of this leading to thoughts of... Adam. I watch these soldiers flying across the screen, the bombs and other incendiary devices exploding, and all I can think about is our guys over in Afghanistan fighting the good fight and hopefully not being wantonly destroyed. This, of course, added to all of the posters, commercials, and billboards for the Army that I am constantly being inundated with. Let alone the fear-fomenting and fulminating Fox News. My optimistic, everything-is-going-to-be-all-right-in-the-world, rose-colored glasses have become somewhat occluded.

Pollyanna just got dirty.

Peter Pan forgot how to think lovely thoughts and how to fly.

I don't like it.

It's not as if I've had my head in the sand or anything. It's just that I try to dwell on the positive. I can be realistic. But what fun is that?

Movies, in general, are escapist. I was trying to escape for a little while and have some fun with my godson.

A nudge in the side. "Are you okay?" the ten-year-old boy next to me says as another rocket explodes on the screen.

I gulp. "I'm fine."

"How come you stopped eating your popcorn?" He points to my hand, where the kernels have begun dropping to the floor.

"I think I've had enough. Shh. Watch the movie." Nice.

My bout with melancholy passed, and I even ate more popcorn and enjoyed the rest of the movie.

I guess the point I'm trying to make is: my life—or at least my perception of it—has changed. I'm constantly being made aware of what is going on in the world and how I, kind of, have protected myself from it. All of those men fighting over there are individual human beings, with individual lives and personalities. They are not THE ARMY. They are individual people. Each and every one of them.

I get it now. How old am I? It's kind of sad. It took my best friend going off to war to make me aware.

This is now my world, and welcome to it.

I have to say, though, that Oz and Narnia and Middle-Earth would be my first choices, but those aren't my options. Nor anyone else's.

Transformers? Transformed?

You better believe it.

No going back to Neverland.

Thanks, pal. [Adam: So, am I to understand that I am being blamed for killing Peter Pan and blowing up Narnia and Neverland?] [Lance: Not at all. I just have a new perspective and awareness level.]

13

POUNDING THE V

~Adam~

"Tear down Little Round Top."

I heard the order, and after a period of deliberation, I came up with a strategy. This thing is supposed to withstand mortar and rocket fire, and they wanted me and four Mexicans to tear it down by hand? We would figure something out.

I managed to acquire bolt cutters and a razor blade.

Little Round Top was made almost entirely of Hesco barriers. Steel fencing wrapped around a thick cloth to hold sand was the entire design, a simple concept that provides a great deal of protection for almost every base that I have been on since my second deployment.

We started using the bolt cutters to clip away one of the sides of each block barrier, then we cut through the cloth. The sand and rocks have been in place for over a year and were not as willing to leave the barriers as we had hoped.

As the sand began to fall, the wind began to kick up. Soon, we were all completely surrounded by clouds of sand. I took my shirt off and wrapped it around my mouth and nose to make sure I didn't spend too much time breathing it in.

After a couple of hours, and only moderate success, we broke for lunch. Davis insisted that we clean up before we ate.

Along the side of the Death Star, we took water bottles and started pouring them onto ourselves. We watched brown water pour off of our arms and chests. Davis started with Alvanez and moved down the line pouring water down our backs. Helicopters flew overhead and must have been confused as to why there were five guys with their shirts off bent over while other guys poured water down their backs. [Lance: It is an interesting image.] [Adam: Uh huh.]

I poured the water into my hair and watched as the clear water turned brown, taking the sand and dirt off my head and running it down my face.

We laughed and made jokes, most racially related. The mood was light-hearted as we moved our—sort of—clean selves over to the meal Davis had prepared for us.

* * *

We were all gathered around the radio up on the Death Star, listening to the sounds of normal radio traffic and swapping stories of sexual conquest and playing the One-Upper game. The sun was just setting over the mountains and the glare was uncomfortable. We all made an effort to sit in little pockets of shade scattered around.

Baltasar, Celaya, Alegria, and I were spread out, seated on ammo boxes, fold-out chairs, and whatever else we found fit to plant our asses upon. The speakers played gangster rap from my MP3 player quietly, something to cater to Baltasar's and Alegria's less-than-savory backgrounds.

"Okay," I start my story, "So, I'm with this chick and—

BOOM!

We lowered ourselves behind the cover of the poorly built fortress walls and all hit the sides to see what was damaged. We all peeked over the edge and saw the smoke coming from next to the little shack the Afghanistan National Army (ANA) used to store their comm equipment.

"Are you okay, sir?" Baltasar yelled to someone walking up the path to the Death Star. It was the Doctor, our pediatric cardiologist turned Army doctor. Who, as Joey put it, was the only adult who enjoyed our jokes. He had picked a bad time to take his evening constitutional to the Death Star. "Hurry up," Baltasar yelled before I started barking orders. Everyone took positions on our optics and started scanning.

BOOM!

That one was to our south, outside of the base and in a riverbed.

Davis had a meeting to go to down in the main part of base and had left me the ranking soldier. The glare on the mountains to the west was almost unmanageable and we couldn't see anything. Several of the guys were lined up along the south wall, scanning. Baltasar manned one of the machine guns. "Can I fire suppression?" he asked.

"Do you see something to shoot at?" I asked back.

"No."

"Well then, fuck no. We still need PID to fire," I responded. The doctor was now up top with us and had taken a position on the wall.

"Where is that shit coming from?" I yelled. I tried to manage the guys and send reports back to command.

Something about it felt like the fire was coming from the south.

BOOM!

Another one landed, now to our southwest just twenty-five meters out from one of our currently unmanned positions.

"V-notch," came over the radio. I looked into the sun at the area where the mountains formed what appeared to be a V.

Those fuckers are using the sun.

"Get those fucking thermals on the V-notch," I yelled. They might not be affected by the glare.

BOOM!

Same spot as the last one.

Mortars.

They were adjusting on us.

WHEEEWWW.

We hit the wall. Those that had done this before knew what mortars sounded like as they flew overhead.

No explosion.

"Anybody see anything?" I yelled.

I only got back "noes."

"We have clearance for fifteen rounds," came over the radio.

As they began their normal radio communications for a fire mission, I grabbed my camera and ran up to sit by the thermal camera. The two of us stared into the glare of the sun as plumes of smoke appeared on the V-Notch in the distance.

Then the sound hit us.

I turned off the camera and jumped back down with the guys. The doctor was watching the Notch with binos. "They are really pounding that V-Spot, aren't they?" He smiled at me.

I smiled at the innuendo. "Yes, sir."

Slowly, the flurry of information that was flying around the Death Star calmed down; radio communications relaxed. I passed information as I saw it. They were trying to get Birds into the area.

Alvanez and Konrad arrived. They had driven Davis down to the base, and must have been on their way up when the attack started.

Konrad put together a fire mission, and I passed that up to command. Everyone pulled back from their observation positions and began sharing what they saw. A picture of what had happened started to form. They talked about rockets and various other firing positions on the radio.

After a while, the Birds didn't see anything that warranted Positive Identification (PID), and they left. I heard a voice on the radio talking about what they thought we saw and really fucking up the story.

"CP do you have any questions about what we observed?" I asked. We weren't about to get fucked on this one by letting them get it wrong. How do they just ignore the observations of the only position on the base that was capable of watching the entire attack?

"Roger. What did you observe?" It was my lieutenant.

I told him about the location of every round and the one that didn't explode. I passed what the Forward Observers believed to be the most likely courses of action that the enemy used against us. Calling in fire is their job. I would hope that counts for something. I also passed on the possible use of the sun to obscure our observations. I hated giving the enemy credit, but they have been fighting wars for a long time, and this was a ballsy, well-put-together attack.

He thanked me and told us to remain vigilant. I hate that.

Davis called up on the radio and passed some information up to us and let us know about another meeting he had to go to.

The Doctor hung out for a while before we finally sent a few guys down to go pick up Davis.

Nobody was shaken up. We were all excited.

After a little while, Davis finally returned.

"Okay, so First Sergeant called all the E-6s and above into a meeting after the attack. He was so mad about this that he was actually shaking," Davis started his brief. The sun had long since set behind us, and through the gray we all watched and listened to what he had to say.

"He was pissed off about uniforms during the attack," he said.

Before he could further elaborate, I interjected, "Just so I make sure I have this right, we have just taken mortar fire inside of our base, and he wants to use this as an opportunity to talk about our uniforms?" [Lance: Amazing. And ire inducing.]

"Yeah, I know." Davis was not happy to have to share this with us. He said his piece, and we prepared for our evening cycle of post.

I asked him to take the first shift so I could get some sleep. The adrenaline in my system from the attack had left and with it any energy I would have normally had. He agreed.

I headed down the steps that were far from straight or level, and made my way to the bunk that would be mine until it was my time for post. Then Davis would occupy it.

We had only enough beds for the guys off post.

I laid my sleeping bag on top and the memory foam pillow on top of that. I took my shirt off and lay down. My pistol was still on my leg, and my boots stayed on.

I didn't want to be caught with my pants down in the event of an attack.

Alvanez's less than graceful feet plodded around on the wooden roof above the stairs. My tired brain kept thinking it was mortars. Finally, I was too tired to care.

* * *

"All right, guys." Davis was busy, so I was left passing the information to the group. "You guys know that the MPs rolled an MRAP, and I know we were supposed to be relieved tonight. But 3rd platoon is going to be sent out to help out with that whole abortion out there, so we are going to have to stay here another night."

"Well, any chance you can have this pushed up?" Konrad asked me, straight-faced. "Any chance we can take a few hours and make an Internet and shower run?"

I paused, looked around to see the faces of everyone, and then I laughed. "You just got here yesterday. You spent ten days in BAF, the land of milk and honey, doing your little class. If Baltasar or Alvanez, who have been here the last six days up here sucking dirt asked, I would take that seriously, but you—no. We will be back tomorrow night. You can wait." His smile faded. Everybody laughed at him.

The next day, as I sat on the radio, I heard Konrad's voice downstairs. "Sergeant Fenner. Sergeant Fenner. I am going to do it. I'm going to be that guy."

"Okay, what is it?" Now, like four-year olds gathered around Mom, they are all standing around the base of the steps.

"Alvanez was going to hit Celaya in the head with a brick, and Celaya was going to let him."

The two of them were smiling. Alvanez, holding a brick in his gorilla-sized hands. "Okay," I said.

"Okay? You pick on me for wanting to get a shower, and when they want to hit each other with bricks, you just say, "Okay?" Konrad raised his voice, obviously flustered but attempting to maintain his composure.

"Yes, because if Alvanez is willing to hit him in the head with a brick, what is he willing to do to the enemy? And if Celaya is willing to get hit on the head with a brick, then what sacrifice is he willing to make for this platoon? And you. You just want to be clean and play on the Internet."

A pause. "You got me." Konrad was less than satisfied with the result of his little attempt to embarrass his comrades.

"So can we do it?" Celaya asked me.

"No. I would love to be able to let you, but as a medic I can't."

"All right." Celaya, Alvanez, as well as everyone else, seemed a bit disappointed.

"That reminds me, Alvanez. Show Konrad how to burn shit. I want that bucket clean when we leave." Konrad was a little hurt by the end result. I began tasking everyone with cleaning details to ensure that when we turned this post over, we weren't embarrassed by the appearance of the Death Star.

Click here for link to photos and/or videos

14

SETTLING IN

~Adam~

As the sun set last night into villages I would like to visit, but as of yet have not been allowed, I stood, my chest heaving, stretching against the small strap clipped to hold my pack straps off of my shoulders. It was leg day, and after a normal work out in the Small Arms Repair Shop, as we affectionately refer to our gym, we decided to fill up our rucks and head up to the Death Star. Well, it was Davis' idea, but he was tired, and I could tell he didn't want to do it.

Neither did I.

After a great deal of heckling, I convinced him that we should suck it up and go. Celaya decided to tag along as well.

So, there we stood, trying to get as much oxygen as we could back into our cells at the almost mile-high altitude that we were still adjusting to. The light from the sun finally disappeared, with no moon to replace it, before our descent back down—which had been agreed on was the more harrowing of the two approaches to the Death Star. The ascent was hard on the muscles, but the descent was hard on one's joints and often one's ass.

If we don't have little adventures outside the wire to fill our time, this is how we'd do it. Either Davis and I will have little pissing contests of masculinity in various athletic events, or I'll lie in bed and read. I found a little electronic reader that has been occupying my time, filling my head with stories of adventures in far off lands like Africa, the Pacific Islands... and Afghanistan. Or I'll study.

I may take a walk over to the MWR to play on the Internet—if there isn't a line. I am impatient, and so, generally, I just get distracted. The base is small, so it seems everywhere I turn there is somebody that I know, and I lose time just talking about the events or non-events of the day. The newest news has been: "Where is Harris?" the chicken-chasing dog that seems to have disappeared.

The secret only a select five of us knew was tossed over the wire and left to rot next to Harris' limp body just beyond the Death Star's field of view: a thin piece of cord wrapped around his neck meant to hold him while Baltasar learned the subtle nuances of canine anatomy and the effects of a NATO round on it.

I felt settled here.

This little base had become, comfortably, my temporary home. As they all tend to be. I was learning all the names and faces. I knew the interpreters by name and actually enjoyed their company. Odie and I had been making an effort to corrupt them with porn and talk of promiscuous American women or Vegas nights, with only mild success. And as we got to know them, we learned which ones we did and didn't like, and they began to see us as people, too. Not just soldiers. We were a team out here. This was their home that we were trying to improve, and to many it may have seemed like we were an occupying force, but it didn't feel that way in their little shack next to the chow hall, where we liked to sit, drink chai, and enjoy some amazing bread, also known as "Nan" (which isn't even a Pashto word; it is Dari, an Indian dialect). I kept thanking Jay, an English teacher, who had a young, thin face with a smile and a poor shave stretched across it. He picked me up when I fell off of a wall in the fields outside of the base.

I expected that from my fellow soldier, but Jay didn't even know my name at the time.

* * *

A pile of letters waited on my bunk for me after lunch. I didn't know anyone who sent them.

I was at a loss as to what to do. It appeared that I had been adopted by a nice lady who is a part of an organization I had never heard of, and that I was unknowingly volunteered for. I always appreciated the effort, but I felt that I was not the right guy for this kind of thing. I was not PR savvy and didn't feel like I should be the one to talk to about this stuff. [Lance: Why are you less worthy than anyone else? Or less PR savvy? They are part of the America that wants to show support and appreciation. Let them. Because they can't do what you do. There are people who care. It is similar to other wars: Civil War—rolling bandages, working in hospitals, knitting scarves. World War II—working in factories on assembly lines. People want to help in the war effort. Unlike the Vietnam War, where they didn't understand what was going on, this war against terrorism, they do.] [Adam: Because I am not here to wave the American Flag and sing songs of freedom for these people. I'm here because I like running around and shooting at shit. And I like this work too much to quit anytime soon. I'm just not a fan of the bullshit my employer bothers me with. Also, you are mistaken if you think the general American public understands why we fight "terror." I've been doing this since '03, and I don't know why I'm here yet.]

They wanted to make a difference in a soldier's life over here, fill his life with a little bit more cheer because he/she missed home. But I don't. I love this work. I would have liked more freedom. And for every inch they gave me, I took a mile. But the only thing missing in my life couldn't be sent in a letter. And as we had noticed, females weren't allowed to stay on this base. They showed up in the morning and did their business before the sun went down.

Don't let the dog into the hen house or the hen into the kennel.

If I was getting laid out here, I wouldn't want to leave. [Lance: Really?] [Adam: Really.]

* * *

"So, Yui is having a little girl," Davis told me, referring to the Thai girl whose company he enjoyed as much as she enjoyed his Baht. (Thai currency)

"That is exciting, is it yours?" I responded, taking a drink of water between sets in the gym.

"Well, the time frame works out for when I was there."

"You know your daughter is going to be hooking in seventeen years, right?" I said to him smiling.

"Yeah, but that is respectable employment out there," he responded with a grin.

Don't let the hens in, indeed.

15

AGAINST MY BETTER JUDGMENT

~Adam~

"Joey, guess who I talked to yesterday?" I asked him in the Aid Station, where I was visiting Bryan, him, and Crockett. Crockett had arrived in Najil to replace Bryan, who was heading back to the warmth and comfort of more civilized facilities in Mehtarlam (or Meth Lab as we called it).

"Lyrik?"

"No. I talked to her on MySpace a little, but that isn't it."

"Okay." He struck his humorously thoughtful, department store pose. "Lyrik?"

I shook my head.

"I don't know."

"My ex-wife."

"Really?" He emphasized the vowels. Joey loved this type of drama. And I liked telling him because he was non-judgmental, which I appreciated. He busted jokes, but was keenly aware and open about his own human faults and poor decisions—especially in the realm of women.

"Okay. So you remember the drama from when I was in Jalalabad about that desperate e-mail she sent me about needing to talk to me?"

"Yeah."

"And how, when I responded, I found myself in a verbal e-mail sparring match with her recovering drug-addict, hyper-Christian, shit-head boyfriend?"

"Yeah."

"Okay. And I told you about how I ended up sending a letter to her folks' house informing her that I set up a secret e-mail account for her with a password only she could figure out and asked for her to use my sister-in-law's name as a subject line to let me know that he wasn't looming over her shoulder as she wrote?"

"Holy shit, yes. You told me all this."

"So, I got an e-mail yesterday, saying she desperately needed to talk, and she included a bunch more stories that only we would know about."

"So, you called her, right?"

"Yeah, I had to borrow a phone card, but I gave her a buzz. She said that this guy was the worst mistake of her life. I told her, 'That is quite an accomplishment.'"

"Wow. You just jumped into this conversation, being a dick, huh?" Bryan chimed in.

I smiled.

"Who is this?" Crockett asked.

"Susan."

"Oh. Wow. Okay." Crockett looked surprised and gingerlishous.

"So, she tells me how controlling he is, how she wants to break it off, and how he has threatened her, her family, and my dog. I let her know that I can't help her this time. She understands."

"You know what you need to do, right?" Joey asked.

"Let me hear it," I replied.

"Send him an e-mail through her account, because he will be monitoring it, telling him that he will be getting his ass kicked when you get back, but the difference between being in a wheelchair or not will be decided on how he treats your dog."

"I like that. I'll let you know," I said.

"Tell him you have been training with a little boy who lives in the next town over and who drags his scrotum on the ground," Bryan snuck a comment in, lightening the mood a bit.

"Joey, it looks like she wants to get back together. She apologized a lot and said a lot of those things that girls like to say," I said as an unnecessary little addendum. [Lance: Adam. Adam. Adam. 'Danger, Will Robinson! Danger!' Use your head here—the one with the brain in it.] [Adam: Life would be so boring if I did that, though.]

"And?" Joey gave me that look.

"I don't know, but I will still be going to Thailand when I get back," I answered in the masculine way that he needed to hear. (Thailand is Disneyland for adults, where anything can happen... anything.)

"Wow, so I won't be able to bat-clean-up for you or Bryan," Joey began the course of our playful banter.

Bryan laughed at the disgusting idea of Joey's apprehension to follow in our shoes with any woman, due to our past sexual history.

Crockett tried not to get involved. Kaitlyn would kill him.

"Sorry, sweetie. You are beautiful and I would love to sleep with you, but you fucked Bryan and he has the HIV." Joey mimicked himself in a fictitious conversation he wouldn't be having in the future.

We all laughed.

"I also thought it was funny that, apparently, her folks are singing my praises for my secret-squirrel actions to get hold of her like I did—this from her mom who repeatedly told me I was going to hell..."

I trailed into my thoughts on religion and its relation to the people who participate in it. We all shared stories and let the minutes slip by, because that was all we could do here.

These are the times where being an avulsed segment of all the platoons I was a part of worked out. I could choose which part of the family I wanted to hang out with based on merit.

* * *

There I was listening to music and staring at my computer screen, sucked into my normal mix so many years ago, by beautiful blue eyes, falling back into memories of a New Year's spent with a bottle of Lambrusco in an oversized hotel room in Wisconsin Dells one day later than anticipated, because someone spent New Year's Eve throwing up in the bathroom at her mother's house while I sat next to her on the cold linoleum floor, not yet knowing she was carrying my child.

I hold on to the hope that this will all work out.

What "this" may be I didn't know, but for the time being I would just enjoy my time here, where I seemed to live my life, waiting for the rest of my life.

16

THE DEVIL'S ASS CRACK

~Adam~

"What is wrong with a concussion shared between friends?"

* * *

I found myself comfortably laid back, staring up at the moonless sky. I was thankful that there were no clouds in the sky to cover what little illumination we were granted tonight by the millions of stars that I so rarely got to see living in a major city. Behind me, my Kevlar leaned up against the same pile of rocks as me. I found this little pile to be quite comfortable, aside from the fact that I am pretty sure it was a grave.

It made an outstanding reclining chair.

Sandy and Finch were in position about fifteen meters behind me doing their sniper thing, and Baltasar was another fifteen meters from them, providing flank security.

* * *

We had spread ourselves out on the northern cliff side across from our little base. The commander finally got clearance to send out four-man teams, and we were his first experiment with that.

So, we picked a spot at the base of the cliff. The commander decided to change that about an hour before stepping-off (departure), to the top of the cliff, which was only six hours after the doctor released Finch from the twenty-four hour observation time that the doctor decided was necessary following any concussion.

He and Davis had been wrestling the day prior, and through a series of circumstances that are still being debated, he hit his head. Hard. And after some nausea and vomiting, he ended up in a chair in front of our doctor getting the look that doctors often give to those who are responsible for their own injuries.

I laughed.

* * *

The night was beautiful. The wind whipped over the cliff and dried the sweat that was hiding under my ghillie and various other pieces of gear. The valley was relatively quiet, and I simply enjoyed lying there, observing the cliff to my left and the area about seventy-five to one-hundred meters below me, experimenting with my night vision and how it might or might not work with the ACOG scope that I am so enamored with.

Earlier in the week, one of the locals fell off the cliff near where I was sitting. The Afghani Security Guards (ASG) watched as he fell, and even more to their amazement, as his mother ran down the sheer, cliff face after him. The ASG did go out to help and ended up transporting him to the local doctor. He died soon after.

These ASG are great. Hired from the local population, I have found that working with them is a pleasure. They fight hard and are as loyal as anyone else on this base. This is their home, and fighting with us is a solid way to defend it.

Finally, after a few hours, we were called back. I breathed in my last few bits of comfort before the descent, which proved to be significantly more difficult than the ascent. Down the Devil's Ass Crack, as Sandy had christened it. The water had washed through the draw and settled all the soil at the bottom, leaving only giant boulders and loose rocks.

As we made our way down in the dark, climbing and slipping and falling the whole way, we did our best to remain tactical and silent, but that was difficult—to say the least.

"Dude, are you okay?" I asked Sandy, after I watched him slip, fall, catch himself, and then pause for an unusually long time.

"Dude, fuck you," he snapped back in an abnormally angry tone of voice for him. I watched, through what little light I could, him pick thorns out of his hand. He did manage to break his fall, but his hand landed on the Afghanistan national flower. The Pricker Bush.

The rocks somehow got bigger on our way down. Baltasar almost plowed me over when he jumped off an unusually large rock onto an unsteady rock, and then bounced onto another unsteady rock, until he finally ran into me.

He replaced Konrad on the team. His motivation and experience have been setting him apart in the platoon—just as Konrad's need for the comforts of home have been setting him apart.

"Fenner, I have rolled my ankle four times in the last one-hundred meters." Sandy looked back at me.

"I'll look at it when I get back, man," I tell him as we watched Finch take a particularly nasty spill.

"That makes me feel much better," Sandy said, stifling a laugh.

I tried to keep mine from echoing down the draw into the town in front of us.

After we climbed out of the Ass Crack, we found ourselves in a particularly scary corn field with massive stalks of corn and only a foot-wide, three-foot-tall wall to walk on while we made our way through to safety.

Thankfully, we only got separated once.

As we limped our way back toward the base, our last obstacle was one last draw filled with rocks. After the rocks was the triple-strand concertina wire, which had been breached by SGT Clemente and SFC Mendoza, the platoon sergeant, who were standing at the top of the hill waiting for us with Gatorade and muffins, along with Crockett, who had been supplementing my position as platoon medic in SFC Mendoza's truck while I was out playing with the sniper team.

Finch fell hard again, he got up, and he fell again. We were all laughing through whispers as he dismissed our attempts to help him up.

"Just give me a moment to collect myself," he said fighting for air, his hand motioned us to carry on without him.

I made my way up through the tangled up wire covering the ground—the last defensive barrier on the base—and finally made it to the top of the hill, where the HMMWV and everyone were waiting.

After some short conversation, we collected ourselves and made our way to the Aid Station so I could check on everyone's ankles and knees.

Out of the Aid Station, Sandy limped toward our debriefing, with ice wrapped around his ankle and his foot awkwardly crammed into his boot. Everyone else had Ibuprofen in their pockets to keep the pain and swelling down.

After putting my gear away, I headed to the shower. I ran into Sandy there, who was already in the other stall. We passed the face-wash back and forth, trying to get the cami paint off of our faces and out of our hair.

* * *

The intent of this mission had been to get all geared up, to let the locals know that these small teams existed. So, we'd gotten all ghillied up and thrown cami paint on our faces. We'd paused at the gate before we'd left and did a little photo session with the local ANA. We'd figured, if they knew, then the locals would know.

They'd taken pictures (got a good one of the team with an ANA soldier holding an RPG in between us), we'd taken our motivational pictures, and out we'd gone.

* * *

Finally clean, I crawled into bed.

* * *

BOOM!

What the fuck?

"I think something bounced off the roof," someone said as the lights went on and we started to get dressed.

The short playlist on my MP3 player wasn't even through yet.

BOOM!

Out we went to watch mortars respond with beautifully heavy volumes of fire on the Jesus Tree where the rockets had been fired from. Somehow, the Jesus Tree, which was named by the previous unit for some unknown reason, has been the reported source of a great deal of Taliban activity. This tree has taken a significant amount of indirect fire and somehow remains standing—which was as strange and humorous as the name.

After a few hours, I crawled back into bed.

After a few hours, gunfire woke me again.

They'd said the election season would be busy, but what the fuck?

* * *

The village was called Dowlat Sha. I hadn't made it out there. It was to the north at the outer realm of the areas that we were allowed to go without significant assets at our disposal. The intel was telling us that seventy armed locals showed up to the local Afghani National Police (ANP) station.

They wanted to help guard the voting booths from the Taliban.

The question I had was whether or not Americans would do that. If there was a threat that a polling station was going to be bombed in America, what would Americans do? How many would expect the police to handle it, and how many would grab a rifle?

Click here for link to photos and/or videos

17

SAMSON AND OTHER PEOPLE I NEED TO STOP COMPARING MYSELF TO

~Adam~

Marquez stood behind me, the clippers buzzing in his hand. He was the only one aside from Jose I trusted enough to touch clippers to my head, a skill he had learned to complement his skill with a tattoo gun. It was all part of his repertoire of ways to make money and still be able to smoke weed, all of which were activities that his new family were forcing him to leave behind in favor of a more domestic lifestyle.

All around my sun-burned arms and shoulders fell two months of hair that I had been growing with great pride. The last time I had gotten it cut was in Vegas by Jose.

Mixed into the gravel, I watched long pieces of my hair blow around. I looked like a reasonable soldier or a borderline responsible NCO.

"How do you want it to look?" he asked me.

"Just pull it off the ears, man. First Sergeant said if I don't get it cut, then I don't get to go on mission. He threatened me with the one thing I give a shit about out here," I told him.

"All right. It is pretty ragged up here," he said as I felt his hand on the top of my head.

"I don't mind. I like looking like one of the mangy-ass dogs out here." I smiled to myself, already missing having my hair hanging off of my ears and seeing the looks of the people I would meet from Meth Lab, when they looked at my week-old shave and two-month-old hair cut.

* * *

After a shower and a much needed shave, that was all supervised by the locals, who won't stop staring at me—or at anyone else it seems—and another lunch consisting of cereal, muffins, and shelf-stable milk, I made my way back up the hill to find Odie getting his hair cut. Apparently, First Sergeant got him too. Odie was only concerned with his Mohawk, which Marquez was more than willing to leave in place.

* * *

Today has been relatively comfortable, an early wake up for an early mission. Baltasar and the sniper team went out to oversee a road where an IED threat existed, while the platoon pressed into a little town called Parmawan just north of the base. Clemente and I climbed one of the hills to sit in our over-watch position over the vehicles while they provided security for one of the Civil Affair (CA) teams and met with the local leaders.

The two of us joked during our stroll through the village, just the two of us talking about getting captured or killed as we moved further and further up, only to find out we were on the wrong hill and had to go back down to link up with Davis and his partner, then up the hill just to the north.

I took pictures the whole way, as I normally do, chronicling this little adventure I am on for whatever reason I can—something many locals don't appreciate when we stroll through alleys and into people's back yards.

* * *

Out here, however, every day is a beautiful day. The sun always shines. The stars are always filling the sky, and some of the local girls are starting to look really good. [Lance: Maybe the resort and spa idea isn't so wrong after all?] The only lives that I think about taking are those of the unwanted, stray dogs chasing Skitz and Coach, who are in heat—and the local Taliban if they ever give me the chance.

I lose myself in daydreams of fire-fights and girls as I lie in my bunk, headphones in my ears, and a "We Love You Adam" sign hanging above me, (inviting a great number of questions), waiting for my next meal. [Lance: So happy you're enjoying your sign. I'd wondered what had happened to it.]

18

"I HAVE A WEIRD QUESTION FOR YOU."

~Adam~

I lick the last bit of microwave popcorn butter off my fingers. I stole a half-eaten bag out of the trash box Clemente keeps next to his bed, while he slept behind a sheet at 3:30 in the afternoon. I have long since switched back into my deployment mode. Every little bit of American-style comfort is capable of making my day—or afternoon—in this case. And with that, the lack of comfort items, like regular showers, a flush toilet, and sheets, don't bother me.

I passed the morning in my bunk, listening to my music, thinking about how I should have been studying and making proper use of my time, but there I remained, headphones on, my head resting on my nice foam pillow, with a T-shirt as a pillow case. My laptop slept on the small table beside me.

My afternoon was relatively simple. I spent a little more than two hours relaxing on the Entry Control Point (ECP, the front gate). My job was to distribute passes to the local workers who were on the base and record anything of interest I saw.

Ultimately I'd end up socializing with the interpreter who was assigned to me.

We'd swap stories and learn about each other's cultures, or as he'd find out, my lack of.

"You are married?" Mohammed asked me.

"No. I was," I answered.

"What happened?" He was curious. None of the locals understood divorce.

"We were both very young when we got married," I tried to explain, holding the nasty details back.

"Women in Afghanistan cannot ask for a divorce. If she wants a divorce, you can shoot her."

"Yeah, women are individuals and can make their own decisions in America. It is very good in a lot of ways. And it also causes trouble."

"If you find your wife cheating on you, what do you do?"

"I would tell her it is over, and we would get a divorce."

"In Afghanistan, if you do not kill her and him, then you would be called a pimp. Pimp is a very bad word."

"Because it means you let other men have sex with your wife?"

"Yes. You should shoot them both."

"We call that murder in America," I told him in a matter-of-fact tone of voice.

I broke the short pause we had, while we considered our cultural differences. "Okay. I have a weird question for you."

He looked at me, not sure what to say.

"One of the other soldiers told me that he saw one of the locals with three dogs," I started my little tale. "There were two male dogs and one female. He threw rocks at the two males and then lured the female over to him. Then he flipped her over and had sex with her. Why?"

He laughed. "That is a sin in Islam. These people are uneducated about Islam, and so when they do not have a wife, sometimes they have sex with dogs or goats."

"Okay. I just had to make sure you guys thought that was fucked up also."

"Oh, yes sir, these people are stupid."

Sitting with Mohammed, as he eye-balled my water, reminded me of the many contrasting cultures running around on this base. It was Ramadan, and no one was allowed to eat or drink anything during the day—the Muslims, at least. I spent breakfast with an interpreter from L.A., who was a former bank manager. Now, he was here in khaki shorts and with a soul patch on his chin.

He was complaining because he didn't have anyone to hang out with, because the local interpreters don't understand why he isn't fasting, and it was hard for him to hang out with the soldiers, because we were generally distrusting of interpreters.

And there I was, sitting with an interpreter who was complaining because many of the ASG and ANA didn't believe that they were fasting. I was even told of a fist fight that Mohammed had with his brother, when he was accused of eating pork because he lived with the Americans.

I am amused by the differences and how the interpreters call it "uneducated." Those people who don't understand are just uneducated.

The goat-fuckers, those who have forgotten that Islam meant peace, and the people who forget that Islam, like Christianity, is about one's personal individual relationship with God and that it was nobody else's business, are all uneducated.

The more time I spent here with the locals, the more I realized how different from us they were. And—I'll be cliché—how similar we actually were.

They thought it was a sin to drink and have sex with girls who we were not married to, but they still enjoyed hearing about it. [Lance: Have you asked them about homosexuality? I know it is against their religion, but wouldn't it be better to have sex with, at least, another human as opposed to an animal?] [Adam: I did. They say there are no gays out here and if there were they would kill them.] [Lance: Oh. That's nice. Guess I'll throw out my tour book of "the places you must see before you die (because you will in Afghanistan)."] [Adam: I didn't say you wouldn't get laid, you just can't be gay. They believe that it is only a sin if you are gay, and you are only gay if you love another man. But having sex with him isn't gay. They won't talk about it, though, but it is an obvious behavior.]

19

WHAT'S OLD IS NEW AGAIN

~Lance~

I stared at the computer. The computer stared back.

Stalemate.

Okay. You win.

I saw an older guy yesterday bedecked in khaki from head to toe and Vietnam patches and verbiage everywhere on him—which made me think of the draft—which made me think of my brother—which made me—

"I have a couple of questions about Vietnam," I ask my brother Rick, the other writer in my family. "I don't really remember it too well. When it was happening, I was too young. But you do." He is appreciably older than I am. "I've tried to remember what I could, but you were actually up for the draft and that lottery thing."

"Yes. And your question is?" He has such a droll way about him sometimes.

Ignoring his wryness, but secretly loving the hell out of it, (His sense of humor is unique and spontaneous. He finds humor in the oddest things, but that's what helps make him a good writer.) I continue, "I remember all the protests and sit-ins and—

"Remember, I was at Akron [University] when Kent State happened. It was only a few miles away."

"Right. Was it weird when that happened?"

"Yes. It was eerie around campus. People didn't know what was happening. We were used to the sit-ins, but they were non-violent. This was something new."

"Now, you were in that lottery thing. Tell me."

"Well, if you were going to school, you were exempt, as long as it was full time. I was on the five-year plan with my double major. But the school said that I didn't need five years, that I could have done it in four, so the Draft Board ruled me available. When the lottery came up, the Selective Service drew lots based on your birthday. Luckily, I came up 342 and didn't have to go. I wrote a short story about it. I'll send that to you."

"Perfect. I also remember there were draft dodgers and people moving to Canada."

"Yes. Quite a few went to Canada. It was not a popular war."

"Didn't President Carter issue amnesty for the dodgers and the... weren't they called... conscientious objectors? I remember studying it in school."

"Yes, I believe he did. But to be a legitimate conscientious objector (from the draft's point of view), you had to have a religious reason for objecting. Even then you might still get drafted but put into a non-combat role."

"I'll have to look it up. I had an English teacher who was an objector, but that's all I remember." (I have since looked this up and Carter did indeed do that on his first day in office to help relieve the ill feelings over the war. It was not popular in all circles.) "Do you think the media played a part? It seems that there are so many ways to get news now, Internet, etc."

"We would hear things in the dorms from guys, who heard from guys who were overseas. That seemed to be a big source of information for us. There weren't many channels then and not everybody had TVs. Today information is everywhere and everyone has a computer."

"It seems to me that the Iraq War, if you will, was unpopular because we all knew that we were there under false pretenses. (Thank you, Bush) But now that the focus is in Afghanistan, where we should have been all along, if anywhere. That's where the Taliban and Bin Laden are. Now, it's like we are playing catch-up. And the public may just be sick of the fighting. So once again, making it an unpopular war."

"We'll see," my brother says, cryptically. "Not necessarily."

"That was definitive."

He gives a short laugh. He loves to expound—on everything. I'm sure a thirty page thesis on this will be a forthcoming e-mail from him. He does love to be thorough—which I appreciate, but don't need right now. I head him off at the pass. "You don't need to research any of this for me. Your story will be enough."

"Okay." I hear the almost disappointment in his voice as his research brain cells power down. "Let me know."

"I will. Thanks again." I hope this curveball works.

Now, the oddest thing is that I took a break from writing this and listened to a little news. (It's still hard for me to get used to watching "The News.") And what's the topic? Right. Afghanistan. Now they are saying that right now is the height of un-popularity for the war. Great. Just when I get on the bandwagon to support the troops (Adam), it becomes unpopular. After all I have read and gleaned from the older generation, I realize that this is a very bad thing. Those men are over there fighting for us, and actually, a good part of the world. It seems that if we'd gone there instead of Iraq, we might be appreciably closer to getting rid of the terrorism threat. Even if we had gotten Bin Laden, as my brother said, the people would feel we had really accomplished something for the 9/11 attacks. But no. We closed the proverbial barn door after the horse—or in this case, goat-fucker (Thanks, Adam)—had escaped.

Outlook: not good.

I also just read in Time that they want to send more troops over there to cover more areas. One of the reasons for this is that we send money to help build schools etc., but the Afghani are using portions of that money to pay off the Taliban in those areas for their protection against attacks, thereby giving aid to the Taliban! Then, they in turn use this money for their own troops.

Must not.

(The following short story has been included, edited and abridged, and used with the permission of my brother.)

* * *

LOSER by Rick Taubold

I rarely win lotteries or drawings. When I do win, it's too little: two dollars on a scratch-and-sniff lottery ticket, or I'll get next-to-useless pens, key chains, or cheap digital watches. I don't consider myself unlucky though, and there's no L-for-Loser branded on my forehead (at least none obvious in a mirror).

Back in 1969, I was in college working toward dual BS degrees in chemistry and biology at the University of Akron at the same time that Kent State University, just thirty miles away, achieved its fame and notoriety. The Vietnam War and the Draft were in full swing. I had a 1-S student deferment: temporary immunity from Selection. I had to work during the summer to earn money for school (this being back when a year's tuition and room and board were $2000 total). I couldn't attend summer school for the extra courses I needed for the dual major, so I had to attend an extra year to make up the courses.

The University was kind enough to inform my draft board that year that five years were not needed in my situation. I was declared 1-A (draft bait) and ordered to report for my physical in October.

"But," I protested (mildly, not by marching or lying in front of vehicles), "I will be away at college then."

"No problem," the lady said. I'm sure it was phrased differently, but I don't recall any ill-will in her voice. "Contact the local draft board." They had answers for everything.

I went for my physical on the day before Thanksgiving (their choice, not mine) in Cleveland, where they declared my 120-pound, 5'10" self Fit To Serve.

During my years in college, two friends had gone to Vietnam and returned. A third went and did not return.

For those who remember it, on December 1, 1969, the Selective Service System held a lottery, based your birthday. Your number determined the order in which you might be called to serve, if at all. High numbers were good. The day after the lottery, one fellow on my floor of the dorm overslept for an exam, locked himself out of his room, and pulled #1 in the lottery. He was in Army ROTC so he was going anyway, but as an officer at least.

My birth date lottery number came up 342.

Some years ago, at my job then, I worked with a Vietnamese lady two years younger than me. We were good friends.

* * *

Thanks, bro. Now I got it straight from the horse's mouth.

20

I'M NOT A BIG FAN OF PANTS

~Adam~

We found ourselves falling into the routine of the relatively non-routine life. We had a general idea of what to expect on a daily basis. Which is nice. Intel said we would get attacked tonight by fifteen men with RPGs. That night I slept soundly. The attacks rarely came.

Nights were relatively late for me. Davis and I made it into the gym a couple of hours after dinner, which was generally an hour after we planned on actually going. Ramadan had affected our lives in ways that had not been predicted. The gym was one of those ways. The ANA didn't eat until after nightfall. So, they didn't lift until they ate. This meant when Davis and I finally made our way into the gym, they were there. Most of the guys used the smell they brought with them as an excuse to work out another day. We had begun to take it as an indicator of our own personal hygiene.

If it didn't stink, then we were part of the problem.

* * *

"So, SFC Mendoza, guess who almost got into a fight with the ANA last night?" I initiated this conversation while we waited for some lunch from Taj. (Taj runs everything out here for the locals. He owns the contract for the Local Workers, runs a restaurant and the shop on base. He is like the local Godfather.)

"Who?" he asked.

I smiled and looked at Davis, who was hiding under his blanket, feigning sleep.

"Oh really. I want to know the story," Mendoza asked, but was met with silence. "I don't intend to correct the behavior. I'm just curious."

"Okay." Davis revealed himself, sat up, and began his little tale. "So, we are working out last night and I notice one of the ANA looking at me while his friend makes fun of him because his arms are not as big as mine. So, I start pointing out other muscles that are bigger—like my thighs and calves."

"And finally your dick," I interject.

Davis laughs. "That shit was funny. So, we go through all of this, and then I go back to my workout. That is when his friend comes up and says he wants to fight me."

"Oh?" SFC Mendoza responded.

"So, I try to go outside with him, but he wants to fight inside. Fenner clears the equipment from the middle of the floor while I take my shirt off and start jumping around the room making animal noises." Davis slowly moved through his story.

"That is important because you like to fight fair," Clemente shot in.

Davis shot him a look and a smile. "I was just goofing around. That is, unless he hit me in the face. Then, I would have destroyed him. His XO was there though, Lt. Said (Say-eed), and he calmed the guy down. I must have looked pretty intimidating to him, though. I have almost sixty pounds on the guy and I was acting pretty crazy. I saw myself in the mirror and scared myself a little."

"They finally shook hands and everyone was better friends for what happened. It was like a party after it was all done," I said.

Davis carried on the story. "Yeah, the only way I can describe them is like the movie Gremlins, when all of them are in the kitchen fucking with the popcorn machine, and the blender, and the microwave. They move all over the place. The one guy is doing some fucked up pull-ups. Another is lying on the incline bench, benching the bar with his uniform jacket hanging off the one side, and that is it; until his friend threw a scarf on to balance it. Finally, Fenner went over to spot for him."

"It was fun. Davis had his Thailand club music playing, and we were all laughing," I concluded.

* * *

The days were rolling by at a steady pace. I walked around performing my daily tasks, generally in my black PT shorts and a tan T-shirt. My sunglasses and a tan ball cap with an American flag kept the sun out of my eyes. And whatever weapon I felt appropriate for my particular errand was how I moved about the base. I didn't wear a full uniform, unless I was going to post or out on patrol. I found no reason to be uncomfortable there.

When I was not on patrol, I was eating, sleeping, or hanging out. Where I hung out was the question. Sometimes, I was in the gym; other times, I was with Joey and Crockett in the Aid Station. Lately, Odie and I had been hanging out with the interpreters getting Pashto lessons. Which was sometimes helpful, other times just entertaining.

Our evenings could often be spent thinning out the pack of dogs that had been terrorizing our COP, threatening soldiers, and getting into our chow. We had become quite capable, an initial shot to remove its ability to run and a final shot to the brain to stifle its last agonizing gasps.

Click here for links to photos and/or videos

21

THINGS THAT MAKE ADAM SMILE

~Adam~

Foreshadowing: Was my challenging Allah to unleash the full weight of his fury upon us, with dark clouds looming in the distance.

* * *

We stepped out on the patrol to see if we could do something about the apparent Anti-American Forces (AAF) that had been moving in the area. I took a look up into the sky. The cloud cover was growing thick, and the span of time between lightning and thunder was getting shorter.

Soon, as First Sergeant and myself sat against a rock in a draw, watching the corn sway in the wind and spitting sunflower seeds, it began to drizzle. The ground was already moist from the rainfall a few days prior.

Fall was coming, and with it the rain.

"Here comes the LT," First Sergeant told me.

I looked back to see him making his way around the bend on the small goat path that wrapped around the draw we were observing. "I'll go see what is up," I said, lifting myself up. I took the path to intercept him. "What is up, sir?"

"Nothing, just wanted to see what you are up to."

"All right. Hey, I see Wills pushed up to a better position to observe. Do you mind if me and First Sergeant do the same this way?"

"Yeah sure..." he agreed, and then gave coordinating instructions.

"Hey, First Sergeant, we are moving up," I told him.

We found a little spot further down the goat path, just past a small pond I remembered from past patrols. We moved around to avoid the tall corn and still keep our eyes on Wills.

"Hey, Fenner. The LT is moving everyone," First Sergeant pointed out.

I settled myself into my position, after my piss in the corn. "Hmm, they sure are." I counted the blinking IR strobes through my Night Vision Goggles (NVGs). "Well, what do you want to do?"

"We stay," he said.

"Sounds good to me." I scanned the area around me. It was just the two of us for a pretty good distance. The rest of Wills' team and the LT were on the other side of the draw about a ten-minute walk away. Davis' and Clemente's teams were close, but I wasn't sure exactly where. We observed and kept Wills' team in view.

Through my NVGs, I could see a laser flashing my way.

A signal?

I flashed back with the laser I had mounted on my M4.

Nothing.

We played this game a few more times, until I heard some movement down the path from us.

I could see Davis waving at me through his NVGs.

"Hey, so what is up?" I asked.

"Not much. They told me to meet up with you guys. You want to see where we have been hanging out?"

"Sure," I said. "You ready, Top?" (a pet name given to First Sergeants)

"Yup."

We followed Davis along the wall through the field until we met up with Celaya in their observation position (OP). We sat on the edge of the wall, feet dangling like kids at the pier. The corn surrounded us, massive stalks to our backs, sticking up from the darkness around our feet.

"This is the best camping trip ever," I said.

We shot the shit for a while, keeping our voices low, watching as Wills and the LT moved the other team around on the side of the cliff.

They gave the word to move.

We all stood and started along the path to meet up with Clemente.

"Hey guys, watch your—" Celaya said as he lost his footing.

We started laughing. Feet and hands stuck up in the air in a patch of now-smashed, corn. About ten-feet down, Celaya lay. We stopped laughing long enough to ask if he was okay.

We got proof of life.

Oh, I'm a medic.

I'm supposed to help him.

I jumped off the wall, which was higher up than I anticipated, but the ground was soft—thankfully. I made my way over to him. He lay like an overturned turtle. "You good, man?"

"Yeah. Can you help me with my rifle? My face broke its fall," he said, struggling to unhook the sling from the NVG mount on his helmet.

"Yeah, I got you, man." We were all still laughing.

So was he.

Finally, after righting him and scaling the wall, again, we were on our way. The clouds had opened up and the moon was lighting our way quite wonderfully. We met up with Clemente's team and moved along toward SFC Mendoza's small group. I wound along the walls, until I looked down, the drop was thirty-feet of rocks, finally ending on a roof.

We took our time.

One foot in front of the other.

Watching my footing.

Wow, that is a long fa—

A hand reached out of the corn and grabbed my shoulder.

I almost lost it over the edge. I looked into the corn to see SFC Mendoza. He was smiling. "Be careful. You almost fell."

"You almost pushed me." I smiled back.

Eventually, all the teams gathered together, after winding through the alleys and empty streets.

The clouds gathered back together as we neared the base, hiding the moon and stars. The rain came in, and the only source of light we were granted was what the lightning offered us.

I realized then that I was smiling. And I have been this entire patrol. I hummed to myself as I walked through the gate. First Sergeant and I checked each other's weapons to make sure there were no rounds remaining in the chamber.

SFC Mendoza was checking to make sure everyone had all their gear and were not injured.

Only some sore knees.

"I'll see you at the top. I'm going to get some supplies for those knees," I said. We pushed toward our barracks.

"Roger that," SFC Mendoza responded.

The medics had been using cord to lock the Aid Station. The rain was coming down hard now.

I managed to break in and get what I needed without waking the soldier sleeping on the cot near where the ice packs were kept. I re-secured the door and headed back up.

Allah finally opened his bladder. If Iraq was Allah's shitter, Afghanistan was the rocky bottom of his piss tube.

I was thoroughly soaked when I reached the barracks. We were all laughing. I managed to get a video of the river, then flowing past our barracks, and the lake surrounding our stairs and the foundation of the building.

We swapped stories about everyone's slips and falls.

Finally, everyone calmed down and the lights turned out.

The rain drummed hard on our tin roof, less than gently, washing the day out of my brain and carrying me into a dreamless sleep.

Click here for links to photos and/or videos

22

ME TOO

~Lance~

I sit here and wait for the e-mail 'ding' to say I have a new message. It's my birthday. September 13. And I'm just hoping...

My sister and her girlfriend (yes, that kind) are visiting, which is great. But the highlight of my birthday is going to IHOP for Eggs Benedict. Whoopee!

I have to work. Ugh! And almost no one has called me to wish me Happy Birthday. What's up with that? Two e-mails and a couple of calls. My tried and true friends who always call, haven't. And even worse, I know I probably won't hear from Adam. It's been a week since his last e-mail. He must be out at the Death Star, so... incommunicado. Even though we had sort of an agreement (at least on my part) that he would call me for my birthday and Christmas, I knew it was contingent on his being able to do it. Ah well, Eggs Benedict, my sister, and a couple of cards will have to do. There's always next year.

September 14: I'm at work. It's 9:15 P.M., or so.

My phone vibrates.

Can't answer, I'm busy.

Glance at the number—404-066. What the hell is that?

Another vibration. A message. I'll check it in a few minutes.

VOICE MAIL:

"Hey, it's me. If you see a crazy-ass number in your phone, it's probably me calling. Yeah, well, I guess I'll give you a call tomorrow. Bye."

Oh my God! He called.

Great. Now what do I do.

Wait. I'll go home and send him an e-mail to let him know I got his message and will be available the next night to talk—no matter what.

September 15th: Now, it's my birthday, or so everyone seems to think. I get calls all day from everyone who spaced out and forgot. Totally weird, but pretty awesome just the same.

I'm at dinner (Tuscany) with Heather (my author friend), who's in town with her clan. We've finished up dinner and still no call. It's getting late. 11:15.

My phone rings.

404-066.

"Excuse me," I say to everyone. "It's Adam." They nod in understanding. They all know him.

"Tell him hi and we love him." Heather says.

"Hi there."

"Hey. How ya' doin? Happy Birthday."

"Now, I'm doing great. Thank you."

"I was at the Death Star this week."

"I figured." Which of course translates to: "I would have called you on your birthday, if it was at all possible." He remembers everything. "So, are you doing okay?"

"Yeah. I'm having fun."

"Fun? You certainly know how to make the best of any situation. Maybe my resort-and- spa idea has some merit after all. Heather and the gang are with me here at Tuscany. They say hi, be careful, stay safe, and they love you."

"Send them mine, too."

The next forty-eight minutes (I looked at the time in my phone.) fly by in un-paused conversation. We talk about everything. Words fail me to convey the actual feelings of our reunited camaraderie. It's cathartic for both of us. I don't get maudlin or teary. It just feels so great to talk to him. [Adam: He has been saving that word "maudlin."]

After almost an hour, I say—but don't want to, "It's pretty late for you."

"Yeah, it is..." I hear the reluctance in his voice.

"You can call me anytime, you know. Just give me a heads-up, an e-mail, and I'll be available."

"I will."

"Okay. I'll e-mail you soon. Be careful. I love you."

"I will. Me, too. Bye."

Me too.

Me too.

Me too.

Me too?

Had I heard right?

Yep.

How does he manage to keep surprising me and know exactly the perfect birthday present to give me?

Happy Birthday to me.

Love, Adam. [Adam: *Rolling Eyes*]

23

HARSH WINDS

~Adam~

Afghanistan again had proven itself to be uncompromising. Both the terrain and weather were harsh. I could see it in the faces of children and elderly, the dirty little boys' faces, smudges of mud hiding smooth, youthful skin. And the beautiful girls who, we were pretty sure—if our fantasies were not lies to ourselves—if they were pulled out of this harsh lifestyle, would grow up to become beautiful women. This was not true here in the valley. The sun beat down hard, the rain harder. If that didn't harden the skin of these people, the long days in the fields and mountains would. Everyone there looked either fourteen or forty. There were no in-between years.

Wills scanned, leaning against the wall of the Death Star, with a pair of self-stabilizing binoculars. His FRACUs (Fire Resistant Army Combat Uniform) were torn from excessive use. Seams were blown. The seat was torn open, and at least one belt loop had quit holding on. His brown shirt floated around him in the wind, untucked and unwashed. He plodded between gun positions, his sandals clacking lazily on the uneven cement floor (which Santana had decided to piss on this morning. At which point, she almost learned to fly, but the animal lover in me conceded to merely throwing my water bottle.)

"Anything good?" I asked him.

"Fuck no."

"Might be too windy even for the Derkas." (A bit of racist slang that we used to describe the locals)

It was pleasantly quiet, aside from the wind whistling through the Mark 19 mount (automatic grenade launcher) looking to our south. It wasn't so pleasant this morning.

An IED split an MRAP from Hustler platoon as they rolled down to Meth Lab. The descriptions of the events I got were pretty choppy. The word was it split the MRAP in half. We knew four guys got Med Evaced (Medical Evacuation) out. Sam was in the group. I heard his legs were broken. Not sure yet. (They weren't.)

Everyone would live, but their injuries were still serious. [Lance: So, everything I have been hearing and reading about the IEDs is true—including this incident I heard about. It's a definite threat and concern. And you knew these guys! And before you interject with some jibe, I know it's part of what you signed on for. Doesn't mean I have to like it.]

Just last week, Sam was up with Odie on a hill operating with the French and Special Forces in the southern portion of the Laghman Province over-watching Sandy, Finch, and Baltasar. One klick, (kilometer) away, they watched as twenty to forty Taliban attempted to overrun their position.

The rumor mill was whispering—loudly—about Finch and his team receiving Silver Stars. They told us stories about French Tigers doing gun runs and the enemy being so close that "Allah akhbar" could be heard through the gun fire as they surrounded their position.

They all made it out unscathed, aside from Sandy rolling his ankle.

I didn't get invited. [Lance: My turn— *Rolling Eyes*]

"You aren't one of the cool kids anymore," Sandy told me, after telling me I would have loved it and that he needs his ACOG back.

I still hadn't given the ACOG back, however.

I learned that there was a fight out there to be had. And for some reason I thought the Army was shielding us from it—for fear of casualties. I didn't want to see anybody on our side hurt, but we had come there to hunt down the enemy. It seemed every time we submitted a mission plan to go after the enemy, it got shot down in favor of relatively meaningless local operations: out to the bazaar to escort CA, or out to the Jesus Tree to set up sensors that didn't work. I know I didn't get to see the big picture, but everything I had been reading about and everything I had seen led me to believe that nothing we did out here mattered, aside from the fact that we existed out here.

Maybe that was why our training prior to arriving was garbage. And the biggest thing that higher-up puts out is what safety gear to wear. It didn't matter what we did there, as long as we were there. The fight was being waged on the news and in conference rooms. Killing bad guys was just a PR and morale bonus. [Lance: Whoa. This is sobering news. I get your frustration and anger. Yet, General McChrystal—who is all over the news—keeps saying we need 40,000 more troops. Why doesn't he utilize the ones he's got to their best benefit? Especially, since guys are getting hurt and killed just by going on supply runs!]

Click here for link to photos and/or videos

24

"TONIGHT, WHEN YOU PRAY TO ALLAH, YOU THANK HIM..."

~Adam~

"Hey, man, cover me. I'm just jumping over the wall," I yelled to my gunner before I dropped off the wall six feet into the river below.

I couldn't wash the blood from my pants. The stains on my knees had held through the repeated trips through the river, whose depth reached past my knees and into the M9 that was strapped to my thigh. But the blood on my newly issued knife, I could get off.

The blood washed away easily from the thick, slate-gray handle, which reminded me of a roll of quarters, bringing with it the pleasant fantasy of punching an AAF in the face and the amusing facial trauma that would follow. Specks of blood hid within the cracks between the base of the blade and the handle where it folded; the cool water washed the majority of it away. The adrenaline was gone, and the shakes with it. All that was left was the euphoria of an exciting day ending as the sun set behind Karandali, about two klicks south of Dumlam.

* * *

We had been assigned to get more MRAPs from Meth Lab. None of us were thrilled. The route was red. Every time someone drove on it, they got blown up. We didn't intend to be like everyone else, though.

We had met route clearance on the road where they had hit an IED and lost an MRAP. We looked into the valley, where only a week prior, Wills had found the trigger-sight for another IED. Those fuckers got us again. This time a group of us had walked across the valley to explore the town we would later learn was named Karandali.

One of the newest additions to the Death Dealers, Smith, stuck close to me, a mortar-man who lived the infantry code, which had been pounded into him for over a decade on the gun line—a code that over time had separated him from his fellow mortar-men. He had asked to become a Death Dealer before tension in the Mortar-Pit boiled over. I watched his thick Hawaiian frame move in front of me as we pushed through the corn and forded the river to reach the village.

We made it back before the sun set. It was just enough time for Davis to find a sand table, and us to have an unsuccessful discussion with the village elder, who seemed confused about the sand table depicting the site where the MRAP was hit.

As the sun set, the LT and I got into an argument about ROEs and Smith's actions while in the village.

* * *

I had wandered off. I normally did. Not too far, of course, just enough to find a good picture or to get a feel for the surroundings. Smith felt obligated to follow, cover my back and all.

We moved up to a small home with a large, flat, dirt yard, square-shaped with an ankle-height wall wrapped around it. We stood a fair distance from the house while I surveyed the area just around the corner from the rest of the platoon.

From the doorway of the house a dog growled, its hackles up. The children watched us from the windows, a mix of fear and curiosity.

"Hey, bro, if that thing charges you, kill it," I told him.

"Roger that, Sergeant."

I turned my back and snapped a picture.

POP!

POP!

I turned to see Smith falling backward, his weapon pointing at the dog, now a foot away from him. He stumbled, and landed on his ass.

I rushed over to help him up.

The dog lay on its side, gasping for air.

The radio exploded with frantic traffic.

* * *

"Sir, he was acting under my orders and defending himself in accordance with ROEs," I told him. I kept my temper in check. I could feel it attempting to boil over, but before the quiver made it into my voice, I shoved it back down.

"What you see is this little bubble around you," he said, showing me a small circle with his thumb and forefinger. "What I am working with is a bigger picture."His hands opened up as if he held a basketball.

"I will never tell a soldier he should get bit by a dog, that is fucked up."

"He should have taken the bite. This was the wrong time for this to happen."

It stung when he said it.

ANP worked through Shamsakheyl, clearing through and managing to find two artillery shells.

I didn't respond and let the conversation fall away as he turned and walked off.

I would tell SFC Mendoza later.

Smith didn't need to know.He felt guilty enough.

Any red-blooded American would—we all love dogs. And he saw in the windows the children who loved that dog, watching as he fell backwards to avoid the charging animal.

He was lucky enough to not hear the children crying. After the radio traffic cleared, and I was able to report the incident up, he was already back down, listening to all the Arm Chair Generals critiquing his course of action. I went back and took a picture, at SFC Mendoza's request, to back him up if it became necessary.

I could hear the children crying inside.

"Dealer Seven. Dealer Medic. He is still breathing. Do you want me to perform a mercy kill?" I asked SFC Mendoza.

"Dealer Medic. Negative. Let's get out of here," SFC Mendoza responded.

That was one of those moments I should have asked forgiveness, instead of permission.

* * *

Mehtarlam was everything I had heard. I was, however, filled with less hate, and more sadness, for those left behind on the FOB.

The command worked them hard—daily missions. Some without warning. We were there for four days; two of them were arriving and leaving. They managed to squeeze two missions in while we were there.

Death Dealers held true to our reputation.

Our nighttime dismounted patrol was an easy four-and-a-half-mile stroll in the dark. And aside from the four locals, who upon hearing us walking past their home decided to charge their weapons, take battle positions, and start yelling at us, things were uneventful.

"We are Americans, mother fuckers," Davis yelled into the dark.

"Davis, calm down." The squadron operations officer attempted to control him.

"Sir, there are only two words that they know: fuck, and Americans," Davis added before walking away.

Eventually, our moderately armed Afghani counterparts put away their weapons and went inside, a decision they made wisely while I watched through my NVGs, with all the Death Dealers' lasers dancing about their thin frames in the dark.

* * *

The next patrol into Meth Lab's bazaar was an adventure and an object lesson on how this war is fought from higher levels.

"That guy has an AK," the Colonel Cunningham's interpreter pointed out.

"Roger. Let's go find out why," Col. Cunningham responded.

As we approached the gunman, he was brushed aside by a heavyset man with a solid beard. I snapped a picture when the Colonel shook his hand and greeted him with a smile.

They exchanged pleasantries, while I took pictures of them and the area, with both his camera and mine.

"You got the pictures, right?" he asked as we walked away.

"Yes sir. A lot of them."

"Good. We are pretty sure that guy is a Taliban leader," he said, without seeming remotely disturbed by the idea of having shaken hands with and exchanging smiles with the enemy.

I would just stick to pulling the trigger and patching holes. It was easier.

* * *

The FOB was pleasant, and aside from the laundry machines, the chow hall, the gym, the MWR, the showers, and the flat terrain, Najil was significantly better. There was an uneasy attitude. Everyone was deathly afraid of getting yelled at for the smallest infractions, and individuality was seriously frowned upon.

Finch mixed well into that environment, being the only one who had told me to blouse my boots. I rogered up, but ultimately didn't comply with the order. The other medics I was actually glad to see.

For the most part, they were content to be where they were in the Aid Station, a few making sure to explain their reasons for not going outside the wire, and how they really did want to.

"You don't have to explain yourself to me," I would respond. I said that more times than I thought was necessary.

Joey likes to say, "Don't hate them for doing a job you don't want to do, so you can do a job they are unwilling to." [Lance: Nice quote. Good perspective.]

* * *

We were finally headed home, after leaving later than anticipated. The ride back was smooth, until we got off the hardball. Just before Shamsakheyl, north of Watangatu and south of the Jaboom CP, in a small town called Nulu, we dismounted. We cleared the road on foot. Clemente took a few guys onto the ridge looking for AAF and wires, while Davis took a team into the corn fields doing the same.

We have been asked why we don't get hit like the other units. Davis always told them, "We aren't afraid to put guys anywhere to get the job done."

SFC Mendoza and I trailed Wills, Smith, and the LT as they pushed along the road.

Before long, we got word that ADT had been ambushed in Dumlam and the Marines were coming to back them up. We would do the same coming from the south.

We mounted up, then flew north, closer to the Jaboom Checkpoint, where another unit was holding.

Again we dismounted.

Into the corn we pushed.

Clearing.

"We won't find shit. These guys are already gone," Wills said.

Regardless, we crossed the first river and entered the corn.

Crack.

Crack.

Crack.

Rounds flew overhead.

"I haven't heard that in a while," I said to myself.

Through the corn, I watched everyone maneuver forward and shoot back.

Wills had entered the clearing on the other side of the corn. I pulled him backwards, up onto the wall, where I was sitting deeper into concealment offered by the corn, just enough to obscure their observations of him and me. Wills changed magazines in the dirt next to me and wrestled with his drop-mag pouch.

We bounded forward.

And pushed through the river.

As I dove up an elevated row of corn, I turned to see Clemente falling in the river.

I laughed.

We entered the corn.

Fire.

Move.

"COVER ME!"

"I GOT YOU, MOVE!"

BOOM.

The ground exploded white in front of me. Sparks shot up from the ground. Pieces of white phosphorous sizzled in the riverbed ten meters in front of Clemente and me.

We paused, our forward movement briefly out of shock.

We collected ourselves and pushed forward, quickly regaining our momentum.

Friendly rocket—a little close.

[Lance: It's very difficult to hear about this after the fact. But I guess that's better than the alternative. Sometimes his tell-all is not so much fun. How many months to go?]

"WHEW, THAT IS WHAT THE FUCK I AM TALKING ABOUT!" SFC Mendoza screamed into the radio, directing the helicopters that continued to hunt our prey with us through the fields.

Further north in the valley, more shots were heard.

Soon, we were just south of Karandali, on the other side of the valley.

We maneuvered around through the corn and the rivers.

Although, I was often knee-deep in the rushing river water, I couldn't feel the cold against my skin, only the force of the water attempting to knock me over, as it did my comrades.

I held my rifle high above my head.

"This isn't Platoon, mother fucker," Clemente yelled to me, laughing from the other side of the river.

I maneuvered, step by step, jamming each foot between the rocks to maintain my footing, and I kept pressing along.

Almost ten minutes had passed since the last round had been fired. In our security posture along the riverbed, the faint smell of cigarettes started to fill the open air. Smith and the other smokers were beginning to light up.

"MEDIC!" SFC Mendoza yelled over the radio.

"Roger. Where are you at?" I picked a direction and ran.

"MEDIC!"

I saw them. In a patch of corn, the circle that always forms around a casualty. I could see the ANA BDU (Battle Dress Uniform, the old style) uniforms gathered next to the Marines in their woodland green digitals. I made out SFC Mendoza's rifle sling, a single piece of yellow duct tape wrapped around the black strap that contrasted the worn gray of his ACUs.

I smashed through the stalks of corn into the center of the circle.

As I approached the crumpled body that lay tangled in the corn, I brushed past an ANA soldier holding a pineapple grenade.

A mask of disbelief and awe was worn by every soldier and Marine in the circle. American or Afghani, both shared the moment.

I looked down at the Taliban's crumpled frame. Half-opened pupils sagged just below the bottom lids, like two suns sinking into the horizon. His hair and beard were a mess of blood. His right arm was tucked under his body, and his left was tangled in a knot with a bent-over stalk of corn on his head.

Dead.

"He's got a grenade," someone yelled.

I shifted my position to better handle him.

"Doc, search his hands," SFC Mendoza's voice directed from behind me.

I drew my nine.

I glanced at it, feeling the weight in my right hand.

Still off safe, and put it between his eyes.

"Get froggy, dude. You won't be pleased how it goes for you."

I felt my pants rip from the strain of moving on my knees, shifting toward him. I looked down to see the hole just below my crotch.

Fucking perfect.

I searched his hands. Empty.

Then his magazine rig. The only sound you could hear was that of his cell phone ringing in his pocket.

Someone was wondering what happened to him.

I fought the urge to answer the phone. ("Hello? United States Army. Mohammed can't come to the phone right now. How may I help you?") [Lance: Brilliant. Thanks for the laugh.]

I pulled out my newly issued blade and cut through the stalk that was preventing me from moving him as I needed to.

I exposed his neck.

Absent carotid pulse.

"Check if he's dead," an unknown voice.

I muzzle thumped his eye with my nine.

Squish.

Still dead.

I began to cut up his gear and clothes.

What killed this guy?

I found the entry wound and the exit wound. His bicep was blown open and revealed to me where at least one bullet had exited his body.

"Dude, you need to put some gloves on." I looked up. It was the Marine Gunny. I recognized his squat, solid figure, even if I didn't make the effort to focus on his face.

COP Najil was like that, a small community, working closely together.

I looked down at my hands. The blood had covered them. The knife in my hand was covered as well, with little bits of red slime hanging where the blood had congealed.

It was too late now.

He is an E7.

I don't carry gloves.

I never want to have the thought of wasting time putting gloves on when it comes to stopping the bleeding of one of my guys. And I didn't plan to treat the enemy.

"I got some, man." Another medic had arrived silently. He reached into his bag and pulled out a pair for me.

I put clean gloves over my bloody hands.

We continued to search his body.

"You done, Doc?" SFC Mendoza asked.

I looked up. All around me, I found glazed-over eyes watching me.

"Yeah, I'm coming." I stood, removed the gloves, and headed to the river. "I need to wash my hands, though..." As I approached the river, I stowed my blade, the blood from my hands and on the blade slid onto the fabric in and around my pocket. I bent over toward the water. My rifle slid awkwardly off of my back and hit my arm.

Breathe.

I took a second, closed my eyes.

Breathe.

I opened my eyes to see the water rushing all around my soaking wet pants and boots.

"Was that your first body, Doc?" Smith said watching my back.

Air whooshed out my nose. "Nope." I thought back to when I was Doc Close's security during the invasion, and another body. My fellow Marines had gathered around a dead Iraqi.

I didn't look up at him.

I knelt down. The river easily moistened the dried blood on my hands and carried it away. I didn't make any effort to clean the blood that had stained my knees. I felt the cool breeze blow through the blown-out seam in my crotch, brushing against my now exposed leg. I didn't realize how badly my pants had torn.

Awkward.

"Fenner, let's go," a voice yelled.

We ran, fighting our way through the water, and soon when we were again halfway up the ridge before we turned around and headed back toward the trucks.

I met up with the other medic. At his feet lay the body of the Taliban fighter, lying limp on a pole-less litter similar to the one tied to my back. A group of us carried him out of the corn.

The villagers of Shamsakheyl had gathered on the roofs of their homes lining the road and pushing up the hillside, along with a large group of others who were stuck waiting in a traffic jam that we'd created on the small one-lane road where our vehicles were parked.

They watched us lift his body onto the ledge along the side of the road. They didn't look away as we rolled him off the litter and gave it to the ANA to get the other body in the field.

The other medic and I moved him around and searched again for more wounds.

I fumbled through the matted hair on his head, pointing out the grazing wounds along his skull as I discovered them. We rolled him over, spotting more grazing wounds along his back. The skin was splayed open in perfectly straight lines of split skin of varying depths.

His stomach and legs had no visible injuries.

"Dude, check this one out," I said, pointing to an entry wound in the center of his back, a small penetrating hole between his shoulder blades. "And this is where it came out." I tried to pull off his shirt enough to reveal his right arm. His contorted shape and blood-soaked clothes made that difficult. I ultimately found the hole in his sleeve and ripped it open.

"Ohhh, shit." My medical cohort turned away, retching.

His right bicep was opened up where the round had exited in an explosion of muscle, sinew, and his humerus bone snapped in two, as a result of having to carry him five-hundred meters through the corn fields with his arm dangling out of the litter—no matter how many times I had yelled at the dead Taliban soldier to keep it at his side.

The sharp pieces of bone erupting out triggered my companion's gag reflex. [Lance: It's so nice you haven't lost your sense of humor.]

I laughed a little before I covered the arm back up.

SFC Mendoza snagged up the Terp (Intepreter) and stood in front of the body.

"We came here to bring you peace. We build you roads, and the Taliban is trying to take that away from you," he starts, while the interpreter translates.

Smith and I looked at each other, wondering how far he was willing to take this.

"America has come here to help you. And today when the Taliban tried to take the peace that America is trying to give you away, we killed them. That man." He pointed at the body. "That man wanted to take that peace away from you, and America killed him."

We were smiling, standing up near the body. We both wanted to hear this.

"So, tonight when you pray to Allah..."

Oh fuck. We fought to maintain our composure.

"You thank him for America, for killing those people who have tried to take away your peace."

I tried to gather myself, but the shock value of his speech was almost too much.

He finished, triumphant, and headed to the trucks.

We tidied up the body as respectfully as we could, considering we left it on the side of the road.

After we were done, we headed back toward the trucks.

Sitting in the MRAP, Smith pulled out the last scraps of the jerky. He offered some to SFC Mendoza, then to me.

I waved him away. "Sorry man, I need to sanitize the Derka blood off my hands before I feel comfortable handling food."

He took a piece out for himself as I turned my head to look out the window.

"Hey." He gets my attention. I look over to see his gloved hand holding a piece of jerky out to me. I happily ate it out of his hand.

Joey likes to say, "There is a thin line between combat arms and gay."

* * *

We finally parked our trucks in their respective locations throughout the COP. We climbed out, yelling triumphantly. Clemente was at the top by the barracks yelling catch phrases from a "Saturday Night Live" sketch. The rest of us just made noises.

We gathered up in the barracks, and while the COP took incoming rocket and mortar fire, we shared our war stories. I hung my torn and bloodied pants out to dry and took off my soaking wet boots.

I passed out the wraps and ice to those who had eaten it out in the river.

"Do I need to be worried? I swallowed some river water one of the times I fell," Clemente asked.

I laughed. "No more than me. I got Derka blood on me."

The euphoria passed and we all settled down.

Tired.

I hung out with SFC Mendoza in Cheap Times until it was late, talking about war and how it affects people differently.

I don't remember who said it, but it has been said that, "The only thing more disturbing than the things I have seen and done is how it doesn't disturb me."

I slept the sound sleep that only soldiers are privileged enough to enjoy.

Click here for link to photos and/or videos

25

LETTERS FROM HOME AND THE WOMEN WHO STARTED IT ALL

~Adam~

"Your Mom saw your photos on MySpace," Lance e-mailed me. "She knows you have been lying to her about what you do out there."

I knew that would bite me in the ass.

They were good pictures though.

"Mom, I'm in a National Guard Tank Unit. How could they possibly send us anywhere dangerous? We wouldn't know what to do. I'm just sitting in an Aid Station taking care of stuffy noses and bug bites," I had lied to her.

"This doesn't look like you are safe inside the base," Mom commented below my pic.

Another soldier snapped the picture. It centered on me. However, all one could see was a soldier's back, with a large pack on it. Rolls of medical tape hung from the back where I had easy access. That was how I knew it was me. I saw the pic and said to myself, "That is bad ass. Hey, that is my bag."

The angle was just right—the kind I couldn't pose for if I wanted. To my left flew the Afghanistan flag, and in the distance to my right, the American, with the sun illuminating it with a soft glow.

I know I wasn't actually pondering the meaning of war and my place in it while I stoically gazed into the distance with a Gatorade in my hand and a pistol on my leg, but that was how it appeared. The rock wall was high enough to hide the landing zone in front of me, but not higher than the mountains reflecting the early morning sun.

It was the morning mortars wanted to take their tubes on patrol and play. We ended up reacting to real-time intelligence of an ambush in the town we were walking toward and found ourselves climbing a mountain, where we took battle positions in an attempt to ambush the ambushers.

That was also where they took the picture of me resting my cheek on Davis' M14 EBR (which he hates.) and observing the possible ambush site through his ten power scope, while he watched with his fourteen-power self-stabilizing binoculars. Coach sat next to me facing my rear, but was looking at me and the camera. My Kevlar was nowhere to be seen. My unnecessarily long hair was a tangled sweaty mess. My bag provided both cover and a solid place for me to rest the EBR.

How could I fix this?

How could I convince Mom that I am safe so she doesn't worry? She has too much on her plate. Dad's health wasn't improving—the opposite in fact. Grandpa was still happily lost in his memory home And she was fighting with a new job and all its drama.

So I lied.

"Mom, that wasn't me. I have just been a ham. I stay inside the wire. My buddy was using my bag and I thought it was a cool picture."

She didn't buy it.

She responded to my e-mail but ignored the topic.

Fuck.

I would have to call her. [Lance: Great. So now I'll have to lie to her, too.] [Adam: Nope, I called to patch things up and she was too busy to talk. So, Dad told me about the weather.]

* * *

"That is the hardest I have ever squeezed a dick before," Sandy said, fixing his shirt and half-heartedly laughing, after a wrestling match with Finch went awry.

"That was the most intense pain I have ever experienced in my life," Finch said, hunched over, moving back to his bunk.

Now, Smith's bunk sat empty, both from their wrestling match, and from his abrupt move to Meth Lab.

* * *

Joey, just before leaving, after receiving a Red Cross message, regaled me with a tale of Aid Station excitement and grandeur.

"So, this kid comes in shot. No more than three years old. The round entered the center of his sternum and was now sticking out of his back—completely intact," Joey said, shaking with excitement as his hands told just as much of the story as his mouth did.

"Major A was on the phone talking to the surgeons in Jaf (Jalalabad Air Field). They were getting mad at him and saying he needed to check an anatomy book to make sure he understood what the sternum was," Hunt added.

"Dude, the round was undamaged. It wasn't a ricochet. And when I played with it, all the kid did was get mad at me. I think he is related to the nut dragger," Joey said.

"All the kids did was look mad that he had to bother with all of this. I'm looking for a chest rig now that can hold a three-year old Afghani boy to my chest, because it is the only thing I know that can stop an AK round," Bryan said, with a smirk.

* * *

It had been over a month and a half since I had last heard from Susan.

All I sent was, "WTF?"

It had been over a month and a half since she had told me how she regretted everything that had happened between the two of us, and how she missed talking to me.

Then, nothing.

Weeks later, I got something.

"I'm so sorry," she said.

She still regretted everything. She had to move out of her home to escape her crazy now ex-boyfriend with a new number and was living with her folks.

Breathe.

Breathe.

Breathe.

"I was worried," I started.

"I am glad to hear from you, but I want to know why you're doing this?" I continued.

"Why do you keep dragging me back?" I asked.

"And that I can't trust you," I finished.

I was sitting in the courthouse in San Diego in 2006, before we were evacuated for a possible bomb scare, the day my younger brother, Evan, got married. The benches were packed. So, while he sat on the bench, I knelt next to him. Susan was in the car with Ryah. She was heading home after the wedding for what, I thought, was a vacation. She almost didn't come back.

"I want you to understand something, and keep in mind my deployment record." I looked him in the eyes as I offered a piece of brotherly advice. "There are days when I would rather charge uphill into a machine gun bunker, than be married." My brother's eyes got wide. "Because at least I can shoot back."

I was starting to remember why I felt that way. At least when I was getting shot at, I could do something easy and solid. These little emotional games are significantly more difficult and harder to gauge the results. And there is no river that can wash away what I felt at the end of the day as easily as I did the dried blood on my hands.

"I want to try again," she says.

Breathe.

"I am willing to try again, but..." [Lance: Yeah. But.] [Adam: But nothing. I do what I want.]

* * *

"Sir, can I ask you a question? I don't want to offend you though," Mohammed asked me as we climbed the hill to talk to my Track Hoe operator as he dug a new range out for us. My COP Mayor duties had me directing LNs (Local Nationals) on work projects on the COP on my week off from missions.

"Mohammed, of course you can. You can't offend me," I answered.

"That is good, sir. You are my brother and I would not want to make you angry with me." His short but strong legs carried him up the hill at my side. Mohammed had become our most trusted interpreter, always willing to help, and he never complained. Two qualities that were rare among the Afghans we worked with.

"So." I smiled at him. "What is your question?"

"Sir, do you jack off?" He made the motion with his hand as if I didn't understand the term.

"Of course."

"No, you don't. You are lying." His tone was jovial, but serious.

I mimicked his accent. "I would not lie to you, Mohammed."

"I do not believe you. You are very strong. I have seen you in the gym. Jacking off makes you weak."

"Mohammed..." I was out of breath from laughing and climbing the steep incline of the rocky road. "Who lied to you?"

"Sir, I was taught jacking off makes you weak."

Our conversation continued up the hill. I was laughing and trying to stay as serious as I could. The world and culture out here was different. For the Terps who work closely with us there was a bit of cultural meshing. They were exposed to different ideas. These people only knew what they had been told and introduced to. This wasn't America with a wide range of different ideas and huge access to different sources of information if it was desired.

Click here for link to photos and/or videos

26

TRICK OR TREAT

~Adam~

Home.

That is all I had been hearing about.

And sore joints.

It was that time in the deployment. It wasn't that our priorities were getting messed up. But we were pushing the midway point and getting closer to setting foot on American soil, back into the arms of our loved ones. Or not.

Sandy was getting a divorce.

And I hadn't heard from Susan in almost three weeks. Last thing she said was, "I'll tell you more tomorrow."

I stayed patient for the piece of me that had made a vow almost three years ago.

My more realistic half plans a trip to Thailand, with Davis and a few other guys, for the type of fun that wasn't legal in America.

And kept loose contact with Angela.

And the occasional call with Kayla.

And whichever other females shot me an e-mail.

Home.

* * *

"Suit up," the LT ran into our barracks to tell us. "COP Keating is getting overrun and we need to reinforce them."

We loaded up but didn't leave. We just listened to the radio traffic and the sounds of gunfire in the background.

Eight of their guys wouldn't get to go home. I also heard a rumor about a Medal of Honor. The rumor came with a good story, probably won't get it. They would bump it down to a Silver Star. [Adam: I hope he does get it.] The same way they bumped down Finch, Sandy, and Baltasar's award to a Bronze star with a V device (Valor). They would have gotten a Silver Star if they had died. We didn't know that was a requirement. [Lance: Ouch. And wrong.]

* * *

Home.

"Your father isn't improving," Mom told me in an e-mail. "I just need you kids to understand that he needs twenty-four-hour care. I'm unemployed, so taking care of him is my job, but if things get worse we will have to put him in hospice.

Grandpa hasn't changed any, still doing well in the memory home and giving the nurses and female residents plenty of trouble." I laughed at the thought of Grandpa flirting with the nurses.

"Kiley went in to the doctor," Kristin, my sister-in-law's e-mail read. "She has type one diabetes."

It wasn't a good week.

The bright side.

"It has taken us some work, but we got her, and she is running around laughing and full of energy again," Kristin wrote me a few days later.

I patched things up with Mom. Sent her a few pictures I took that I thought she would like of a scarecrow I found, some dishes next to the river, and some flowers. I told her a story about how I told the villagers who tended those flowers that my mother has those same flowers in her garden: marigolds. At the time I was pretty sure it was a lie. Turns out it wasn't. Nice way to connect everyone.

Behind the poncho that was my door, I took a breath and gathered it all together. I no longer noticed the weight of my kit. It felt like any other part of my anatomy—even if it did weigh an extra forty pounds. I slung my rifle, threw on my desert ball cap with a subdued tan American flag on the front and deep black stains from the black ink of my Kevlar pads, grabbed my Kevlar, and headed out to the flight line for roll call.

Time to work.

* * *

It was our first all-dismounted patrol in a while. We had been driving, parking, and walking from there. But this isn't the type of place where you park and walk away. Normally, the drivers and the gunner stayed in the vehicles. Deutch would stay to keep control of the trucks and control the major radio traffic with Punisher base and whoever else might have wanted to talk to us. He sounded like the Hamburgler on the radio, but he always knew what to say. He jokes about how even his fellow police officers like to insult him about it back home.

We stepped off.

Up through Dumlam, on the main road Route Nebraska, we walked north. Finch, Sandy, and Deutch broke off to go sit on the cell tower above Dumlam to provide over-watch while we kept going.

We crossed the Gonapah Bridge and started heading south again.

"Dealer six, you want us to go around or through the village?" Wills asked the LT.

"Roger, let's go through," he responded.

The village was like all the others: rock and mud walls. There is no trash on the ground. These people are so poor everything becomes of use. Small windows with faces obscured by the shadows within were sparsely scattered on the different walls with no apparent pattern.

The men, if they were around, would come out, followed by the boys. The women and young girls always hid or went about their daily business, pretending we were not around. Each village was surrounded by trees for visual cover from outsiders, and a few scattered trees were within the village for shade.

The buildings themselves were built directly into and around the mountains. There appeared to be little to no pattern as to how they built their homes. Some stood independently two stories tall. Others were built directly into the sides of the mountain. The villages were rarely the same elevation from one village to the next or from one home to the next.

Aside from the occasional ornate window frame and the window panes themselves, the homes were built from materials found in the immediate area. The villages close to the river had rounded stones to build their homes. The homes set further into the mountains were built with the sharp rocks that were scattered around seemingly everywhere. [Lance: So the idea of planned communities hasn't reached their area yet.] [Adam: I haven't seen any Del Webb signs, if that is what you are asking.]

"Hey, Fenner, you might want to come check this out," the LT said over the radio.

"All right."

I walked over to him. As I did, I heard an unusual sound.

Children chanting.

I went closer, my camera ready. It was a classroom. Sort of.

Under a small roof, held up by crooked pieces of wood, a small boy stood. He didn't stop yelling when I walked up. And the group of small children, boys and girls, were sitting in the open air under the shade of a tree. A large woven plastic mat had been laid out for them to sit on, and along the wall their small shoes had been left. I stepped up and quietly greeted their teachers, who beamed with pride for their pupils, still repeating whatever the small boy said.

"Hey, what are they saying?" I asked the Terp.

"The Qur'an, sir."

"Can I take their picture?"

"Of course. Why not?"

I snapped a few pictures as best I could with my point-and-shoot digital camera without being intrusive. I would later find out that my helmet camera wasn't working.

I stood on the ledge watching them for a while, and finally, respectfully, we left. A handshake, a thank you, followed by my hand to my heart.

We headed south to the next village. No school.

We walked out of Kowta to the Jesus Tree. Heading west, we walked though the Sherwood Forest area, which was nothing more than a copse of trees two hundred meters west of the Jesus tree. Into Seqanwatah we walked, another small village built into the mountain, with a deep cut separating the town in half, but not appearing to affect day-to-day life for the residents at all. [Lance: They sound like American Indian tribe names, Kemosabe. Couldn't resist.]

My camera was starting to run out of battery.

Out of the town we started heading east again, back toward the COP.

Pop.

Pop.

Pop.

BOOM.

BOOM.

Pop.

BOOM.

"That is coming from the OP," someone yelled.

We booked it.

About a klick and a half away, we moved as fast as we could without losing anyone in the platoon.

It took a while before we heard Finch on the net.

"Thanks for that Two Oh Three, Davis," Finch said over the radio. [Adam: M203 Grenade Launcher]

"Dealer Eye, I need a Sit Rep," the LT asked him.

"We are ex-filling down the hill to the base of Dumlam at this time. We will meet you on the road," Finch briefed the LT.

We met up with them on the road below Dumlam.

"Dude, there was like four to six, two hundred meters north of our position. They just opened up with PKMs and AKs. I dropped my sniper rifle and grabbed my M4 and dumped a mag," Finch told us as we walked up on the three of them on the road.

"Fenner, Davis, I dumped a mag of M4 and just started dropping Two Oh Three rounds. The first round landed like thirty meters in front of us." Sandy made his little "I fucked up" face. "So I decided to aim a little higher, then I was dead on target. I started with nine rounds, and I only have one left."

"Yeah, we dropped rounds while Deutch called in a fire mission, which got fucked up somewhere. Then we beat feet. Classic Battle Drill 1 from sniper school," Finch added.

"This guy and his fucking Battle Drills," Sandy said, picking on Finch.

"We are going to maneuver on the enemy," the LT passed his orders over the radio.

"Good," was the consensus.

The platoon split. One group went back up to the cell tower; the other went around to flank the enemy if they were still there.

Before I knew it, we were next to the cell tower. Davis, Clemente, a few other guys, and me set in among the rocks, avoiding the dog that was tied to the other side we set in.

When we finally caught our collective breaths, I heard Davis. "Fenner, where did you get the SAW?" (M249 Squad Automatic Weapon)

"One of the guys was falling back, so I took it." I looked up at him. My left hand was on my knee. My right was holding the SAW over my shoulder trying desperately to get air into my lungs.

He was smiling. "You are such a fucking Jarhead, man. SAW good. We need SAW. I carry." He did his best caveman/Marine impression. "A medic with a SAW, fucking stupid."

I smiled. "Look, the best preventive medicine is superior firepower, plus I prevented a possible heat casualty."

He shook his head and laughed to himself.

"Dude, did you see that fucking dog?" Mike asked me as the wind started to cool our uniforms down.

"You mean fucking Cujo back there?"

"Fuck, I threw a rock at him to shut him up and he ate that fucking thing. What the fuck, dude?" he said.

"Fuck, I don't know man. I just work here." I smiled at him.

It didn't take long before the others were in place.

It did take a while for the ANA to reinforce us. It took even longer to get the fast movers (fighter planes) to drop their big bombs.

Fighter planes are cool.

Big bombs are cool.

Fighter planes flying only a few hundred feet above the ground— very cool.

"Those planes were a waste of our fucking time," I said to Davis.

"No fucking shit, man. I'm ready to get the fuck off this rock. I'm freezing my nuts off," Davis responded.

"ANA are heading back. I think it is time for us to head down," I added.

"We should probably go around the non-dog side of the tower," Davis said.

"Fuck it, man, take the bite." I smirked at him.

As we piled in through the gate, with Clemente counting us to make sure we had all made it, SFC Mendoza made his announcement. "Good job out there guys. Who wants to know what our mileage was for the day?"

We all looked at him.

"Eight miles for the day," he said.

"All right guys, who is hurt?" I yelled to the platoon as they cleared their weapons of any ammunition.

"Sergeant, my knees hurt," several soldiers spoke up.

"Hurt not hurting," I responded.

"Umm..."

"Come see me when you drop your gear," I told them.

* * *

I didn't know where the week went: two nights in a row sleeping in our uniforms waiting for a fifteen-minute alert for a possible mission, some small missions, then today doing route clearance so the Hooligans could go back to Mehtarlam after dropping off supplies the night prior.

"Let's do something with this mission," we said after arriving at our southernmost point, Watangatu. We stood just outside the school that is on the plateau where we were parked, waiting for the Hooligans to roll through so we could head back.

"It is Halloween," I said.

"I got candy," Clemente said.

"I got cigarettes," Wills offered.

Slowly, everyone started to reveal the goodies they had brought from base to munch on while on the road.

Someone had brought a box of bags of candy for Halloween and had left it in the chow hall. Everyone had snagged one up, including the Terp.

"Let's go talk to the kids, pass out candy, and tell them about Halloween," SFC Mendoza said.

"Sounds like a plan to me." The LT put his seal of approval on the mission.

We made contact with the principal, who guided us from classroom to classroom to talk to the kids. The rooms were solid concrete, no lights hung from the ceiling. Sunlight streamed through the broken windows. There was no chalk on the concrete sill of the concrete blackboard.

The younger kids were too afraid to ask us questions about anything. Except they asked for pens, pencils, and notebooks. And we spent some time showing them some of the gear we had.

SFC Mendoza spoke to classes, asking what they needed and told them, "I will tell my boss what you need."

"We have heard all of this before. You can make promises to me and break them, but not in front of these children," the principal replied at one point.

SFC Mendoza was taken aback. "I can speak only of what I can do. I will do what I can within my power to help you."

As the children got older, they got braver, asking more questions.

To the kids, we passed out candy.

Because of a combination of their maturity and being out of candy, the older students only received a message.

Davis, being the self-nominated speaker of the group, passed the message that apparently no one before us has. "We are here to help you help yourselves. We will fight the Taliban when we meet them, but we can't be everywhere, and it is up to the Afghan people to kick the Taliban out of Afghanistan. And when you work together you can defeat any foe."

We finished visiting with all the kids and headed for the door where Clemente, Wills, and the LT sat with some other kids.

The principal offer us chai. We graciously declined and headed back to the COP.

27

PISSING OFF THE EPA BUT NOT THE AFGHANS

~Adam~

I stood atop the Hesco wall, my feet damp from standing on the tarp where small pools of water sat from the previous night's rain. The world buzzed below me as I watched the carnage swirl. Below me, the fueler divvied out fuel to as many as he could while the ANA ran in every direction with anything that could hold liquid, spent artillery cases, water buckets, and the fifty-gallon trash cans from in front of the chow hall.

Diesel leaked out of the Hesco wall through the tear in the tarp that held the fuel bladder. "Those look like cuts to me, man," one of the mechanics told me.

"Yeah, they do," I responded. He was soaked with diesel up past his ankles from having walked down by the bladder, attempting to ascertain the source of the leak.

"I just turned on the fuel this morning, and it just blew," the fueler told me. The line was destroyed; the massive heavy hose was opened from one end to the other. It looked like a clean slice. First Sergeant disagreed with me. I'm not a fuel guy. I really don't know.

"I guess those fuckers got what they wanted," the fueler said, looking down at me. He was a dark green soldier, standing well over six-feet tall. He looked down at everyone. The whole week we had been fighting with them about how much fuel they needed for the heavy equipment operators and the other Afghans we worked with. We knew they siphoned the majority of it off and sold it out in town. So we had been giving them the bare minimum required for them to do their jobs.

They furiously drove around in their ANA tan pick-up trucks, heading off the COP with our gray trash cans full of fuel.

"Hey, Gunny, your boys took all my trash cans," I told the Marine Gunnery Sergeant who supervises and acts as a liaison to the ANA.

"Yeah, they took mine, too. Except mine has a one inch hole in the bottom of it," he replied.

They gathered every drop of fuel they could. They had pulled fuel off the ground as it ran along the dirt road into make-shift dams of mud to slow its escape. The whole road was soaked with diesel. The smell hung heavily in the air.

The mechanic stood atop the Hesco wall near me, just above the ANA, like flies on shit, at the point where fuel poured out. His tattooed, light-brown hand held out his lighter, a smile across his face. "Watch this."

The flies scattered.

We laughed.

The spill was quickly contained. What fuel could be saved was, and what ended up in the ground the ANA and my LNs strained out of the dirt itself to sell off.

I would normally not have been there, but my mayoral duties brought me and a group of my workers in to help. I quickly sent them away, realizing our presence was hurting more than it was helping.

Back to work.

Back to trying to figure out how to explain what I wanted done, without being able to talk to them. Aside from a few of the younger kids, no one spoke English. They were mostly the shit burners or involved with the trash, and the orphan who looked fifteen had been married twice. His English was garbled by a combination of a thick accent and a speech impediment.

The LNs my age were either high on hashish, lazy, or both. The really old men were the hardest workers.

* * *

I bent down to help an older squat Afghan man sporting a thick white beard and sun-worn skin pick up a larger rock.

"Na, na," he told me gently, brushing me aside.

Baba, as he is often called as a term of respect, placed himself between the rock and me. He motioned to the other workers, who quickly got up and moved over to the rock pile and moved them. Qasim, a taller and more intelligent Afghan, began to whistle with a smile on his face.

"Na, na," Nasim responded, frustrated. He is generally the subject of a great deal of ridicule and actually named by his co-workers as "crazy" because of his behavior and also because of his one lazy eye.

"Mohammed, can you tell Nasim that I like his shirt?" I asked.

"Of course, sir."

"I want him to know that the company that makes that shirt is my favorite beer company," I said with a smile.

Mohammed translated and everyone had a good laugh, smiled, and shared positively toned words.

* * *

Clemente had been Mayor since we got to COP Najil, but has been busy lately and unable to do the job. So, I have been stepping in. The locals love us, telling us that we are the good Mayors and the others are "no good, no good." Clemente's police experience gave him the patience to work with a variety of different people. It helped out there. People's hatred for the Afghan people could be quite transparent at times, which was a difficult trait to have when one's job was to supervise them. [Lance: Mayor Fenner has an interesting ring to it. But then you do like to call the shots. :)]

I refused to believe that these people were any different from us, and I wouldn't blame them for my presence here.

It was too easy to join all the people who said, "Fuck them," when they needed help. That was why we were here after all.

As I changed into PT shorts, at the end of a long day as Mayor, I heard a knock at the door.

I opened it to find Mohammed standing there. The other interpreters send him if they need anything because they know we like him.

"What is up, man?" I asked.

"Sir, I am sorry to bother you, but the light in our room went out," he said.

I looked back into the empty barracks. Everyone was down getting dinner. I was pretty done with the Afghans after a long day.

I looked back at him.

"All right, Mohammed, I got you, man," I said, pushing aside my frustration. "Just let me finish getting dressed and I'll get you a light."

I looked at the laptop, the caret blinked waiting for me.

After the gym. I closed the laptop.

28

TAKING THE HIGH GROUND

~Adam~

Another maneuver week was already dragging on, grinding itself into my knees and ankles—reminding me I'm not eighteen anymore. But I was not that old either. Growing old, or hiking the mountains of Afghanistan, was taking its toll. I could feel it in my knees when the weather was cold. The early mornings were the worst. [Lance: Not eighteen anymore. Please.] [Adam: Oh, I know. You weren't eighteen anymore when I was still two separate sets of twenty-three chromosomes.] [Lance: Now you're just trying to be clever.]

Zero three (3:00 AM) comes quickly every morning. I awoke and slid out of bed, grabbing the 9mm that lay next to me, stumbling out to let the last of the excess amount of water I drank in the gym out. My knees ground and took a moment to warm up as I climbed down the stairs and headed toward the piss tube, enjoying the moonlight and the cold air. I rushed back into my warm sleeping bag and got to enjoy the last few hours of sleep before my day started.

We were barely half-way through the week. The first night was an overnight stay on the ridge just south of Galwatah.

"Dude, are you seriously bringing that big bag out there?" the LT asked me as we stepped out the gate.

"I feel like I made the right decision, sir," I responded.

The moon was setting behind the mountains. The sun would soon be out, but the light had not yet broken over the peaks to the east. The cold wind whipped up and over the small rocks that surrounded our battle position overlooking Galwatah. I looked over at the soldier sitting next to me, shivering where he slept.

I smiled to myself.

Ten hours later, while Deutch and Finch headed to their OP, the rest of us passed out candy to the girls, telling the boys to go away, spreading the word about our made-up holiday: Afghan Ladies Day—like Mother's day, but for all the women and girls of Afghanistan. We were noticing they were beyond neglected out here. They didn't understand the concept. They wouldn't though. They believed women were unclean, something about their menstrual cycles and a series of cultural misunderstandings caused by following a religious text that even many religious leaders in the region couldn't read.

* * *

We again found ourselves meeting up with the ANP at the Jaboom CP for a mission down in Karandali. We had left the Jaboom CP and had made our way, relatively slowly—as slowly as Wills was willing to walk. Soon, we were standing in the riverbed, about to cross.

Pop.

Pop.

Pop.

From behind us.

We turned and started moving.

"Mother fucker, come here!" I screamed at Mahmoud, our new Terp, who was busy hiding behind a rock in the riverbed.

I stayed online with the platoon as we pushed forward to the elevated ground, trying to take cover and figure out where the fire was coming from.

Something felt wrong.

I didn't feel like we were in danger.

There was no snap of the rounds as they flew overhead.

Pop.

Pop.

Pop...

Someone must have seen something. One of our guys was shooting.

I still couldn't see anything.

I kept moving. Below me, the guys still tried to find high ground. SFC Mendoza was right behind me.

Through my ACOG I scanned. Nothing.

SFC Mendoza saw a guy on the road and called him over to us. I scanned him from a distance. He didn't have a weapon that I could see.

I kept scanning as he passed me, and SFC Mendoza started searching him.

The LT's radio was down, and he began to relay his plans through my radio to the team leaders on how we would maneuver on the possible enemy.

"Get on your fucking face," I heard SFC Mendoza yell from behind me.

It didn't take long before the guy was standing up and we were brushing him off.

Wills handed back his pistol with an empty magazine that had been fired into the hillside. Our now very frightened friend was ANA and had decided to test fire into the hill.

The ANA took a big dip of a green tobacco-like substance as we handed him back his identification and weapons permit.

"Yeah, man, do what you got to do to cool off," we told him.

We sent him on his way.

"Who fired their rifle?" SFC Mendoza asked the group.

Silence.

"I did," one of the mortar attachments finally said. We were hurting on bodies to fill patrols and needed supplements. Mortars had been providing for us since so many of our guys had been hurt.

"What did you shoot at?" SFC Mendoza asked directly.

"I was in fear for my life, Sergeant."

"Okay, so what did you shoot at?"

"I was providing suppressive fire."

"So, you didn't see fucking anything?" Wills said, a now lit cigarette in his hand.

"I saw a guy on the hill with an AK."

"I just need you to understand what PID means," SFC Mendoza reaffirmed with him.

"Roger."

We pushed on, back down the riverbed, until we found a suitable spot to cross the river.

"I don't believe that mother fucker saw shit," SFC Mendoza told me, once we got moving again. "Are you with me?"

"Oh yeah."

We visited a few villages, passed out some candy to the kids, slapped hands with the village elders, as SFC Mendoza likes to put it.

And asked about some local Taliban, who no one had ever heard of.

"It is just like fucking Iraq. No one knows shit about anything," Finch said.

"I'm starting to feel like these fuckers are just playing games with us," I told SFC Mendoza while we sat overlooking the same home ANP had had us search two times already, because this was where the Taliban lived.

We watched as the LT and the interpreter questioned the same old lady we had questioned the last two times we had come through this village.

"Yeah, I feel you, man," he told me.

"These people don't give two fucks about anyone but themselves and their little fucking villages," I said aloud. "We are just another means to an end for them. They don't give two fucks which side wins as long as they can eat."

The LT and the ANP, dressed in their blue jump suits and sandals, walked away from the old lady, looking beaten.

* * *

Within COP Najil I stepped out of the MRAP after we'd parked. There was the ANA soldier who we had rolled up earlier in the day.

"What is up, man?" I yelled to him as he walked with a friend.

"Hey, Jour-aye," he yelled and waved back in a traditional Pashaye greeting, with a smile.

The next day when we were sitting just outside the gate, talking to the locals as they passed, we caught that same ANA not standing his guard duty, as he was assigned to, and seriously compromising the security of the base.

And then arguing about it with us.

All the while Clemente, Wills, Finch, and I were arguing and questioning SFC Mendoza as to why we would be unfit to date his sixteen-year-old daughter.

We have repeatedly found the gate unlocked and unmanned. Weeks earlier, we had to break into the COP after a patrol, without being noticed as I climbed the wall, opened the gate, and the whole platoon walked in. Without a word of protest from the ANA on post.

We needed help out there, but we didn't have the bodies. And they just pulled the ADT and PRT elements off base, stretching us even thinner.

"What do we do for QRF if we get hit, sir?" we asked the LT.

"The commander already knows, man. We will just have to fight through."

"Okay."

Click here for link to photos and/or videos

29

MUSINGS AND THANKSGIVING

~Lance~

We e-mailed just about every day. I told him what was happening over here. He told me... nothing. The e-mails were short, and if I didn't ask specific questions, he didn't volunteer much. He sounded fine, though. I hated having to wait for the next book e-mail to find out all that was happening there. He kept saying he would write it all in the book. Aargh! I stared at the blank page before me. Daring me to write.

Aha!

E-MAIL NOVEMBER 23rd:

LANCE: Is this deployment easier on you because you have better

communication with home?

ADAM: Nope, it is a constant reminder that I am not back.

LANCE: How is it different?

ADAM: Different people, mission, terrain, culture.

LANCE: Is this a better situation?

ADAM: Just different.

LANCE: What are your thoughts about writing a book while you experience it?

ADAM: Gives me a chance to vent.

LANCE: Is your mindset different?

ADAM: I'm older.

LANCE: Are you more prepared mentally?

ADAM: For what?

LANCE: What are the differences between the two places, the cultures, the natives' reactions?

ADAM: Similar culture as far as the things that I am exposed to.

LANCE: How are the guys different?

ADAM: Different motivation.

LANCE: What's the difference being a Sergeant?

ADAM: More pay.

LANCE: What's the difference being Army instead of a Marine?

ADAM: Uniform.

"And that was Lance Taubold, reporting live from Afghanistan with guest, Sergeant Adam Fenner."

It was slightly enlightening, slightly amusing, and a whole lot irritating. Guess I won't try that again. He needs to work on his elaboration skills.

In his defense, however, he was always genuinely interested in what I was doing and what our friends and Richie were up to.

On another note, I sang for the Vets again on Veteran's Day, same place as before, a lot of the same Nevada politicians spoke. It was moving, of course, but not like Memorial Day. I was much better this time. I didn't want to cry at everything. I felt the pride and courage of everyone there and could identify.

It's pretty amazing what a new perspective can do.

* * *

Thanksgiving. Well, actually the day before Thanksgiving. We always celebrate it then. We pre-empt everyone else's Thanksgiving, and everyone is available. Richie and I are always off and it just works out better all around.

"It's too bad Adam can't be here," my cousin Gloria, an amazing older lady, said to me as I poured her a glass of Beaujolais Nouveau. "I know you miss him. I do, too." She always asks after Adam and wants to know the latest. She's one of my favorite people on the planet because she genuinely cares about people.

"Yeah, you know I do, but he said he's going to try to call, and barring any mishaps, I know he will. He's good that way. He says he would like to talk to you all." I took a slug of some kind of new martini I'd created, which seemed to be a big hit with people.

"Oh, I hope so. He's such a sweet boy." She clinked her glass to mine. I knew what her toast meant.

"Yeah, he is." I finished off my martini. "I hope Richie's almost done with the turkey (deep-fried). If I have many more of these, I won't be coherent when Adam calls."

She laughed. "Just save room for lemon pie." She makes the best I've ever had.

"Always room for that." I refilled my glass. One more couldn't hurt. I'd eat a lot. And they were pretty good.

~Adam~

Thanksgiving brought real turkey and a pumpkin-pie-like desert (which was a disgrace to the pie), which has similar ingredients and the same name. I called Lance in the morning. [Lance: Ah, there I am.] He loves Thanksgiving and I knew I was missing his big Thanksgiving bash, which I have attended for the last three years, although rarely sober.

This week was light. It was also the holiday known as Ead to the locals, so our Terps all went home for the holidays, leaving us inside the wire instead of outside exploring. It is apparently like Christmas. But it is to commemorate the Abraham's willingness to sacrifice his son Ishmael as an act of obedience to God.

* * *

"Oh, Akhmed, RPG rounds. You shouldn't have. I got you something special; I hope you like it."

"Oh praise be Allah, are these American white phosphorous rounds? Mohammed, you dog you, where did you get these?"

"Allah provides, what can I say? Just don't forget to pull the pin out. Last time you forgot, and all that happened when it landed in the infidels base was a puff of dirt."

"Enshala, enshala. Merry Ead everyone, merry Ead."

~Lance~

Thanksgiving was great and satiating. The food was all put away. The dishes done. The house back in some semblance of order, thanks to a couple of hangers-on who generously helped out. I had just said goodnight to the last of them—and to Richie an hour before that.

My phone rang. It was almost 11:00 P.M. my time, 12:30 in the afternoon his time. (I still hadn't figured out how there could be a twelve-and-a-half hour difference. Hadn't the Afghani heard of Greenwich Time? Who was I kidding? They've never even heard of Greenwich.)

406-065 lit up my screen.

A little late, but all right.

"Hey. Happy Thanksgiving." The pleasure in my voice was apparent.

"Happy Thanksgiving. Sorry I was a little late."

"That's okay. Just happy you called."

"Was it fun?"

"Almost perfect." My subtext not so subtle.

"Right. I know." Of course he did. "Who was there? What food did I miss?"

And we talked for another hour and fifteen minutes. Nothing of import—just connecting.

Happy Thanksgiving.

30

SEPARATING THE MEN FROM THE ISAF

~Adam~

"Yeah, roger. I got Dealer Medic seeing if he can dig it up right now," Davis passed to SFC Mendoza over the radio. I pulled out the pickaxe from the MRAP and made my way over to the area in the road that was of interest—a large spot of disturbed dirt, looking like someone had just been digging in that spot recently.

"Hey man, just dig around it," Davis told me.

"Sounds good." I buried the sharp end of the pickaxe into the soft dirt to the side facing the outside edge of the road. I was looking for wires. This was the most likely place they would have been laid.

About six inches down, still no wires.

So I dug on the side next to the cliff.

Still nothing.

So I centered myself into the pile and went down.

Still nothing.

We marked the grid and passed it up as an area that appeared to be clear, but the dirt was disturbed.

Later in the patrol I listened to SFC Mendoza and Davis in their usual banter.

"I'm just saying that I would not have tried to dig an IED up, especially with a pickaxe," SFC Mendoza said. [Lance: Maybe you should listen here to what he says. Sometimes being, Mr. "I do what I want" can have its downside.]

"And that is what separates the men from the ISAF (International Security Assistance Force)," Davis responded. That got SFC Mendoza hot. The argument raged on.

* * *

Months passed since I had picked up that pickaxe, and the leaves had fallen off the trees and snow was visible on the distant mountain peaks. I had to wear a fleece out, and I brought gloves with me on patrols. And still I got to listen to SFC Mendoza come up with different ways to pull himself out of his ISAF status.

The kids joked, referring to it as, "I Suck At Fighting." This was the organization that our unit fell under that has provided a significant number of rules to control our behaviors and how we fought, preventing us from chasing the bad guy and entering homes.

* * *

SFC Mendoza planned training to fill the open time during a more relaxed week. I had just wrapped up a medical review class with the guys, and was relaxing on my computer.

The bay was silent. Deutch and Clemente were in the gym. Davis was tapping away on his computer, while Wills was watching a TV sitcom DVD series on his computer. Finch was out and about. Sandy was still at home with his son on leave. (Complications from Swine Flu had put his son in the hospital.)

Boom. I heard faintly in the distance.

Hmm. That didn't sound like mortars.

BOOM.

Hmm. That didn't sound like outgoing.

I ran over to Cheap Times to check with SFC Mendoza who was monitoring the radios while he played on his computer.

"Yeah, that is incoming," SFC Mendoza said after a little bit of wresting with the radio.

I ran into the barracks to throw my gear on.

Clemente and Deutch came running in.

"Dude, get dressed," Clemente said, correcting my laziness. I looked down. I was wearing PT shorts, running shoes, and a green fleece. Dammit, that whole professionalism thing.

It didn't take long before I was at the trucks.

1630. Everyone was waiting for word. Outgoing mortars rang out on the hill above us. We watched the explosions off in the distance peppering the hillside that fifteen minutes ago had been where they attempted to do the same to us.

"LZ 1700, we are going out there to check that spot out," SFC Mendoza passed to the NCOs.

Hmm, I could use some more comfortable socks.

I changed my socks and planned for a long walk up a mountain in the dark.

"It is about two and a half klicks there," someone said back on the LZ.

"Two and a half klicks?" one of the junior guys whined.

"Yup, but it is a good two and half klicks. It is all uphill." I smiled at him. LT laughed and proceeded to brief us on how the operation was going to go.

Above the black hills, we needed to move. The sun was just setting.

It didn't take long before we set up an OP near the base of the black hills, but by no means the base of the valley. It had been hard walking for around an hour to get to that point already.

"You want to come with us, dude?" the LT asked me, assembling his small team to go investigate.

"Fuck yeah, sir. You can't keep me off this shit."

We plodded up the hillside. The ground suddenly turned black under our feet. As I stared at the ground, careful of my footing, I tried to figure out what had caused the color change, but the moonlight wasn't enough to reveal any answers. It cast a pale blue light all around me, allowing me to see onto the hills that surrounded us, giving me the illusion that I could see the enemy if they were nearby.

Another twenty minutes and we had climbed past the blackened portion and were on our objective. We searched the area, looking around the spires of rock and the small nooks that might reveal a mortar tube, a rocket launcher, or maybe some bodies.

"Dealer 3, Dealer Eye, did you guys find anything?" Finch asked Clemente from the OP.

"Just some big rocks," he responded, hushed over the radio.

"Don't forget we found small rocks too," I turned to whisper to him.

We uneasily made our way down. "This is your favorite part," Clemente laughed to me from behind on the climb down all the rocky faces we had only recently climbed up.

"Yeah, no shit."

Clemente and Davis take a great amount of pleasure watching me slowly make my way down hills, falling further and further back from the man in front of me. They can't beat me up the hill, but they sure do move faster down.

"Up wears me out, but down just hurts," I tell them. We all understand the impact it causes on our joints.

"Do these cursed black hills never end," I whispered in the dark to Clemente, shaking my fists at the sky as we slowly neared the OP.

He laughed quietly in the dark.

We made our way back down the hill, through the crags and villages, until we reached the fields. After a long jump, I found myself kneeling in the soft dirt, a mix of manure and the silt brought together and molded by the hands of the local women. They created small rows, each by hand, all over the steps that formed these fields. And we stomped all over them on our way to and from the hills, expecting to hear some complaints the following day, "Your soldiers stomped on my fields, and we would like money."

"How about you keep the Taliban out of your town and not let them shoot mortars at us from up there and we wouldn't stomp all over your fields, dick?"

The fields provided no amnesty from the impact on our knees and ankles. Somehow, we still were jumping off walls and climbing toward the road.

This must be where my grandpa went to school. It is uphill in every direction, and even downhill is miserable.

There was no reprieve until after I'd climbed the wall to let the platoon in the gate and finally took my boots off next to my bunk, not without the ANA threatening to shoot us if we tried that again. We laughed as we walked past him.

We were just waiting for the day they really did fire on us, so close had we already come, as tensions mounted between us and them. After the incident at the fuel point, we now posted a guard on it. Wills and Alegria actually managed to catch some ANA soldiers stealing our fuel. They have moved to pulling it directly out of our generators. Not good for international relations.

Finally, the mission was done. We all lay in our bunks nursing our swollen joints.

"I feel good about this one," Clemente said.

"Yeah, I don't mind going out and not finding anybody. If we were going to check out the site, this was it. We were out that gate forty-five minutes after their rounds had left the tubes. At least we tried to catch them."

"Is anyone else really sore?" Finch yelled from his bunk.

"Oh yeah, but ours is because we hiked that hill. Yours is because your time has come, old man," I responded.

Everyone dove on him; he was a wounded gazelle for a pack of lions.

* * *

Another patrol out to the bazaar had finally broken SFC Mendoza's resolve.

"That is the last time. Fuck those boys. I am never giving any more boys candy ever again. I hate the men and the boys of this fucking country. Some fucking adult came up and smacked the fuck out of this little girl who was following me, and then grabbed a handful of rocks and threw it at the other girls who were in the area. Fuck them, man. Fuck them," he said after we had gotten back into our hooch and dumped our gear after the patrol. "And then the ANA pull fucking guns on us over a fucking rock. They point AKs and RPGs at us—over a fucking rock!"

SFC Mendoza was hot. Relations between the ANA grew even worse after one of our more brilliant soldiers threw a rock at an ANA vehicle and broke a window because they were driving too fast.

"Just stay away from the ANA," LT told the NCOs. "That soldier will be leaving the COP. Just be careful for right now."

"What about the fact that they pulled weapons on us over a fucking rock, sir?" SFC Mendoza asked, trying to keep his temper under control. "And on the Marine LT."

"The commander is working the soldier issue today, and tomorrow he will address the weapons issue," LT responded.

"Are they going to address them threatening us the other night?" SFC Mendoza asked.

"Yes, he will."

"Those fucking guys have never moved that fucking fast before. They were probably at the ECP (Entry Control Point, the base's front door) with shit left on their dicks," Davis interjected.

"We all have to figure this out. We aren't going anywhere and neither are they," LT said, showing exhaustion from the conversation and the situation that brought it on.

"And you wonder why I sleep with a loaded nine next to me," I said to SFC Mendoza. [Lance: I don't. And I'm glad you do. Your well-honed, gregarious skills appear to not be working. Must be a cultural thing. Is this the turning point where you decide you don't want to be a linguist?]

Click here for link to photos and/or videos

31

AWARDS I NEVER WANTED

~Adam~

The morning sun hadn't quite crested the mountain behind the small village of Tamia, set in the valley east of the Jaboom CP. The snow could be seen in the mountains to the west and north of us, where the elevation was higher and the clouds still hung tightly to the individual peaks.

"You guys like candy?" I asked the village kids, knowing they didn't speak any English, but understood they might get something when I reach into my cargo pocket. Patti (Lance's singing friend) and her friends in Pahrump, Nevada had been sending me packages full of candy, toys, and small stuffed animals to pass out to the local children.

The older boys laughed at me but encouraged their younger brothers to take the suckers and various other treats I passed out. To the youngest, I gave a stuffed purple dolphin. I tried to show him how it swam in the water. But he would never even see a picture of a dolphin, let alone understand all the fun facts about them that American children learn. To a similarly aged boy, I gave a small tiger. The two of them ran off down an alley playing with their new toys. I managed to capture them on my helmet camera nervously taking the toys from my hand—and the smile that quickly grew across their faces before they ran off.

When my pockets were emptied, I joined Davis back on security on the road. We were supporting the ADT while they passed out money, seeds, tools, and advice to the locals. We chatted about plans for vacations and trips we wanted to take when we returned to the States, and the women in our lives.

"Dude, those little fuckers are throwing rocks at us," Davis said as another rock bounced along the ground near our feet.

"This would be a bad time to shoot them, huh?"

"Look, they have their scouts watching out." I turned to see a small group of pre-teenage boys watching us from a back corner. They snickered to each other, then turned away quickly. "I'm going."

I watched Davis hustle down the road and circle around a building, now out of their field of vision. I stepped into the street to keep their attention and draw fire.

Within moments, I saw the kids come running out from around the corner, half excited and half scared, like this was a fun game we were playing.

I soon saw Davis standing on the corner of the mosque where they were hiding, a modest building of stone and mud with a well-constructed wooden porch and a green speaker system on the top with a tree in the courtyard. The front had a small metal door to let the smoke out, which had blackened the wall above it where "Allah" had been written in Arabic all around it.

"They were throwing rocks at Alvanez, too, but he chased them off with a stick," Davis yelled to me. I met him at the stone stairway built along the road.

"That is funny."

We relaxed a little.

"That guy sure headed into the Mosque in a hurry." Davis pointed out an older gentleman, rushing into the Mosque with a cell phone in hand.

"He is probably calling the Taliban, telling them to set the ambush."

"No shit, huh," I said. We exchanged an uneasy laugh.

It wasn't long before ADT was finished and we were heading back to the trucks. We mounted back up. Wills took the lead in his MRAP with ADT behind them in a HMMWV. I was with Davis, SFC Mendoza, and the PA (Physicians Assistant) Maj A, who had jumped on the mission last minute in the rear vehicle right behind Clemente and his crew in their MRAP.

We slowly made our way back down the road, a narrow dirt road hardened from years of travel and barely wide enough to pass the MRAPs through. To our south was a steep hill with sporadic agricultural steps built into it. To the north was a cliff where millions of years of running water had cut a deep valley. We drove along the highest point. Our drivers were thankfully seasoned enough to understand how to move these lumbering vehicles around on this terrain.

POP.

The thick MRAP windows and armor diminished the sound and reduced the concussion from the blast.

"What the fuck?" someone yelled.

I turned and looked out the window behind me. All I saw was a puff of smoke coming from one of our vehicles.

I don't remember opening the door, and I barely remember grabbing my kit as it sat at my feet. It was too big for me to wear and still be able to sit on the small hard seat. But I did open the door, and I did grab my kit. I threw it on while I ran and dodged past Clemente, who was climbing out of his vehicle as the spare tire skidded to a halt in the valley below, over a hundred feet down and few hundred feet away. The six-hundred-pound tire became a black speck leaning up against a rock.

I realized my M4 was still in the truck.

Fuck it. I ran.

The hill pulled me down to the lead vehicle, past the ADT HMMWV, and to the back of Wills' truck. Under the back wheels was a crater. The LT and CA's LT COL were already getting out. "You good, sir?" I asked.

"Yeah," he said, obviously shaken up, but alive.

I ran to the driver, and opened the door. Normally, I would have to climb up the wheels to do this, but the engine compartment was no longer attached. The driver's compartment was nose in the dirt. The hood lay twenty-plus feet away, where it had landed after flying high into the sky, its heavy bulk upside down along the side of the hill and just south of the MRAP.

"How you feeling, Bacon?" I asked the oldest member of the platoon.

"I'm good, but my leg hurts." I took a glance at his leg. He was moving it but was still obviously in pain.

I saw Wills in the TC seat, his face locked in a grimace. I ran around the fragments of the engine to his side. He had already opened his door. "Dude, my ass hurts," he told me.

"Alegria is unconscious," I heard from the back.

Fuck.

Fuck.

Fuck.

I ran to the back and helped one of the ADT soldiers—another former Marine who decided to throw on ACUs—grab Alegria's body. Alvanez passed him to us as we laid him on the ground.

I began to strip Alegria's gear off him.

His pupils shook underneath his eyelids.

I put my hand under his nose to feel for his breath.

Good.

The ADT soldier ran around to check on Wills. He found him face down on the ground where he had gotten out of the truck. "They got me. They got my ass," Wills told him.

Then, in a blur, I found everyone at my side. I could hear SFC Mendoza barking orders, "Search the hills. I need security out."

"Sir, can you check on Wills?" I asked the Maj A.

"Roger," he said in his calm Filipino voice, which showed his years of combat experience.

"Davis, can you grab my bag from the truck?" I asked.

"I got you, man."

Davis ran back to the truck to get the rest of my medical supplies. I began directing everyone around me to open litters and get me supplies.

I started checking Alegria for any obvious injuries. He was still unconscious. I started at his head.

I thought back to several conversations I had had with the LT. "Sir, I won't accept a Combat Medic Badge unless I put someone on a bird. It is a disgrace to every medic who has earned it before me, covered in his buddy's blood, if I get it on some bullshit technicality." The award requires only that I do some amount of medical care while under fire. It could be as simple as me yelling from my bunk to the guys in the barracks, "You guys good?" during a mortar attack.

I didn't want this. I held Alegria's head in my hands, feeling for trauma, watching his eyelids flutter.

Everywhere I touched on his body, he grimaced in pain, but I couldn't find anything broken.

I noticed blood on my hands.

Oh fuck, where is he bleeding?

Then I noticed the small nicks and cuts on my own hands from the day's events.

Breathe.

"He is going to need morphine. You have to get an IV, Fenner." I looked at Maj A as he said it. Fuck. Earlier in the week I had to evac Baltasar for a medical problem and had to try three times to get a stick in him.

Alegria was starting to come to. He started talking, however barely audible his voice was. Bacon and Alvanez set in close to me on security. It didn't take long before the people around me had opened up the necessary litters. SFC Mendoza called Deutch with the MEDEVAC request. Deutch used the vehicle's radio and pushed the message up to higher command, along with coordinating the other incoming units.

My hands shook as I slammed the first needle into the dirt behind me.

Fuck.

The second needle I flung down the hill. Let the kids find that one. Fuck 'em.

"Breathe, we need you." SFC Mendoza's hand rested gently on my shoulder, and he used his comforting church voice, the kind of tone that only a person with Jesus in his heart can use.

I grabbed another needle and switched to his other side, a fresh arm.

"I'm sorry, Alegria. I'm going to get this mother fucker," I told him as his level of consciousness continued to creep back.

A third needle.

The needle slid smoothly into the vein. I saw flash. Blood from his vein quickly filled up the ampoule at the end of the needle.

Drop the angle.

Fuck. I looked into the bevel, now out of the skin. "Fuck it." I never claimed to be the most doctrine observant medic. I angled the needle back down, slid it in. More blood filled the tube. I dropped the angle.

So far, so good.

The catheter slid smoothly into the vein. I released the constricting band, put on my saline lock, tossed the blood-tarnished needle into the rocks, and started pushing morphine slowly into his body.

Davis ran over. His experience as an ER tech was a welcome amount of help out here. He prepped the various equipment and assisted the PA and myself.

"Alegria, now in the event you go home, is there anything in your room you need me to take care of?" Davis said, inches away from his head.

"No," he said softly.

"You sure? Drugs, alcohol, gay porn?"

He thought a second.

"No, there isn't anything."

"All right, man. I know you got a girl in JAF. So, your back may be a bit fucked up, but at least try to get a BJ out of the deal," Davis told him.

He smiled.

We packaged everyone up for transport. The ANA arrived just before the bird. Their individual soldiers filled the area, some set in security, and some helped us move the casualties.

The bird came in with gunships circling around. The flight medic was lowered down and he ran over to us. We exchanged information and started planning the evac. My request was to hoist them out.

It was finally agreed to put them onto the back of the small ANA pick-up truck and drive them down to the new LZ, which ANA and ETT (the Marines) had prepared.

As we rolled down to the secondary LZ, I sat on the back of the trucks, the litters hanging off with ANA running behind, making sure nobody fell out.

"Wills, when you get home, make sure you send us good packages," I told him.

"I don't want to go home," he replied. For a moment he wasn't angry at the world like he always was. He was human. Maybe he just needed a smoke.

The helicopter flew away with Alvanez, Bacon, Wills, and Alegria. We began cleaning up the area. It looked as though a grenade full of medical wrappers had gone off.

"Fenner," Maj A yelled to me.

"What is up, sir?"

"You did good out there. After that IV incident in the Aid Station earlier this week, I was nervous. But you got that stick under combat conditions. A lot of guys can't do that. You are a combat medic now. I'll put you in for that CMB when we get back," he said. I put my head down and thanked him.

The sun didn't make it over the hill to brighten the day. It was around ten in the morning now. Instead, a blanket of clouds had rolled in. The sun was dim, and the sky seemed to weigh down upon us.

A group of us returned to Tamia after EOD (Explosive Ordinance Disposal) arrived with reinforcements from Hooligan element, who had responded to the incident on QRF (Quick Reaction Force).

"Glad to see you, man," I told the medic who greeted me next to the wrecked vehicle.

"You too, man," he said.

"So, what has been going on in Meth Lab?"

"Dude, nine people got killed during a riot. They may have been Taliban, but we didn't shoot them. But the locals are pissed," he said grimly.

"Fuck man, everybody is having good days then," I said.

It isn't what happens on ground that wins a war; it is what is viewed on the television screens back home that matters. [Lance: Seems pretty cowardly of the almighty Taliban. But then what else could you expect from those sneaky murderous fucks? I remember 9/11 vividly. I used to live in New York and have a lot of friends there.] [Adam: With the understanding that there is nobility behind looking one's enemy in the eye and entering into mortal combat with him. If they were to do that, they would lose. No one can argue that that is why they have chosen this method. It isn't like they are losing this war.]

We sat outside the village, calling for their elders. They said ten minutes. It took thirty. When they finally arrived, "We see nothing. We hear nothing. We know nothing." [Lance: See my above comment.]

"Dude, I am so sorry," the ADT Sergeant told me while the officers and the village elders lifted up their shirts and rubbed their bellies together until everyone felt warm inside within our circle of security.

"Don't be, this wasn't your fault," I told him.

"This was our mission, and your guys were the ones who got hurt. We really did think this was one of the good villages after all the things we had done for them and the time we had spent here," he said, shaking his head. "I'm so sorry, man."

I could hear the conversation behind me as I pulled security from where the CA LT COL and the elders were talking. "Because of this incident, we may not be able to bring you any more support, because we no longer feel safe," he told them.

"This town is very safe. We did not know. We are deeply shamed that this happened so close to our village," they responded.

"These mother fuckers. There is only one road leading in and out of their village. How would they not know there was an IED buried in their road?" I said to Davis, who was posted on security near me.

The young boys, who had earlier been throwing rocks at us, were now standing on the outskirts of the town near us, laughing and pointing.

The elders scolded them only after we pointed out the behavior of their future leaders.

* * *

We weren't cracking jokes about how old SFC Mendoza was or looked on the slow drive back. We weren't smiling or laughing. We talked about the events of the day, trying to stay positive. But the clouds still hung over heads.

Before Bacon drove that MRAP over the small mine attached to all that HME (Home Made Explosives), I honestly had no hate in my heart for the Afghan people. But after that mine went off, igniting all that HME, it burnt a small part of my heart:

For the small boys who only know how to take and will knock over and strike their sisters for a sucker.

For the men who would rather fuck each other in the bazaar while their wives toil in the fields than treat her with some fucking respect and love her the way she deserves.

For the snickering school boys who have not been taught respect by their elders.

For the men who will lie to our faces, but approach us with hands open, demanding aid. They do not understand loyalty to anyone but their own families, and they take from anyone willing to give, Taliban or Coalition forces. It is all the same.

And for the fathers who will walk in the rain with an umbrella in hand while their wives walk behind them, carrying their infants in their arms, absorbing every cold drop into their burqas.

When we returned to the barracks, everyone passed out from exhaustion. Davis didn't even make it home before he fell asleep, snoring into his headset on the drive back. I stayed up late and barely slept that night.

I was aware of what happened to a person, physically, following traumatic events, but it didn't make me immune.

The next day I couldn't eat. I was deeply affected by the malaise that existed within the barracks. I couldn't sleep. I lay in bed for hours holding back nausea, hoping I would fall asleep, so I wouldn't have to fight the waves of nausea anymore. I finally woke up in the middle of the night, threw on my sandals and a fleece, and grabbed my pistol. I took a piss in the rain and found a spot to evacuate what remained in my stomach. Bent over, with my nine against my stomach, I threw up bile and undigested cheese from the burnt pizza we called dinner. It filled my nose while the rain pounded the back of my neck and soaked my short hair.

Get it all out. Keep my weapon dry.

Fuck this place.

I'm ready to go home now.

* * *

"Sir, don't tell me I'm going to fight a war, then tie my hands so I can't fight. And then don't tell me I am here to help these people, but don't let me help. Not that it fucking matters anymore. I find a way to offer good will in my own way by passing out candy and stuffed animals. Then, no more than an hour later, I am pulling my friends' limp bodies out of an MRAP after it hits a mine. Fuck these people," I vented to Maj A, while I restocked all the medical supplies for the remaining MRAPs and my own aid bag and kit.

Click here for link to photos and/or video

32

THE WORLD NEVER STOPPED SPINNING

~Adam~

"Stay safe. I hope you have a great day."

Every e-mail I got said that in the days before Wills and Alvanez returned, and it just made me angry.

The manuscript lay hidden within its respective folder.

Not right now.

Davis badgered me in the gym for being weak. The mother fucker. The traditional strength I have to beat him was missing.

It didn't take long before it was back—not with the symbolic return of half of our injured party and all the relative good news about our boys who were MEDEVACed, but with my slow return to being me. Everyone kept telling me I did a good job. The LT kept thanking me, and I kept asking how he was doing. The light in his eyes was slowly returning, like a piece of himself was coming back to him as I pulled myself together. I tried to deal with it alone. The older guys recognized it.

"Stop being a bitch, man. You did good out there," Finch would say.

"Do you ever go to the gym?" Clemente would ask. Then he would look at my arms. "You look like a bitch."

"Doc, you were so fucking fast," Rabbit said before he began to bend the time-space continuum with a variety of movements and noises that seemed to defy logic as he described how he saw me. For the kids, I faked my moods. I played it tough. They had to believe that I was some sort of action hero, and that no matter what happened out there, I would save them, so they could do what they do without fear. Or with less fear.

The following day, we were out again, supporting ADT who was still apologetic as they did their piece for the local farmers.

The patrol finished off at the top of the hill, just in front of our barracks. "Fenner, you got your nine?" Clemente asked, looking at a tan dog covered in mange, standing where the kids burn our shit.

"Yeah," I replied.

"Can you handle that one?"

"Yeah, whatever."

SFC Mendoza got clearance from the CP, and I fired.

The first round slid cleanly into his back and entered the dirt behind him with a puff of dust. We watched his back end droop from the impact of the round before he started running off. I took a few more ineffective shots. He escaped running down the hill and onto the road heading toward the ANA.

That was the last straw for the Commander, however. The animal lovers' protests were finally loud enough, and before the sun set there was a memorandum describing the requirements to kill a dog. It was now easier to call for fire.

The cats and dogs that once lived in fear on COP Najil now had their chance to stake claim to our home.

The next day, we helped the ANA check vehicles just outside the COP.

And the next day, we were promised a chance to rest and recoup.

However, RCP (Route Clearance Package) hit an IED near the Jaboom CP and we walked out to help. We vented our frustrations on each other in a local vegetable garden while we pulled security. The laughter didn't linger in the air, but the scent of pepper and smashed tomatoes did. It clung to the ground and stone walls. And it clung to Clemente and a few other guys' gear and faces.

As we settled back into our rooms, before we had the chance to begin complaining, RCP lost another MRAP. The sun was setting as we prepped ourselves to meet them in Watangatu. It ended in a less-than-pleasant walk out to the Najil ruins, just south west of Galwatah, only a few klicks away, to set in a blocking position for possible reinforcements that might be moving to attack RCP as they recovered their vehicles to head back to Meth Lab. The moon didn't light our path, and we all came back with bumps, bruises, and hilarious stories of our slips and falls.

Odie and the PA kept me company. We were short on bodies, and I asked for help from the medics. They were the only ones who even looked at me when I asked for help.

We finally got our day off the following day.

Me returned to me before I realized it. Soon, I was talking shit in the gym and laughing at Sandy as he tore down all the pictures of guys in their underwear that I'd posted on his walls—finally, back from leave.

Of course, soon I was standing on the top of the Death Star, staring off into the valley, watching the snow cover the mountains and push our way along, and feeling the blood pull out of the tips of my fingers into my core. And Allah's cold breath found every exposed nook and cranny of my uniform to chill me to my bones.

I looked forward to the coming patrol week. I found humor again when they told us we would have Christmas off. "Really, you know we are getting attacked right," I told Davis.

He nodded. "Yeah, it's true."

I looked forward to the idea of handing out candy again. I don't expect to win this war by killing the enemy. But maybe when these kids grow up, they will remember when infidels gave them chocolate and plastic dump trucks.

The light of the white page filled my small room. I stared blankly at it. The air slid out my nose slowly, and I began to type. "The morning sun..."

[Lance: Glad you're back, pal.]

Click here for link to photos and/or videos

33

STOPPED HEARTS

~Adam~

Mission week flew by, sort of. Our first day was supposed to be a walk out to Watangatu—secure the road for RCP and Hooligans.

It did end up being a walk in that direction, until ANA and Hooligans came under fire at the school on the plateau above Watangatu. We maneuvered through the fields of wheat grass to assist those under contact by flanking the enemy. We covered the two- kilometer distance quickly and managed to dodge ANA's fire as well as avoiding our own incoming mortar rounds.

We pushed across the river and into Karandali before Punisher Six (the COP Commander) could give the order to stay on the road. We broke up into smaller teams to clear along the ridge and villages.

The intelligence we gathered on ground led us into a valley that was apparently considered one of the worst valleys in the area. Abandoned baskets just big enough for a child to carry full of firewood lined the trail as we pushed deeper in.

The terrain was rough—the worst we had seen—not even a visible walking path.

"I'm feeling an ambush coming on," I told SFC Mendoza.

"You nervous?" he asked, looking at me.

I smiled. "No, but they definitely own this valley, and we are walking right into it."

We pushed until we were only half a klick away from the village.

SFC Mendoza asked for a Show of Force (shoot something big without hurting anyone.) The chain gun was accurate. The missiles they launched, however, were not.

I watched debris land all around me.

I turned to see the point of impact seventy-five meters behind us.

"They missed," I heard someone say.

As we exited the valley, one of the younger soldiers started to wobble a little more than normal.

"What the fuck is wrong with you?" Clemente asked him.

"I'm just a little dizzy, Sergeant," was his reply.

"Dealer Medic, Dealer Three," Clemente called over the radio.

"I'm already on my way," I told Clemente.

My blood boiled as I approached him. This was the easiest injury to prevent and can be the most fatal out here. "All right, man, what is up?"

I didn't pay attention to what he said, only how he said it while I looked into his eyes and read his body language.

"Let's take some of his gear and keep him moving," I told Clemente and updated SFC Mendoza on the situation. "I'm not going to stick you out here because of where we are. I don't need a bag hanging from your arm if we get ambushed, so you need to keep pushing," I told the soldier.

"Where the fuck is your water?" Clemente asked as he took the soldier's Kevlar and swapped his own M4 for the kid's SAW.

"I drank it all, Sergeant," he said.

"And your food?" Clemente asked.

"I didn't bring any." His tone showed he was realizing this wasn't going to go well for him.

"How the fuck do you come on a patrol with no fucking food and improperly hydrated prior to stepping off? We all knew this would be a fucking long hike," Clemente yelled through clenched teeth. There was a bit of a young Marine Sergeant left in Clemente also.

"I don't know, Sergeant," was his only reply.

"Fucking walk," Clemente ordered.

As we approached the Jaboom CP, the only thing he was still carrying was his plates. We had passed off all of his ammo and weapons to other soldiers to carry.

The Hooligans sent out a small vehicle-mounted patrol to meet us at the CP. Taj, however, beat them to it. He had MREs and water in the back of his sedan to help us out.

The kid drank water and ate until the HMMWVs arrived to take him away.

"What the fuck, man? You cold?" I asked with a smile as we approached.

Sandy, with a beanie on his head and his gloved hands shoved under his armor, was visibly shaking under his fleece. "Dude, it was cold as fuck up here all day, but we aren't even going to talk shit. You guys fucking earned it today," Sandy said through chattering teeth. Finch nodded.

I was sweat-soaked and comfortably warm from our hike. "Yeah, fuck that being cold shit."

"You know that was your boy, right, Deutch?" I said, looking down at the vehicles as we returned to the COP.

"Nope. Mendoza's boy," Deutch responded.

"Kid rolled out without a full Camelbak and no food. Thinks he is a fucking hero because of how he pushed until he dropped," I told Deutch.

"The kid can be retarded, man," he said.

"Did you hear Konrad and Sergeant Mendoza tried to kill us?" I said.

"Did you hear what the helicopter pilot said?" Deutch asked, equally cold. His deep voice shook as he did.

"No, I was on Dealer net," I told him, referring to the internal platoon radio frequency.

"After this mother fucker launched the rocket," he said, 'Whoops that one got away from me.'" He smiled.

"What the fuck, man? That is hilarious." I laughed. "Fucking whoops, huh?"

They all nodded. We laughed about the day and took a few pictures before the sun got too low on the horizon, bringing the cold wind to chill our sweat-soaked uniforms. Soon, we were all shaking in the twilight together.

We slowly walked into the barracks at the end of the day. I could barely lift my arm to unsling my rifle, my muscles were so sore.

"You guys want the pace count?" SFC Mendoza asked the NCOs.

"Fuck it, give it to us," I yelled from my room as I arranged my gear onto its stand.

"Over thirteen miles," SFC Mendoza told us. His pride was still visible through his tired features.

Davis walked through the door and into his room. "You guys know that is a COP record, right?" His uniform was fresh and clean. I had taken him off this patrol because of an injury he had earlier in the week. He had spent the day in the CP following our progress and helping where he could.

"Oh, Deutch, I checked on your boy's progress."

"Yeah?" was the response from his room.

"Joey and Hunt told me he almost died. He was so dehydrated, all his muscles locked up. If his electrolytes would have been any lower, his heart would have stopped," I told him. "He had to have stepped off dehydrated."

Everyone in the room expressed their disappointment and anger.

Deutch just shook his head with the resolve that this would never happen again.

"His stubborn immature attitude almost got himself killed and could have hurt the platoon as a whole. That is fucking bullshit," I said to the group. "I'm so mad at that kid I can't even look at him."

* * *

My inbox had been looking empty lately.

Every inbox.

I was sending e-mails but not getting responses anymore.

Phone numbers had changed, and I was getting more voicemails as of late.

I was starting to feel like the only people that I had left were Lance and my family.

* * *

It was over a year ago I found myself with my face in my arms, crying on my kitchen table—the first time in almost fifteen years that I had cried.

The last time was when the magic in my world was taken away: there was no Santa.

This time I was trying to break up with Angela. I wanted to reset my life. I wanted to deploy to Iraq. Get away from the world that I was fucking up. I felt as though I had fucked everything up, and I wanted to be forgotten.

Angela hit me, a couple times—a solid fist into my shoulder. My arm ached. She wasn't the type of girl who was unfamiliar with how to throw a blow.

She didn't let me off that easily. I was a fuck-up, but she didn't let me quit. A few months later, I found my way out, and she couldn't hold on anymore.

She called me a sociopath on the way out.

That I couldn't feel.

I had heard that before.

Why do I smile when I walk into incoming friendly fire, and laugh when I play with the limp bodies of my enemies, but I am afraid to care about the people who care about me?

* * *

I did it this time, not by choice, but I did it. Everyone was forgetting about me. I was losing friends. I had fallen out of everyone's lives. My life would reset, with only Lance and what was left of my family to welcome me home.

I got what I wanted.

I guess.

* * *

Dad had another stroke.

His obvious mortality was wearing down on Mom.

"I'm not ready," she told me.

I'm not qualified to tell my mother how to handle the imminent death of her husband, my father.

I faked it.

Click here for link to photos and/or videos

34

A MOST UNIQUE CHRISTMAS PRESENT

~Lance~

"When Adam came back from his second tour to Iraq, he was so angry," his mom said to me in a conversation we had a while back. I don't ask. She loves to volunteer information. I'm sure Adam will be thrilled to know that. "I used to hide in my room from him," she continued. "I was genuinely frightened. I was afraid of my own son. His wife, actually, brought my son back to me."

I found that a little hard to believe, having known her.

"He wasn't like that after the first tour?" I asked.

"No. This was different. He yelled all the time. He was so angry. I couldn't talk to him."

"He must have seen some bad things," I said, really curious now.

"Well, the first dead body he saw was liquefied."

Okay then. My fault. I pushed it.

"And he told his brother about the skull tattoos some of the guys would get to represent kills."

Did his brother really feel he had to tell his mother that? I thought I'd heard enough. But did I say that? Nooo. What she'd said instantly brought to mind the tattoos he already had on his body: the angely thing, the dragony thing, and the Iron Cross thing. And he was talking about getting another one of the vertebrae of his back inked onto his spinal column. Ugh. Did I say "Ugh?" I meant Ugh! Not a tattoo fan, but I have to admit the artwork on him is good. Besides which, Richie had gotten a rather large tattoo of a scorpion this past year on his upper arm. He's a Scorpio. And once again the artwork is superb.

But on this body? Not in this lifetime. [Adam: He is using the voice you imagine him using also when he says that.]

Now, as the monitor before me tries to melt my eyeballs, (It's some god-awful time in the morning.) I'm re-reading and reliving Adam's latest traumatic event with the blown-up MRAP and his expert medical treatment. This is taking vicarious to a whole new level. [Adam: Borderline competent medical treatment.] [Lance: That probably saved their lives.] [Adam: Eighty percent of all patients will survive no matter what treatment they receive from a medic.]

I was very proud when I heard how he had helped the wounded men.

I was very concerned, though, when I heard how it had affected him. He does care a lot, maybe too much, to do what he does. It reminded me of the conversation I'd had with his mom about how angry he was after his second deployment, and a conversation he and I had had a while back about PTSD (post traumatic stress disorder).

"Yeah, I think I had it," Adam told me.

"What do you think was the cause?" I prodded.

"I told you about Corey."

"Yeah, but not much." I'd remembered Corey was the only one of his platoon guys who'd died.

"He was trying to get to his post at Sadaam's palace in Babylon. He was going across a ledge sixty feet high. He slipped and fell."

"You were there."

"Across the river, I had turned just before he slipped and didn't see it."

"I didn't really know what had happened. That's so tragic."

He said nothing.

"That's why you were in therapy after you got back?"

"No. All the guys have to go. It's part of processing out. I went once a week, but all I did was complain about Susan for a solid hour."

I didn't want him to have to go through it again.

E-MAIL FROM LANCE:

Hey A

If you want to talk about it at all, I'm available, just call me.

—L

E-MAIL FROM ADAM:

Hey

Thanks. I'm just waiting for the guys to come back and move on.

—Adam

I tried.

But he seemed to have snapped back, and his men were recovering and would be fine and returning to the unit.

He was back handing out the gifts to the village kids, which gave me my next brainstorm.

Santa Fenner.

I had just sent off my own package to Adam: books, DVDs, tuna, jerky, and some awesome hot sauce from New Orleans from my recent visit there, and I was talking to my friend Patti. She had said that she'd just sent some more boxes over also. That's when I decided it might be a nice idea if more people did this. The newspaper might a good place to start, and we do live in a city of over one-and-a-half million people.

A quick call to the newspaper, an enthusiastic request for a press release from me, and the juggernaut was in motion. [Adam: I was effectively under the bus.]

Now, it's just three days before Christmas. The reporter from the Las Vegas Review Journal was very excited. He wanted to interview me. He wanted to e-mail and talk to Adam. He wanted pictures ASAP. I gave him Adam's e-mail. I e-mailed Adam to warn him. Oops. Too late.

E-MAIL FROM ADAM:

Hey

I will have to give you a call it seems. I got the e-mail from the RJ and will e-mail him back after I talk to my command. He asked a couple questions.

I also need to know how far this donation thing has gone. It seems like this has gotten out of Patti's hands. I need to prepare logistically for that level of distribution, especially if there are another 20 boxes on the way. You need to keep me updated on this, me hearing it through my mom, who talked to you, stresses me out. What I am worried about is people giving so much of themselves to this cause and me fucking it up or letting them down.

Like I said though, if you are going to do anything, just give me a heads-up first. I have a large amount of bosses out here that I have to keep happy. And it doesn't make things easy when the base commander walks up to me with a printed copy of an e-mail from the squadron commander and the subject line is simply "Fenner." I like to know what is coming first. I appreciate all the efforts. I just like to be prepared, and I can already feel the command breathing down my neck and getting involved in this whole RJ affair.

I will try to call in the next couple days. I can't guarantee Christmas.

—Adam

E-MAIL FROM LANCE:

Hey A

I was hoping you would get back quickly. Sorry if I've caused you any undue stress. I'm sure you don't need it. Things have been happening quickly here. I'm trying my best.

You just keep doing your best in distribution. Don't ever think that you're not capable or that it's overwhelming.

Personally, I think your command should be proud of you. You've already done more for good will than most anybody, and if we want the people there to appreciate our efforts to help them, this is a great way to show it. I don't want you to get into any trouble, but I really don't see how you could. You're doing good things.

I want this to be exciting for you and not a pain in your ass. I'm working hard, but I want it to be right for us. If you get this soon write me back.

—L

E-MAIL FROM ADAM:

Hey

Keith just asked me what I think about passing out the candy out here.

I'm hoping it is a small thing. I don't know how I'll pass out more stuff. This is really cool. It is just not what I am used to and, it is adding a different element to my deployment. It doesn't sound like my command is pissed. They are happy to get any press that they can—as long as it is good.

I am all random right now and about to go to bed, so bear with my thought process. I also forgot to tell Keith about how the only toys I have seen that the kids have out here is a metal ring that the kids roll around on a metal stick, like I think I have seen from the Fifties, and they play hop scotch, but no stuffed animals or little toys.

Let me know. I'll try to call tomorrow.

—Adam

That night. When I was out at dinner, I thought he had meant my tomorrow. But no.

Ring: 406-065

Crap. I had been drinking, and it was loud in the casino.

"Hey, I didn't think you were going to call until tomorrow?" I yelled over the noise, my brain a little befuddled from a couple of drinks. But Richie was driving, and I was celebrating. "How are you? Is everything okay with your command? Everything happened so fast. It's not like I can just call you. But it's great to hear from you." I rambled.

"Everything's cool. My command is okay with it. They were just a little surprised. I'm fine."

"Great. I'm glad. I didn't want you to get in trouble. I'm just really excited. I hope you are, too."

"Yeah, it's cool. I just didn't expect it. I know you didn't have time, but a little warning would have been good."

"Next time, I'll try." I knew I was talking loudly, but it was noisy, and I didn't care. "But I'm glad you're happy about it. We'll see what happens next."

"Okay. Let me know."

"I will. Merry Christmas."

"Merry Christmas."

He was okay with everything. The phone call was great—my Christmas present.

Christmas Eve day. The newspaper editor loved the article so much that they were going to run it as their feature story on Christmas day! I couldn't wait to tell Adam. This was amazing. Keith, the reporter, said he had a surprise for us, too. Couldn't wait to see it.

Christmas day. I ran out to the nearest mini-mart and bought six copies of the paper. There it was, in the Nevada section: From Nevada, Kindness Flows Overseas—Medic giving gifts to Afghan children. There was a huge 5" by 9" picture of Adam in his Army garb handing out gifts to the children and a smaller photo of the two of us together—full color, of course. The article covered almost the entire page. It was more than I could have hoped for. The article compared him to Santa Claus and talked about how he was trying to help shape the minds of Afghanistan's future leaders and give them a positive look at the Western world.

This was my gift to him. I hope he liked it.

Merry Christmas, Adam.

35

FALLOUT

~Lance~

The calls and e-mails came pouring in. It seemed that AP (Associated Press) had picked up the article on the wire, and it had also appeared in many papers around the country. Fan-f-ing-tastic!

His mom called me and she was very happy about the article and the pictures. "I can't believe that's my son doing that," she told me. "That's not the Adam I know."

"I guess he's changed," I replied, feeling somewhat awkward. "That's the Adam I know. He's a great guy."

"I guess. I just never thought my son would do something like that."

"He's grown up—and met me," I wanted to say, but it would probably not have been appropriate. Or even accurate. It was all him. He's done this on his own.

"And you're writing a book?"

"Uh, yeah." Awkward. Again. I'd forgotten she didn't know about that. Blunder number— I think I've lost count. "Yeah, Adam and I are chronicling his experiences over there and mine here at home. We thought it would be good for people to hear about it." Another thing for Adam to explain. Wait till she reads the book. Ow.

"Okay. I didn't know about it."

Silence. What could I say?

"Oh, my sister is here," she said. "I have to go."

Thank God for the sister.

"Okay. I'll talk to you soon. Bye."

That was close.

I am really glad, though, that Adam's dad got to see the article and can be proud of his son, especially since his dad is not doing well. I pray he will last till Adam comes home. Becky says anything could happen to him at anytime. Right now, he is holding his own. She is taking it day by day.

I dodged that bullet—but not Adam's.

E-MAIL FROM LANCE:

Hey A

How did your command like the article? I hope it helped you.

—L

E-MAIL FROM ADAM:

Hey

No one has really said anything about it. I doubt they will. The thing you didn't account for that I saw coming is that I am in an all-male unit, and the Army is very homophobic. And that article came off gay. Take that for what it is. I don't care what they think. You just didn't account for how that is going to affect how I am treated by my command and fellow soldiers. And by the time I knew about it, it was too late. I appreciate the effort, I really do. But no one cares here that I pass out toys. They hate these people, the kids included. So now I have two strikes, possibly gay and Afghan sympathizer. Please, next time you do something, notify me. I expect most people to not say anything, to not have the balls to say anything to my face and to whisper behind my back. But I still have a few months left, and I would like to leave the battles outside the wire.

—Adam

Buzz kill.

I certainly hadn't expected that. Well, marshal on.

E-MAIL FROM LANCE:

Hey A

I'm really surprised by the backlash. I had no idea. I figured the most they would be is jealous of your recognition, not thinking you're gay or an "Afghani sympathizer." It makes me kind of sad to hear that the rest of them hate all the Afghani people—kids included.

All the media does say we are there to help the Afghani help themselves and to promote some good will and nice thoughts in their minds. The article doesn't really come off gay, I don't think, nor does anybody here, unless you want to read something into it. But I'm sorry for you. I'm glad you don't care what they think, though.

Anyway, all of the forthcoming things I will run by you. This all happened so fast, I couldn't tell you all in advance. TTYL

—L

~Adam~

Christmas came and went without incident.

The day after Christmas took us a few klicks to the east. We hadn't been out there since the night of the Black Hills—after Thanksgiving. The powers that be don't like us going east.

I took a pocketful and emptied it on our way through Kanday. The girls were shy, and the boys rushed me. I passed the boys and handed two stuffed animals to an elder with his daughters behind him. He passed the small toys to the young girls, who held them close to their chests.

They followed us out of town and watched as I tossed small pieces of candy to the little girls watching us from their porches. They chased the candy and ran back to the edge to see if there was more.

After our OP was collapsed and we strolled back through, I tossed the last of my bag of candy to a mother on the roof with her children. Mohammed translated, "For your children," for me.

They smiled enough for me to see, but not enough to get in trouble.

The next mission the LT gave me. He said it was my mission to help quell the rising tide of packages of toys in my small room.

* * *

Deutch, Davis, and I loaded our bags up with toys and candy.

The article had compared me to Santa Claus.

The reporter obviously never met me.

It was funny though. So, I emptied my green laundry bag and filled it with toys.

"Doc, you look like Santa," Konrad told me as we stepped out the gate.

"Yeah, but I carry a gun."

The kids started following us when we entered the town.

The open area we pass through every time on our way to the bazaar was soon filled with children.

Lots of children.

They swarmed us. Every bit of control was lost. Finch and the LT frequently requested different items that I was barely able to get out to them; I had to throw the toys over the kids' heads to them. They were inconspicuous and able to move freely, while I drew the children's attention. Finch got some stuffed animals for the girls on the hill too shy to get into to mix. The LT got some purses and hair scrunchies. The kids followed me around the area as I chose different children to give toys to. Sporadically, the adult males would swoop in and start slapping the kids to behave.

"I would like to give each child a present," I told one older gentleman with orange ink on his palms.

"I can't control them," he replied with a laugh.

In the end I was defeated by their small hands.

I limped back to base, my empty bag slung over my shoulder.

"I have not been beaten by the rivers or the mountains of Afghanistan. But today, those kids kicked my ass," I told Deutch. He was still smiling. He had been spraying silly string on some of the kids in the street as they ran around and laughed. I babied my knee up the hill, until I got to my room. I found a small scrape from where it hit a rock. I had slipped moving around some kids.

Lance had proudly posted the article up on Facebook for everyone to see. I read through to the end—the end where our friend Ed had posted his comment. He said he knew me. He said it was all a lie to sell the book.

I fumed.

Click here for link to photos and/or videos

36

WE ARE SOLDIERS, NOT MONSTERS

~Adam~

I spent Christmas sitting next to Deutch in his room, enjoying a "Die Hard" Christmas marathon.

~Lance~

New Year's Eve.

11:00 A.M., my time.

"What are you doing? As if I didn't know," Richie says, as he pops into the office.

"Staring at a blank screen." I ignore his snide dig. "Is that coffee for me?"

"No." He takes a sip from the cup he's holding. "You know where it is." True love. "Since you're doing nothing, except pining away for your boyfriend, I thought you might like to hear about something that happened at work."

"This must be good." I smoothly ignore the 'pining away' barb. "You never talk about work."

"Unlike you." Ow. "This woman called me the other day asking if there was any possible chance of getting a room for her son and his friend." (Richie is an Executive Casino Host at Harrah's, and that's part of what they do.)

"New Year's in Vegas? And she calls at the last minute? Right," I said.

He glared at me for interrupting. "And she said that her son and his friend had never been to Vegas and were due to ship out to Afghanistan soon."

That got my attention—as he knew it would.

"I explained to her that it was a very busy week, but I would see what I could do."

"Did you get them rooms?" I knew this story was leading somewhere.

"Of course. There are always rooms available if you know what you're doing," he said.

I could feel the suspense building.

"So, on Wednesday, this Army-looking guy comes into VIP looking for me," Richie said, grinning. "The guy was a hunk, and I told him I would comp the first night's stay for him." (That's my Richie, altruism personified.) "He said that was fantastic and that he and his buddy didn't have much money. Then the guy gave me a huge hug and said, "Don't tell my Army buddies I hugged you." (Ah, the innocent.) "And I said, oh, screw it. I'll comp your whole stay. I asked him what he did in the Army, and he said they were like the Green Berets, but better."

I like to think that Richie was doing his bit to help out our troops, and maybe knowing Adam had something to do with it. I'm sure the "hunk" part helped, too. But, whatever, it was a nice gesture and made me proud of him.

Ring.

406-065.

"Happy New Year," I answered. "It is your New Year, I know."

"Happy New Year. Things okay?"

"Everything's great... now. I'm glad you haven't had any problems with our article."

"Yeah. They don't care. I'll just keep doing what I do."

"Good. You should."

"I see you posted the article on Facebook and told people to send things to me. I just wanted to add something about not sending any more packages after February. Is that okay?"

"Sure. That means you're still coming back in April?"

"That's the plan."

We're back.

It's going to be a great New Year.

~Adam~

Before I knew it, it was two weeks after Christmas and we were finally opening two months worth of backed up mail containing Christmas presents and the various other and sundry items that we had sent ourselves.

The miles wore our boots ragged, but the distance we traveled was a pleasant distraction from my world back home spinning away without me.

Although, the word wasn't getting better coming from Mom about Dad and Grandpa, they held on. I guess my progenitors do not like to go quietly into the night.

The nights found me in my bunk, when I wasn't walking among my fellow Death Dealers out to rescue Hooligans or RCP. I gathered my thoughts and my metaphorical balls. I weighed the consequences. My list of things that I had to lose was running short.

I thought back to when we were still at Camp Atterbury.

* * *

The cold from the metal picnic bench had soaked through my gym shorts, and the cold Indiana night wind had raised goose bumps on my legs. Joey was twenty meters to my left, arguing with his wife about pre-deployment preparations, pacing back and forth in the dark. I was thinking about my post-deployment plans and enjoying a trusted female voice resonating through the small speaker of my phone.

"We can keep doing this because I know you won't fall for me." Angela's voice came in clear through my oversized outdated cell phone.

I caught the lump in my throat and let what I wanted to say drift away into the place of my heart where I like to tuck away all my "should haves."

"No, worries. I know this isn't your normal style," I responded.

* * *

"I'm sorry..." I e-mailed to her. "I want to try again."

I got back the expected defensive response.

It took over a week of exchanged e-mails and a few online chats, but I wasn't getting a no—a few threats on my life, but I could work with that. [Lance: I have something to say, but I won't—which is kind of like saying something. I'm staying out of this one. For now.] [Adam: Not interested.]

* * *

"I don't understand why anybody keeps clearing this road and not bringing any supplies up with them. We keep having to walk out here to support whoever, after they get blown up. I don't mind helping guys in trouble, but don't put them in a situation to get hurt for no reason. This whole idea is like trying to teach a dog not to eat meat by feeding him steaks," I told one of the Hooligans, standing over another blast hole next to another wrecked MRAP.

Sandy was leading an OP, in lieu of Finch, whose body had finally given up earlier in the week, after a decade in combat arms, to watch over us as we searched both Bandeh and Shamsakheyl, but Sandy got hurt on the way up and had to be helped off the mountain. I met him at the bottom and assisted him to one of my younger medic's HMMWV. Sandy couldn't make the four-mile walk back, but he could survive a truck ride to Mehtarlam.

"Fenner, hurry up," the Captain's voice barked behind me. Through a variety of circumstances I ended up, also, his guide to the Death Dealer's location.

"I'm loading a casualty, sir," I told him, trying not to lose my temper. My inflection betrayed me slightly. I made no effort to hurry as I briefed Sandy on the situation and made sure to insult him a little bit.

We found no bombs, no unusual amount of weapons. These people were too poor. All we learned, as we rooted through their homes with ANP, is how little they had. They weren't maliciously hiding Taliban equipment or members. They were either getting paid for help or silence, or they couldn't fight back against the insurgency.

They were just trying to make sure they had a home and a family to go home to at the end of the day.

Fuckers.

* * *

"Listen, mother fucker, you can't come through this road unless you are bleeding to death. If you have a problem with that, go talk to your governor. He issued the order," SFC Mendoza pushed through his teeth, then waited for the interpreter to translate.

One Afghan lifted up his pant leg to reveal a scabbed-over knee.

"Are you fucking kidding me?" Davis said, lifting up his own pant leg to reveal a larger scab from a night QRF the previous evening, where he took a header off of a wall and into the boulders six feet below. The interpreter didn't need to translate for the crowd to understand and laugh at him as he lowered his pant leg, defeated.

We were to spend all day and the night blocking off the road before Shamsakheyl and after Bandeh, per the governor of Laghman province, in order to prevent any more IEDs from being emplaced in the road. So, there we sat, occupying this area with ANA in a joint operation that also involved the ANP, until they got bored and walked off.

"Listen. This is your decision. But I strongly encourage you to stop letting your cousins and family through the gate. Every time you let one of them through, somebody who shouldn't come through thinks they have a chance and won't leave us alone," Davis tried to explain to the ANA we were working alongside.

The cars continued to roll through the gate, and slowly, in frustration, what started as a group of American soldiers working the gate with SFC Mendoza, Clemente, and me, dwindled down to us three and an interpreter. This promised to be a long twenty-four hours.

Four hours in, our frustrations were beginning to peak.

An ANA soldier in civilian attire (AKA man jammies) strolled up through the gate. We waved to him, and he walked around. Our hands extended to shake his as he approached. A fellow ANA intercepted him with an open-mouthed kiss. They enjoyed the kiss long enough for us to pretend our handshakes were natural movements into our pockets, and we simply verbally greeted him again before he continued on his way back to the COP. [Lance: Is this the normal greeting or only if you've been intimate?] [Adam: Umm...]

"No, he can't go see the witch doctor. Being in pain from the rods in your formerly broken legs is not an emergency."

"Being blind is not a fucking emergency."

"If he is so fucking sick, take him to a goddamned hospital— and that is the other fucking direction."

SFC Mendoza had me checking the legitimacy of every medical emergency.

I had long since lost my patience when he walked up to the concertina wire. He was tall and lean with a well-groomed beard. He had a dark vest over his deep-red slacks and matching shirt. "My wife is dying. She is pregnant."

"Then take them to Mehtarlam where there is a fucking hospital," I screamed from my spot.

He walked away. A few minutes later, he returned.

He and SFC Mendoza argued for a few minutes.

"Let's go check her out, man," he said. His hard edge was softened only by his Christian beliefs and empathy toward fathers and husbands.

I lowered my rifle from where I had centered the arrow of my ACOG onto his head. I walked around the wire and out to the van, where I found his wife.

She sat in the back seat in the center. Her blue burqa covered her head as she leaned on the shoulder of another woman's covered head. I couldn't see through the screen, and I knew cultural taboos wouldn't allow me to do an exam. Her belly bulged under the burqa. She was probably pregnant.

"If she is dying, she needs to go to the hospital. Go back to Mehtarlam." I told the Terp to translate, and walked away. I brushed past the crowd of rubberneckers and headed back to the other side of the wire.

I turned to check on SFC Mendoza as a fight broke out between the husband and another Afghan, who was laughing at his plight.

I walked back to the group to guard SFC Mendoza, now consoling the man apart from the bulk of the Afghans.

"I wish there was more we could do. I too have a wife and children," SFC Mendoza told the man, who was obviously shaken. "If your wife goes into labor, my medic can deliver the baby. Otherwise, go to your wife and hold her while she dies."

This was the first time I saw an Afghan man feel for his wife in a way other than as an object he possessed.

As SFC Mendoza talked to the man, we learned that his wife had already delivered a week early. The baby had been stillborn, and the doctor had sent her home to die.

We had our orders.

Not long after everything calmed down, I headed back to my own truck to try to take a nap. Sleep didn't come—only SFC Mendoza—with a hiss as the pneumatics engaged opening the MRAP door.

"I hope you don't think I was being too hard on you," he said.

"Not at all. I made the call. I accept that. I take that responsibility. I just needed a nap," I told him.

"Good. I had to leave after the LT tried to let the butcher's son through," he said, climbing into the truck.

"Makes sense."

"Yeah, where do you want to crash tonight?"

"I was thinking the ground next to the MRAP. It will be too cramped in here with the dog handler, dog, and the interpreter."

"All right, bro. I'll wait till you get off the OP tonight before I crash out," he told me.

Long after the sun set behind the mountains and the cold crept into the valley, I climbed with Konrad, Clemente, an ANA soldier, and the interpreter up to the OP that Clemente and Davis had chosen while the sun was still up.

Clemente wasn't his normal energetic self. He kept pausing to sit as we climbed the steep grade and moved along the winding foot paths.

"You good, man?"

"I'll make it."

"You still feeling like shit, I take it?"

"Yeah."

"You could have taken those pills I gave you."

"But they make me drowsy."

At the OP site, he started retching. Davis sent him back and volunteered to take his shift on the OP.

Davis, Alegria, who was happy to be back out, and I covered the back side of the ridge, while Konrad, the ANA, and the Terp covered the front side. I changed into my cold weather gear and wrapped myself in a small blanket Grant had sent me.

I spit sunflower seeds and kept asking Alegria if he was awake, while Davis went to go sit with Konrad. After, he found out that the interpreter and the ANA soldier had curled up under Davis' poncho liner and gone to sleep. We over-watched the ridge where Gunslinger, first platoon out of Mehtarlam, had been attacked the night prior. We kept hoping for the chance to ambush the ambushers this time, but the time moved by and we were soon heading down the hill.

For the most part, it wasn't the Taliban but the terrain that was beating us, slowly breaking us down over time. I could feel it in my knee. I kept banging it on everything. It was a gentle ache at all times, but it held weight. I carried on right next to every member of the platoon, who were experiencing the same aches and pains that I was.

The countdown to go home had long since begun. We enjoyed the days when SFC Mendoza didn't have to calculate our miles traveled—and RCP didn't get blown up. We fought to be heard by those above us, pleading for common sense and changes that could help us on our journey home.

We fought for adequate chow. Breakfast we had given up on and relegated ourselves to bagels and cereal, having become long since tired of soggy eggs and burnt breakfast burritos. There was rarely lunch and dinner was...

"First Sergeant, I looked into one of my guy's watery eyes as he handed me a can of parmesan cheese. He said it was the only way he could eat the food, it was so spicy," I told him.

He replied with a shrug, reassuring me that it would never happen again...

"Why are we here?" I mused to myself.

"To secure the road," I replied.

"Why do we secure the road?" again I asked.

"So we can get supplies. Duh." I answered, chuckling to myself.

37

THE HORSE THAT WOULDN'T DIE

~Adam~

WAAABOOOOM!

I lay in my bunk, a cave of darkness I created with a wool blanket to hide the light from bothering me, while I slept during the day. I pretended that didn't just happen as the various items on everyone's shelves crashed to the floor.

"That didn't sound like outgoing," Finch said.

"Maybe the D30s," Deutch said, referring to the ANA Russian-made artillery pieces.

"No, that was definitely incoming," Finch finally said. "You guys good?"

"Yeah, you good?" I asked back. "I'll go check on the kids."

"Is this a time when I can wear my gear?" Finch asked. His injury had prevented him from donning his gear in all but extreme situations.

"Yeah," I said, walking out the door.

I found two of them at the top of the stairs, "Everybody good?"

"Yeah."

"Good, get your shit on."

I walked back into my room. Finch ran out wearing his armor. As I got dressed, I turned my radio on.

"Punisher Base. Dealer Medic."

"Dealer Medic. Send it."

"Hey, was that incoming or outgoing?"

"That was a controlled det. We have been announcing it for an hour now."

"Roger, we had post late last night, so we were sleeping."

"Oh. The blast knocked our doors off the hinges."

"That is exciting. It just knocked our shit off the walls."

I let everyone I could find know to stand down and crawled back into my bunk. I knew I wouldn't be able to sleep, but I could at least let the last bit of sleep hormones drain out of my brain.

* * *

I made my way down to the MWR to check my e-mail. The offset sandbag on the stairway constructed of rocks and sand bags leading down to the MWR taunted me, reminding me of the ache in my knee, when it gave way in the dark and I ended up on my face, before I limped the rest of the way up to the barracks to nurse my wounds.

I found an empty seat in the small room in a booth next to some of my fellow COP Najil compatriots.

Now, that is a name I didn't expect to fill my inbox.

Susan.

Fuck.

She threw herself at my feet. She sent pictures of our wedding... and Ryah.

It took two days before I responded. [Lance: Really low. Wedding pictures? Ryah? I'm glad you resolved that.]

The infantry corporal in me stirred. This was his favorite part. I began to type.

"Four fucking months... How dare you throw those memories in my face.

"I love you, I do, but there are two types of love, the youthful kind that is like a drug, and the kind that develops through mutual respect and admiration over time. You are like a drug to me.

"I tried to keep e-mailing you for a month. After two, I stopped trying. At three, I found someone who could tell me you were safe. And I realized that you didn't care enough about me to spend any time communicating with me.

"You're too late. Two weeks ago, I went back to the one person who did love me, but was too afraid to commit to, the person who I did share that mutual respect and admiration for. And I committed," I e-mailed her back my response. I felt finally free.

* * *

"First thing, gentleman, the National Guard unit that was coming to relieve us has been redirected to another mission." The crowd was silent while the commander spoke. "As for your next question, I do not have an answer to that. Now, your next question will be: Will we be extended? I do not know. They have not said either way."

Fuck. Fuck. Fuck. [Lance: Fuck.]

The individual leaders at the meeting began to grumble. I hung in the back. I was just passing through to go to chow.

Dinner was breaded catfish.

38

FUCKING GUMP MAN

~Adam~

I stood on the road snapping a picture of the brown helicopter with a red cross just before it lifted off. Below me, was the MRAP on its side. The sun was just beginning to set behind the mountains in front of me. This promised to be a long night.

* * *

I woke up. This time, SFC Mendoza had just turned the light on. Streaks of light lit my small cave, and I began to stir. I had been hiding from the day long enough.

I grabbed some cereal, a carton of shelf-stable milk, and turned my computer on.

I got ready, while enjoying an obscure conversation with Mom, Crockett's wife, and Angela.

The birds chirped and the sun shone as we stepped off just after breakfast time. We were all in a good mood, the first chance to head north in a while. Intel said we might find a fight if we looked hard enough. ANA led the way as we pushed up to the Gonopah Bridge and split off on our own path. We marched up the hill through the village and further up the mountain, keeping pace with ANA, who remained on the road.

Already high on the mountain, we met up with ANA. We coordinated for a bit, and they pushed a small element around the hill, as Clemente, the LT, and I climbed as high as we were willing to, to "observe" their movement.

"Who gave you the idea to come up here, sir?" Clemente asked, when we finally stopped, our calves burning and our lungs gasping for air.

"It was mine," the LT replied.

"No, it wasn't. He did this, didn't he?" Clemente pointed at me.

"Oh yeah, you did mention this earlier," he said, smiling at me.

The LT and I laughed at Clemente, who started his one-man bitch session.

"So, we are up here for a dick measuring contest?" Clemente asked.

"Marines said they went up 1826 meters. We are only at 1740," the LT said, pointing to the spot they claimed to have reached.

"Sir, to start off, that point is lower than us. Second, who gives a fuck?"

We laughed and argued for a bit, and as the LT finally pulled the right strings and we were gearing back up to continue to the top, we got a call from Davis to head back down.

My knee ached the whole way. I finally started complaining after we met back up with the platoon and began to move to the valley floor. Clemente chose a route that led us along a cliff face and through some very serious terrain. After a great deal of complaining, we were finally on the ground.

We gathered ourselves and pushed to the road.

One last stop when we got to the road. I adjusted my gear, checked on our gunners to see how they were feeling, and we pressed on. The ANA was waiting for us at the bridge. We let them pass us and take lead.

Crack.

Crack.

Crack.

Alvanez dove while turning to see where the fire was coming from. Somersaulting for cover, he began to unload his first hundred rounds.

"Sarjeent, ees my ass bleeding?" he yelled, his Salvadoran accent thicker than ever.

"Whaaat?" Davis yelled back.

"Sarjeent, I think they shot me in the ass."

Davis looked to see red spots forming through the gray of his ACU trousers. "Yeah, now load another belt," he yelled back.

"Oh, I got the Forrest Gump wound." He loaded the next belt and unloaded another two hundred into the hill, while Celaya dumped Two Oh Three rounds. Deutch was already wrestling with permission to fire mortars, and the rest of the Death Dealers tried to match Alvanez's fire.

I ran for cover behind a small rock wall. I jumped. In mid-air, I looked down at the six-foot drop on the other side. This was going to hurt later.

I found a spot of cover and started scanning the ridge where all our fire was being concentrated. Explosions, M4, and machine gun fire peppered the hill. I wrestled with my camera, trying to get it back into its bag. Finally secured, I was able to pop some rounds off.

I listened to the radio chatter, still no casualties.

With a momentary lull, I yelled, "Everyone good?"

No response, only more weapon fire.

A good sign.

"Alvanez's asshole is bleeding," I heard Davis say over the radio.

This mother fucker, even in a firefight he is making gay jokes.

In my head, I pictured myself running over to find Alvanez fine and Davis laughing.

"All you heard was asshole and you came running. Fucking fag."

"No really. We need a medic," Davis reiterated.

I jumped out of my position and started running down the street. I kept my eyes open, looking for a hint of where he was hiding.

As I passed a large boulder, I felt the air from rounds whizzing past my face. Out of the corner of my eye, I saw the muzzle flashes from Alegria's SAW, set five feet back behind a wall. My legs stopped moving, but my momentum carried my torso forward. It bought him enough time to lift his finger off the trigger. I used the momentary pause. My legs caught my body as I stumbled forward and broke into a sprint. I heard his fire resume from behind me.

I found Alvanez passing off his weapon off to Clemente. Reynoso, one of the Aid Station medics who came to help on this mission, guided Alvanez to the ground. We rolled him over to find the blood. Reynoso began to cut into his pants with his trauma shears. I dove in with my seatbelt cutter. We exposed the wound and started dressing it.

The shots were beautiful through-and-throughs. We talked about the wounds casually with Alvanez, while we wrapped him up and began to search for more injuries. Clemente wrestled with his machine gun a few meters away, with Alvanez offering up his advice.

"Sarjeent, you need to pull the charging handle back," Alvanez yelled from his supine position.

"Mother fucker, I know," Clemente yelled back, trying desperately to pull the handle to the rear, to no avail.

"We need a saline lock man. You want to do it or you want me to?" I asked Reynoso.

"I got it," Reynoso said. He rarely ever spoke to anyone. This was probably the most I had ever spoken to him the whole tour. He and Alvanez chattered away in Spanish, while I watched the needle move unsteadily toward his vein.

I stole a move from SFC Mendoza's playbook. I reached out, and through the gunfire and mortars raining down on the hillside, grabbed Reynoso's shoulder. "Hey, take a breath for me."

He paused for a moment. I watched him take a breath and skillfully guide the needle into the arm.

No initial flash.

He guided to the right.

Flash.

The blood filled the small capsule at the end of the needle. He was in the vein.

"Take off the constricting band," he said.

I released it, and he clipped the saline lock into place and secured it.

A little bit of morphine and Alvanez was as cheerful as ever.

"Hey doc, I learned what placebo means." I laughed. Rabbit had asked me for a placebo for his shoulder. I'd obliged with some vitamins that aid with sleeping and told him that they were powerful, would make him drowsy, and were very addictive, so he needed to be careful. Within days, he was singing my praises for helping his shoulder." Fucking kids.

"Oh really."

"Yes, Sarjeent. It is a drug that doesn't do anything."

"Yeah, it is, just don't tell Rabbit. Hey, I want to apologize, man."

"Why, Doc?"

"I jinxed you. Last week me and Deutch were watching Forrest Gump, and I said that you were him."

He laughed. SFC Mendoza and I had long since coordinated a MEDEVAC out. Somewhere along the line we were getting both a bird and a vehicle.

"Doc, I can walk back."

I looked at him. His pants were in shreds around his ankles, his bloody underwear hanging over his bandages. "No, dude, you don't have any fucking pants."

He laughed again, that big throaty laugh that makes us all smile.

WUMP.

WUMP.

WUMP.

I looked to our south to see an MRAP speeding toward us, peppering the hillside with the fifty cal. Reynoso and I helped Alvanez to his feet and ran him toward the truck.

The door swung open. I saw Joey in his shorts, a T-shirt, and armor, with Wills beside him. He was still too injured from the IED and unable to do long patrols. I smiled at Joey and let him know what was up with Alvanez while we helped him up.

Before we knew it, the MRAP was flipping around.

"FIRE AGAIN!" SFC Mendoza yelled.

Rounds peppered the hill while they drove away. Burning brush covered the ground at the base of the hill from the white phosphorous rounds that were used to screen our movement earlier.

A tree burned brightly, the corn stalks left as animal feed had gone up in a blaze. Our adrenaline ran high along with our spirits. We began our walk back.

"The MRAP rolled," came over the radio.

Fuck.

"Let's go Reyn-man (a pet name for Reynoso)," I yelled as I started jogging down the road.

"I think it may have been the Mad Dog element," Clemente said. They were down by Jaboom CP, too far to run. We slowed to a trot as we rounded the corner.

In the distance, I saw a tan spot lying in the field, with smaller dots running toward it.

Fuck.

"Reyn-man, through the fields. Let's go." We ran as fast as we could through the field. Thankfully, our adrenaline carried us further than we normally would have been allowed.

When we arrived, I saw Wills next to the MRAP. He didn't even look shaken. Other soldiers I had seen on the inside were walking around looking at the damaged vehicle lying like a dead animal on its side. The road above them looked like a dirt slide. Joey was right behind Alvanez as they climbed the slide to the road, where a HMMWV was waiting with members of Hustler platoon. I got to the top in time to say hi to Joey, to see that Alvanez had no new injuries, and to see the MEDEVAC bird come circling in.

It landed in the field in front of the MRAP. I helped Alvanez down to the bird and talked to the flight medic as Alvanez walked over to the helicopter and took a seat.

"He has a gunshot wound, and he was just in a roll over."

"What about the other people in the roll over?"

"I don't know. It just happened." I could tell he was confused. "They all seem fine. I'll go double check."

I jogged back to the group. Everyone was fine. I climbed to the road above the MRAP and snapped a photo before the bird lifted off.

As things calmed down and we really began to assess the damage done to the MRAP and its passengers, we did find the gunner to be a little sore. Joey drove him back to the COP in one of Hustler's HMMWVs.

The sun had sunk behind the mountains. I could feel the cold settling into my bones, and I began to check on the rest of the guys. We had been running around for eight hours and we were running short on water. I tossed around bottles of water and some Gatorade from the MRAP.

"Dealer two. Dealer Medic," I called Davis on the radio.

"What up?"

"Where you at?"

"The other side of the river. We set in an OP over here."

"I'm bringing you guys some water. How many guys you got?"

"Fo."

"Was that a fucking number? How many guys?"

"I said four, mother fucker."

"Copy."

I snagged up four Gatorades and a case of water. The LT walked with me to the edge of the river, until he decided that he might actually fall in, which he decided was not a preferable option. He tossed the bottles he carried. They landed softly on the bank.

I looked at the rocks, spaced throughout fast moving, assuredly cold water, "Dealer two, Medic."

"Yup."

"Did you guys find a way to cross or just push through?"

No pause. "We just pushed through, man. All our boots are wet."

Liar. "Roger."

I walked north until I found a suitable rock path across. I saw boot prints I recognized on the rocks that I jumped to and from.

"Medic, Two."

"Send it."

"I got two guys coming to meet you. They have a guy with them that came running off the mountain we got shot at from. He was all running and singing Taliban songs, until he saw us and slowed down."

"Copy."

I met up with Alegria and Baltasar. I passed them the bottles, and they turned over their detainee to me.

"Mother fucker, walk," I said to him, pointing at the wreck.

He took the lead, guiding me back over the rocks.

I turned him over to SFC Mendoza, who began to interrogate him with the interpreter. The interpreter had miraculously survived the firefight. We thought he had died. Immediately after taking contact, he began to play possum in the middle of the road, until the LT pulled him to cover.

"He is deaf, sir," the interpreter told SFC Mendoza who was working a thorough search of the individual while I provided security.

"Hey, Dealer Two. You managed to catch Greased-Up Deaf Guy."

"I bet he's deaf after all those mortar rounds landed next to him."

We turned him over to the ANA with no results.

Different elements arrived with different ideas on how to recover the MRAP.

Wills, now a part of our element, after arriving to help us with QRF and now stranded with the MRAP, sat with SFC Mendoza, Clemente, and me on the east side of the river, watching the village. We placed bets on how long we would be out and complained about the cold. The last bit of the sunlight caught the red of Alvanez's blood, still on my hands. I laughed to myself.

Finally, with the Commander on the other side of the river talking to the villagers and offering them money for their damaged trees and fields, our LT made a decision.

They found a low spot where the road was almost level with the field and drove in. They shredded the ground as they drove through it. The wrecker backed up to the MRAP, and soon had it on all four wheels.

As the bulldozer arrived to help make a road to drive out on, the MRAP was started. Bulldozer's tracks ripped deep holes into the field while it guided the MRAP, now on its own power and three good tires, drove out of the field. We cheered as it drove down the road. [Lance: You really are in the thick of it, doing the job now. Way to go.]

We followed in tow, laughing in the soft haze left behind from the sun. We would make it back in time for dinner.

"Right in the fucking ass, man," I said to SFC Mendoza, laughing. "Right in the fucking ass."

* * *

"Que pasa, Dahctor?" Alvanez said, pulling me out of my daze, as I prepared lunch the next day.

"Welcome back, man."

Click here for link to photos and/or videos

39

COMPLACENCY-ITIS—THE SILENT KILLER

~Lance~

I lay in bed, trying to fall asleep last night, and couldn't stop the nagging thoughts I'd had from a conversation a few hours earlier with a co-worker of mine. So, I got up and went to the office.

Her boyfriend is a Marine stationed on a ship in Kuwait, and, coincidentally, due back in mid-April. I asked her how her boyfriend was doing and she replied, "Oh, he's fine," without much enthusiasm.

"Don't you miss him?" I asked.

"Yeah, I guess. But he'll be back soon, and I've got my friends, and I go out."

A klaxon sounded in my head. The past few days Adam's and my e-mails had been short and uneventful—and not even every day. He'd been at the Death Star, and I'd been busy.

Wrong.

What was I thinking? Actually, I wasn't thinking. I was just doing—going about my day-to-day business. Yes, I still think about him a lot. But it's different, I realized. Why? I'm not like that girl, who said, "Oh, he'll be back soon" am I?

No. I couldn't be.

But what do other left-behinders think? I'm sure a lot of them do get lax or forget. It's wrong, but I see how it can happen.

And that made me think. What about years ago when communications were only by letter? I could really see how apathy could set in then. It's a virus—and possibly a deadly one. All of the wives and sweethearts with their undying protestations of, "I'll write every day" and, "I'll wait for you forever."

I'm thinking: not so much. And some of those men were gone for years—not ten months. Then again, those were different times. Everything moved at a slower pace. Snail-mail was basically the only means of communication. But people knew that and waited for correspondence. They went about their lives, hoping and praying that everything would be all right. The men overseas could only hope that everything back home was fine as well and that sporadic letters meant everything to them.

Nowadays, we live in the age of instant gratification. We shoot off a quick text or e-mail and get a swift response—hopefully. And when we don't, we think something is wrong, or that they're busy. So then, we get busy and forget to shoot off an e-mail. Then a day passes, then two... Complacency-itis has struck.

Of course, there's the whole, quote-unquote, friend, thing. I don't wonder now that Adam's acquaintances are not so responsive anymore. I do wonder sometimes that he is pulling away and keeping things from me. He's not sharing personal feelings. It has taken a few months, but I do feel he's withdrawing from me.

Yesterday:

E-MAIL FROM LANCE:

Hey A

Would you give me a call? I'd really like to talk to you. It's been a while. Thanks.

—L

Today:

E-MAIL FROM ADAM:

Hey

I will call you when I want to. Don't beg me. Even my mother
doesn't ask me to call. I'm not feeling it right now. Don't ask me.
Everything here is fine.

—A

That was one of the meanest things he'd ever said to me—and
in an e-mail no less. I certainly didn't think my request warranted
that vitriol. Something was up.

E-MAIL FROM LANCE:

I'm not your mother. I'm your best friend, you asshole! I'm not
one of your bimbo/bozo acquaintances who doesn't care if you live
or die. I may be the only one who does care, whose life would
genuinely be affected by your death. Think about it. Then tell me
not to ask you to call. And that's all I did was ask—not beg. Keep
pulling this type of shit and you will be alone.

—L

But I didn't send it. (It'll have to do just to write it.)

* * *

I thought about him being over there, fighting and alone. That
would have been cruel. He may have hurt me, but I wouldn't enact
revenge on him. I always have to remember not to distract him. It's
not about me. Doesn't stop the hurt though.

But that leads me to...

Acquaintances. They are especially susceptible to complacency-
itis. (Known fact.) People have their own lives and day-to-days. Out

of sight, out of mind (a known symptom) has never been more apt. Adam doesn't know this. He can't. And he couldn't really get it unless he'd been there and done that. He hasn't been on the other side. He only knows that no one seems to care anymore. It's not true. It's the nature of the disease. He does probably understand it a little more than some of the other guys he's with, since he's done two previous tours. But what about the new guys? Some of them have never been away from home before; they're the instant gratification generation. They are not immune to home-sickness. Video games and porn only go so far.

[Adam: It is immature for anyone deployed or away from their families to believe that those left behind are sitting at home pining over their missing loved ones. And, as we have passed along to the kids who are experiencing the same thing, "If they aren't able to put the four minutes of effort into writing you an e-mail, then they aren't worth bothering with when you get back." Deployments are very good at the depressing task of solidifying the blurred line between friends and acquaintances. And video games and porn can go very far.] [Lance: In which case, there aren't very many of us to bother with.]

People here don't realize the effect they're having on the people over there.

It scares me. I'm consciously fighting to not be like that. He's my best friend, for God's sake!

Every day—every minute! It's a life threatening situation for him. [Adam: HOLY SHIT! NO ONE TOLD ME I COULD DIE!] And I can't find a couple of minutes each morning to shoot him a, "Hi, how ya doing—I'm fine," e-mail?

I would say that, in my defense, he tells me: "Things are fine" and, "Nothing crazy here." They are his leitmotif. But then I hear about what's been happening in his life, and I know that's not the case.

But that is no excuse for my complacency-itis. I know the symptoms now.

So, I have to thank my co-worker for the wake-up call. I will again e-mail Adam every day. It doesn't have to be earth-shaking news, just a simple hello and maybe a tidbit or two about my ordinary day. I know that I look forward to his e-mails, as I'm sure he does mine. And I'm equally sure that his attempts at withdrawal are his self-preservation tools. It is the connection that's important. I need to remember that. And I won't let him disconnect.

I know things will be different for a while when he comes back. He's going to be re-establishing his life and will probably be leery at first. I should be one thing he doesn't need to be leery about.

But he knows this. Death, taxes, Lance.

Until then, it's back to regular e-mailing.

Complacency-itis. There is a cure.

40

A PINHOLE OF LIGHT

~Adam~

E-MAIL FROM SUSAN:

Adam

"I don't know how you just write me off..."

"I hate you..."

—Susan

* * *

E-MAIL FROM ADAM:

Susan

"Hate me, if that helps you to become the woman that I needed for someone who deserves it."

—Adam

* * *

Snow crept down the mountain toward the Death Star, where I snuck into the wooden box that was our shitter, placed four feet from the edge of a hillside set at a forty-five degree angle, dropping down almost a thousand feet in elevation. I battled the wind outside to get into the relative safety inside the small wooden box filled with large cracks and openings to allow air to flow freely through, with my little MP3 player full of dirty movies to relieve some pressure.

This was the closest we had gotten to snow. Thankfully, it didn't reach us. Only the rain covered the top floor in a thin layer of water that took days to dry up.

Rumors of going home and dates had been flying for weeks now.

"Don't believe anything is going to happen until it is over," I told some of the kids, who clung to every little rumor that got passed around.

The best we could get was finally being relieved on the Death Star and heading back down the hill.

* * *

"Happy birthday, beautiful," I told Angela. I was sitting on a table next to the phone in the MWR.

"Thanks, Sweetie, but you are a day late." Off to a great start.

"Hmm. Did you at least get your presents?"

"Yeah, I did. Thank you." [Lance: I had asked him to bring me back a pendant of one of the indigenous minerals there. I wear a lot of them. It would be a great souvenir. We'll see.]

"Did you ever tell your mom that we were back together?"

"Yeah, she was wondering why I was bringing trash back into the house."

"I hope I can prove her wrong."

"Me, too."

The conversation moved onto more pleasant topics. We play argued about things that didn't matter for well after my allotted time on the phone.

Time wasn't moving fast enough out there, but it was moving.

* * *

Dinner had thankfully settled in our stomachs long enough for us to get to the gym. Mine was now deposited in the bottom of the trash can, but we drove on nonetheless. Davis and Wills were playing video games with the kids. So, I was working out with Deutch, Clemente, and Rabbit. Rabbit and Clemente bounced around the room, while Deutch and I laughed and listened to the music playing on a pair of off-brand speakers purchased from Taj's shop.

BOOM!

"Maybe that was a door closing," Clemente said as he went to check with the CP, just next door.

WABOOM!

SFC Mendoza burst through the doorway. "Suit up. Get to the trucks."

I grabbed my stuff and ran up to the barracks to get dressed. A layer of dust filled the air. My headlamp could barely cut through the fog. I could taste gunpowder and sand as I moved further up the hill.

A soft blue light caught my eye off to the left, near Hustler's living area. "You good, man?" I asked as his figure became clear.

"Yeah. That shit landed in front of me." I now recognized him as one of the Mortarmen I frequently saw in the gym.

"So, you are good?"

"Oh yeah," he laughed. "I was just trying to take a fucking piss."

It didn't take long before we were geared up in front of the MRAPs, watching our own mortars explode on the hill. Konrad had luckily been on post and seen where the rockets were fired from. This afforded him the ability to accurately call in the necessary fire mission. Sporadic AK fire could be heard from the ANA side of the base, peppering Dumlam village and the surrounding area for no known reason.

I ran into Odie. He was still with the sniper team, but now working out of Meth Lab with Sam. His team was operating in our area on occasion, lucky for him.

It didn't take long before the show was over and we returned to our barracks. We dropped our gear and swapped stories about the event. However, two voices were not heard. Sandy and Finch had gone home in the weeks prior. Non-combat related injuries had taken them out of the country and back into the arms of their loved ones. Baltasar and the other IRR soldiers had also gone home, their contracts finally up. The platoon was getting light, barely able to make the minimum manning requirements to leave the wire. And taking our injured soldiers into account, our numbers further dwindled.

I kept stressing to the LT, "Sir, you know I love to explore, but let's just get home."

As Hunt so aptly puts it, "It is time. I'm ready."

Click here for link to photos and/or videos

41

SLEEP DEPRIVATION AND COYOTE TRAPS

~Adam~

The sun was just rising when we returned. Sam, Odie, and whoever else felt like being involved in the sniper mission had been handed off to the Hooligans, north of Watangatu. We had dropped them off around eleven that night.

The mission, aside from being all night, had had its perks. We drove down a bit south of the Jaboom CP and everyone able dismounted. We did a local area patrol, leaving the snipers behind, and made a small noisy stop in Bandeh.

"Let them know you are here," Sam and his fellow snipers told us.

"Roger." We smiled in response.

We flashed our lights and threw some smoke grenades.

After an evening of sitting in the MRAP on QRF for the snipers, we were back.

How the coyote trap ended up in our barracks is a moot point. And how the coyote trap ended up the subject of conversation this early in the morning is a point of equal value.

"You aren't fast enough to hit that and escape," Davis told SFC Mendoza in a casual tone.

"You think because I'm old I don't have any quickness left in me?"

"Three hundred dollars for you to try."

"This won't break my hand will it?"

"Not at all. It is designed to grab, not break."

"All right. Three hundred," SFC Mendoza agreed while Davis ran to his room to grab the money.

SFC Mendoza slid a small set of drawers into the center of the hallway and set the coyote trap on top, its silver maw open and springs tensed in anticipation.

"I recommend you not do this," Deutch said behind his camera.

"I also am advising against this." My voice was monotone. "But if you are going to, I recommend you let it bite down at this angle. So you should turn the trap this way." [Lance: You are so thoughtful.]

He adjusted the trap to reduce its possibility of injury.

Clemente worked diligently to get into SFC Mendoza's brain to dissuade him. SFC Mendoza focused on the trap, throwing a few practice jabs into the air next to it.

Davis stayed positive but looked away.

SFC Mendoza drew a deep breath.

SNAP!

He looked up; his face was a contorted mess. It quickly morphed into a look of relief and victory as the trap clanged to the ground near Davis.

The room quickly filled with the sounds of excitement. We replayed the scene and our impressions.

"Dude, that would have broken your hand," Davis said.

"It did scuff you a bit," I said, pointing out the grazing marks on his knuckles.

We tested the power of the trap on our individual hands, easing it closed, to show its potential crushing power.

"Yeah, that would have broken your hand for sure," I said. "But I did have ice and a cover story on hand."

"Here, you can have this back," SFC Mendoza said, handing Davis his money.

Davis was surprised, but he didn't argue. The rumble of voices slowly calmed down as we headed into our respective rooms and fell asleep. [Lance: I know I could never be that bored. This is entertainment? Whatever happened to staring at a wall, watching paint dry, and looking at the stars?]

* * *

"Hey Two, Alegria found some wires up here," Wills asked Davis over the radio.

"Roger Five, push past and start looking for a trigger, man. Three, can you grab a couple guys and get them to clear this?" Davis responded.

"Roger, I'm coming up now," Clemente answered back.

I grabbed SFC Mendoza and headed up behind Clemente to the possible IED site. Clemente grabbed the mechanic and the two cooks who were helping us out on patrol. It was the cook's first patrol since we had arrived in COP Najil. Not a good way to warm them up.

"Hey Three, Punisher base wants us to clear that IED if possible. You are the most qualified guy we got—after that correspondence course you took," Davis said over the radio.

"Roger that," Clemente said, guiding the mechanic and the one cook up the small cliff to get a different angle on the pile of dirt the device was hidden in.

"Aren't you going to go up there?" SFC Mendoza asked the remaining cook, who lingered on the road. He looked at SFC Mendoza. "Go on, get up there."

The nervous cook climbed the cliff, chasing after Clemente and his IED defeat team. I scanned the field and kept my distance. But not too much.

"Holy shit. I see it," SFC Mendoza said. He backed away from the dirt mound with his camera rolling. "Right there." He pointed it out to Clemente, who climbed back off the hill after looking at it through his ACOG.

Before we knew it, Clemente had his team huddled around the battery and circuit board, with the wires running in every direction. The mechanic and Clemente had wire cutters out and were deciding which wires to cut.

"What the fuck are you doing?" SFC Mendoza yelled at the cook as he pulled his camera out. "I'm documenting this. You are on a fucking IED! Get your head in the game."

Clip.

Clip.

"BOOM!" SFC Mendoza yelled. They stood jumped to their feet

SFC Mendoza began to laugh manically.

Realization replaced the startled looks on their faces.

I gathered them all together for a group photo. "Afghanistan, you got Punk'd," Clemente said. [Lance: The humor still eludes me.] [Adam: …]

Click here for link to photos and/or videos

42

MORE POO

~Adam~

"I don't know. They just gave us these awesome mittens, like the kind of thing you need in Korea," I told Angela around one in the morning, my time.

"All I got when I was in Korea was a garbage pair of mittens," she responded. Her office phone rang in the background. "Sorry, can you hold on?"

"Sergeant..." I could hear her talking in the distance through the phone.

WABOOM!

BOOM!

Fuck.

"Sorry, Sweetie, I got to go." I didn't even listen for a response before I hung up.

I grabbed my pistol, flashlight, and ran out the door.

WHEEEWWWWW!

Something flew over my head as I ran up the sandbag stairs and headed toward my Barracks.

Mortars began to respond in full force on the site of the North Ridge, where we had taken rockets from the previous week.

"Was that incoming?" SFC Mendoza asked when I ran into him, just before I arrived at the barracks.

"Oh yeah."

"Let's all take positions by that Hesco wall," he said, pointing to the wall just north of the barracks.

I took my position, enjoying the show, and directed the kids as they slowly started showing up.

WABOOM!

The rounds would exit the tubes in a flash, occasionally offering a glimpse of the round as it flew into the air.

Within a minute, the round would slice through the darkness. A shower of sparks and flames would splash across the ridgeline. A second later, the sound would hit us.

Soon, we were all gathered against the wall. I made my way over to SFC Mendoza. "Pretty good first night for the new unit coming in." The first part of the advanced party for our relief had arrived earlier that day.

"That is right," he said. "WELCOME TO COP NAJIL, MOTHER FUCKERS!" he yelled into the darkness.

I looked at the time. It was pushing close to my shift on tower guard.

SFC Mendoza and Clemente took the kids to go look for impact sites on the base, while I gathered what gear I needed and headed to relieve Deutch and Rabbit on post.

It promised to be an exciting four hours with the LT.

"So. How about those command Climate surveys, sir?

"I haven't even filled mine out yet," he replied.

"I figured I would fill it out while I was still heated."

"Yeah, I want to be honest, but it asks for rank, and there are only three of us officers on the COP. Kind of narrows it down."

"That sucks. You could always just lie." He nodded and shrugged. "I got pretty mad when they asked for three improvements. So, I just said that this survey could have helped out six months ago, not during RIP (Relief in Place)."

"Yeah," he said in a quick bark.

It was our fourth day in a row sharing post together. He would tell me about his trials and tribulations as Death Dealer Six: all the behind-the-scenes things that had happened that I hadn't heard about, all the fights we had run headfirst into—while his boss had told him to fall back—and all the times he had to take heat from majors and lieutenant colonels who didn't like being corrected by us, his NCOs.

We laughed, swapping stories about how many things I had said that had gotten him in trouble and how our antics had affected operations.

The radio crackled to life. "Punisher Base. Death Star."

"Death Star. Send it."

"Hey, we have a guy moving around at the POO (Point Of Origin) site."

"Roger, stand by."

"Death Star. Punisher Six." The COP Commander jumped on the radio.

"Send it, Six"

"I need you to continue observing and report any unusual activity."

"Roger."

I looked at the LT. "You want to see about putting some fire in his ass, sir?"

"Yeah, I'm going to go talk to him."

The LT stepped out while I continued to watch the local area.

"That didn't take long," I said as he returned minutes later.

"Yeah," he said with a bark.

"Nothing, huh?"

"Nope."

"All right. This is why we don't always call shit up that we see. Nobody ever does anything about it."

"I know."

We talked local politics and vented about failed operations.

"All right, sir, I got a good one for you."

"Okay."

"What was our mission out here, our commander's intent for COP Najil?"

"I don't know. I used to ask, but I never got an answer."

"That makes it hard to plan operations."

"Yeah, and I used to throw out a lot of ideas, but those would get shot down. He said I was too aggressive and didn't understand why we wanted to go the places that we did."

I shook my head.

"Punisher Base. Death Star."

"Death Star. Send it."

"That guy finished picking up what he was going to and headed back over the ridge."

"Roger."

"He is so afraid to kill the wrong guy that we won't take action against even those obviously doing the wrong thing."

"Yup."

Eventually, our four hours passed. We said our good mornings and headed our separate ways.

* * *

"Hey, sweetie."

"Hey." Angela's voice sounded cheery on the other end of the phone.

"I just wanted to call and apologize for hanging up on you. I had to go take care of something."

"That is okay..."

We drifted into playful banter. She hadn't heard the explosions. I was in the clear.

"Have a good night, beautiful."

"Get some sleep, crazy."

43

PROFESSIONAL COURTESIES BETWEEN ENEMIES

~Adam~

"Remember gentlemen," the LT COL started before we stepped off on our mission. "We have historically taken contact in this valley. So, when you are walking, always be on the lookout for your next piece of cover."

He stared at us as if this was our first time in the valley or as if we weren't the ones who had taken contact. Clemente, Davis, SFC Mendoza, the LT, one of the cooks, and I were escorting engineers, ADT, and some Civil Affairs elements on the Gonopah Bridge, Jesus tree loop. Deutch would take a small crew into the hills to set up an OP. This was an officer-heavy patrol and we weren't looking forward to it.

It didn't take long before the pattern emerged: a large crew of officers walking in a tight group with us enlisted Death Dealers and about 100 meters behind them.

"I don't want to be anywhere near that RPG magnet," Davis said.

"In their defense, the safest place to be is where they are aiming, and that is where I would aim," I said.

"How about some fucking dispersion!" Davis yelled ahead. No one, however, seemed to notice.

The patrol went slowly. A lot of tourists who were not used to the terrain kept the pace slow. It didn't take long before we passed the spot where Alvanez had been shot, just before the bridge.

"Hey, Reyn-man, I found some trash from your saline lock," I yelled ahead to him.

He turned. A smile stretched across his young Hispanic face.

We crossed the bridge over the branch running north to south, then turned south and crossed the west-to-east running branch of the river. We carefully maneuvered through the rocks, trying to keep our boots dry. I took my last step, flinging myself forward and arriving safely on the other side of the small river. I pushed forward to allow SFC Mendoza and the cook to cross.

The two jumped to safety and took their first steady steps on dry land.

Snap.

Crack.

Crack.

Crack.

Crack.

I dove against the wall to my left. I saw the rounds impact in the riverbed ten meters to our northwest. I looked up through my scope and fired toward the flash. All around me, soldiers fired on that location. It didn't take long before the noise settled, leaving behind the faint echoes of gunfire traveling in every direction of the valley and the gentle scent of gunpowder hanging in the air.

"Is everybody all right?" SFC Mendoza yelled.

I listened for a response, looking back.

The LT was sharing a small tree with another officer for cover.

Information flew around on the radio, reporting the incident and coordinating mortar fire on that location.

It took a while before mortars started landing near the POO site. Adjustments were made. Slowly, the rounds started landing further east of the POO site. "They need to go down," Davis yelled to SFC Mendoza. SFC Mendoza tried to call it up, but the round continued to push further east.

"Hey, Sergeant," LT said to the ADT team leader, as he ran over. "I need you to take charge of your guys."

I didn't hear him respond by saying, "So, how is that different from the rest of the patrol?" I was laughing too hard.

The LT missed it too, "What are you laughing at, smart ass?"

"Hey, Sergeant, you know those guys that are yours? I need you to take charge of them," I mimicked and continued laughing.

The LT made his way back to check on the pile of officers.

"You know that was really nice of them," SFC Mendoza said in a matter-of-fact voice.

We all looked at him, our confusion easily visible on our faces, as he looked at the hill where the attack originated.

"They waited until I had crossed the river before they attacked. They went up a point in my book today."

"Hmm," I replied with a smile and a nod.

We decided to continue the mission. ADT and the Engineers did their inspections of all their projects, current and prospective, and we stayed to the back enjoying the show.

Deutch organized a show of force from some jets, which turned into a few flares flying over the valley—another waste of time.

"You were looking a little tired out there," SFC Mendoza told me as we climbed the hill to our barracks. "You all right?"

"Yeah, I'm good. Kind of tired of this. I thought last week would be our last mission week. I'm ready to be done with all this walking."

"Yeah, I agree."

We returned in time for a late lunch of warm deli meat and stale bread.

I overheard the LT COL tell another officer that when the attack kicked off, he couldn't find any cover. I smiled.

That evening I bumped into Maj A in the showers before I jumped in for a lukewarm shower. "Hey, sir, what was up with your boys out there?"

"You know they asked me why you guys were hanging so far back from the group," he said. "I told them it is because we were all jacked up and you guys didn't want to be anywhere near us." He finished off laughing. I joined in.

* * *

I e-mailed the most recent manuscript to Lance and opened an e-mail from mom.

Ethan is getting married.

My nineteen-year-old brother is getting married.

I had tried to talk to him about pushing the date back, "Wait a few years. Live together first."

He stopped returning my e-mails.

Mom says be supportive.

Angela says it is his choice to make and I need to support his decision.

I'm hypothetically biting my tongue so hard I can taste the imaginary blood.

Click here for link to photos and/or videos

44

COMFORTABLY DRESSED FOR A PROPER SEND OFF

~Adam~

I had just spent the week up at Death Star, slowly transitioning over to the new unit. We passed it along. No one from the Cav was left up there. The changeover had been slow, but larger and larger groups had been showing up. My bunk welcomed me back with its familiar unforgiving springs. I was enjoying some casual trash talking with the new occupants now occupying Finch, Sandy, and Wills' newest rooms.

"Hey, gents, they just arrested three guys with RPGs above the Death Star." A tall young LT ran into the door to pass the latest word, all geared up.

We asked all the right questions until we got the details we needed. Three guys with RPGs behind the Death Star, and Mortars were working a fire mission.

Davis, Deutch, and I debated going up to reinforce. I was hoping this would pass quickly, so I could call Angela.

Crack.

Crack.

Crack.

Suddenly, it sounded like the whole COP opened up outside the door.

"Holy fuck!" someone said as we grabbed our kits, weapons, and ran outside.

I racked my weapon and hit the wall just outside the barracks, overlooking the valley. PKMs and RPGs flew at the COP, while M19s (Automatic Grenade Launcher), and the M2 (Fifty-Caliber Machine Gun) returned fire. The mortars joined in the fight as well.

I watched as rounds flew everywhere. The newest denizens of COP Najil, fully loaded, hit the wall around us. I popped a couple rounds at some flashes I saw on the North Ridge. The whole picture of the attack formed as different posts and units called in on the radio. On the hill above, the Death Star was engaging and dodging RPGs.

It was a coordinated attack from at least three different locations. I had to give them props.

Boom. I saw the flash from the North Ridge.

WABOOM!

I watched an RPG land on the south road below Punisher Tower.

My legs started shaking. I looked down, PT shoes and shorts. It was cold.

WABOOM!

Another RPG. I saw the flash explode behind us. It looked like it hit Cheap Times. I sprinted over to check for casualties. Some new guys stood shaken near the building, but were unharmed.

I ended up near the wall again.

I watched over the Hesco wall, enjoying every impact as the sound waves shook through my chest.

"What the fuck are you looking at?" a booming voice came from behind me. It was one of the new platoon sergeants, a solidly built, older gentleman who had decades of experience as a Marine sniper to harden his attitude and features.

I didn't even notice the soldier cowering at my feet against the wall. He was turned, facing the barracks. He had made himself as small as he could to avoid the fire. He didn't respond, aside from shuffling to his feet.

"Are you fucking kidding me? What goddamned good are you down there? Get your fucking weapon and eyes facing out," the sergeant screamed at him.

I smiled to myself.

Slowly, the fire calmed down. I jumped in with Clemente and SFC Mendoza and started walking around the base. The radio net filled up with random garbage. I could hear faint gunfire in the distance. I looked up to the Death Star where it was originating. Nothing came over the net about it. After a few minutes, the net cleared up long enough to get a word in.

Finally, they did report their status to Punisher Base.

Still no casualties.

I walked around, said hi to the different people. I did a small patrol around the COP with some of the new guys.

"If I haven't said it yet, welcome to COP Najil," I said as we walked around. They chuckled.

Sporadic fire randomly filled the air. Tracers flew overhead. The One Five Five artillery pieces out of Mehtarlam's impacts echoed loudly from the Death Star. Eventually, Air Support came into the area.

"Punisher Base, this is One-Two. Punisher Base, what is your status?" The fighter pilot's voice slid beautifully through the air, as we imagined the sexy mouth that was speaking into the radio.

"Dude, she sounds fucking hot," we all said together.

"Roger, One-Two our current status is..." Deutch reported to her, and began his coordinating instructions in his Hamburglar voice. We listened intently.

He had headed directly to the CP to make sure that all the mortars, artillery, and air support were properly coordinated.

"Ask for her number," Clemente joked.

It took a few hours, but eventually things calmed down.

"We need you to stand up QRF. Hooligans are coming up," became the latest word.

"Wait, why do we need to prepare QRF for them when they are the ones reacting to an attack on us?" I asked aloud. Everyone was asking the same question.

We prepared our trucks and listened on the radio as Deutch argued to get them to turn around. Eventually, they headed back to base after arriving at Watangatu.

We returned to our normal base defense posture, and I got the chance to make my phone call.

"Still trying to get out of here, sweetie. Nope, nothing crazy here, pretty quiet," I told her.

* * *

Birds kept coming, dropping off guys and taking more of our own out. Soon, all that remained of the Death Dealers was SFC Mendoza, LT, Davis, Deutch, Clemente, and me. Hustler had even less. The turnover was almost complete. We were just doing a few patrols to familiarize the new unit to the area. They were an infantry unit, trained in the mountains. They possessed more combat experience than we did and were receptive to all of our advice and experiences. It looked as though they would do very well.

45

A STRIP AND A C-130 ROLLING

~Adam~

I was pleasantly enjoying some conversation with Dilay in the Aid Station, while the new medics were out on a patrol, when First Sergeant came in. "We have Blackhawks coming in and I need you two to go," he said.

"Hey Top, you know they only have two total medics on the COP without us?" I asked.

"Yeah, we are a crutch for them and we need to knock it out from underneath them. They need to stand up on their own now."

"Roger that."

Dilay went up first. My bags were almost packed. So, I knew it wouldn't take me long to get ready.

It didn't take long before Top came back into the Aid Station. "I have someone coming down to relieve you. You have to go pack and get on those birds," First Sergeant said.

"Roger."

A little while later, I was on the flight line saying good-byes to Davis, SFC Mendoza, and Deutch. Mohammed came down as well after we had grabbed some fried chicken and beans from his cook, the best lunch we could have to remember the COP for.

"What is up man?" I asked Mohammed.

"Sir, I am happy for you. You will go home and see your families. For this I am happy. But, Sir, I will miss for you," he said, barely able to look at me.

"Mohammed, you will be in America before you know it." I had started his visa paperwork, and it was taped firmly next on the wall for the new COP Commander. "We have told the new guys how good you are, and as long as you keep up the good work for them like you did for us, we will be able to see you soon."

"Thank you, brother. I am going to miss for you so much," he said, fighting his tears.

We all chatted for a while, until Mohammed excused himself to get some lunch, but not before he gave us hugs, something we don't normally do with Afghan males. We don't want to give them the wrong idea after all.

The birds landed, bringing with them a cloud of stinging rocks to pelt us as they settled on the landing zone.

We were heading to JAF. I took pictures along the way. We spent extra time circling RCP, who had just hit an IED south of the Jaboom CP, before we finally made the relatively short flight.

JAF welcomed us with overcrowded tents and overused cots. It was just Clemente and I from Death Dealers, aside from a few of the kids who we kept pushing ahead of us to make sure they made it to their intended destination. I ran into the other medics from Meth Lab. It was a surprisingly pleasant reunion. Like nothing had changed. Joey, Hunt, and I had spent a lot of time talking in Najil about how we had spent too much time apart and the rift that would result. There was no such rift, as long as we didn't act like children and have dick-measuring contests about our exploits throughout the last nine months.

Before long, we were in Bagram Air Field, crammed into a giant shell with enough beds for over four hundred soldiers. We took it in stride, taking care of our required tasks to get home. We filled our noses with the unfamiliar scents of women, who were suddenly all around us.

We gorged ourselves in the chow hall. Clemente and I ate more ice cream than was necessary, and I was able to have salads with all the fattening accoutrements that I enjoy. New greasy foods and dessert tables welcomed us. Fast-food and brand-name coffee garbage were commonly found lying around our bunks, along with new magazines and candy wrappers.

We tried to adjust and not hold this lifestyle against our fellow soldiers, with success for the most part.

46

CUTTING THE FAT

~Adam~

Again, we have returned to The Land of Milk and Honey. I said it on my way in, and I wholeheartedly agree with my earlier comment, "This is these people's combat deployment. They get paid the same as we will, sucking dirt up in the mountains."

Before it was a prediction, now it was our reality. Deutch and I scheduled massages for a reasonable price, and we had an option of which spa to go to. We went to a carwash earlier in the week to have the bus we borrowed washed by local laborers. I had eaten at multiple chow halls since I had been there, including one specializing in barbecues, and I had happily walked past a Burger King without temptation. I had had the privilege to complain about long lines in the PX, where I could have purchased plasma TVs and condoms. There was a club on base, and I had not only talked to two young ladies on separate occasions, but turned down their flagrant sexual advances.

This wasn't Bagram, Afghanistan, partially covered in minefields and littered with Russian equipment long since bronzed by rust. This was Bagram, Colorado, where I could go to the club, pick up a young lady, and take her back to her room where we could both enjoy the fifteen-dollar vibrating condom I purchased from the local pajama-wearing shopkeeper.

I had once again begun to lose the filter on my mouth that prevented me from screaming about the blatant lack of enforcement on height and weight standards. It started as casual friendly comments directed at the senior enlisted soldiers I did know. Soon, I was actually screaming, "You fat fuck," at Staff Sergeants I didn't know.

How did this happen? While we were hoarding muffins in Najil and vomiting up rotten chicken poppers in the trash cans at the gym, just trying to get enough calories to make up for what we used on the last patrol, they were gorging themselves on bread bars and Dairy Queen Blizzards.

This was why I got angry when I heard phrases like, "I believe everyone who puts on a uniform nowadays is a hero."

Maybe I held that word to a higher standard, but it was hard for me to believe that the soldier who shut down the MWR because they were missing some webcams was a hero. I wouldn't pretend to have the education or authority to define the word hero. I did believe that there were those who were essential to the cause—essential to the defense of our nation—and for this they should all be thanked and admired, but that didn't make them heroes.

More than likely you would never know when you met a true Hero, because they themselves did not know, or believe that they acted heroically. They just did what they thought had to be done and put no more thought into it.

I firmly believe that it takes a little more than surviving boot camp and wearing a camouflage pattern to earn the title of hero.

Click here for link to photos and/or videos

47

ANTICIPATION VS. TREPIDATION

~Lance~

March 15—The Ides of March. (I hope it's not an omen.) Just read the newest stuff and know he's making his way back. I got an e-mail after not hearing from him for a couple of days. "Was in JAF now in BAF. Nothing crazy here. Just getting ready."

I have to remind myself that JAF is Jalalabad Air Force Base and BAF is Bagram Air Force Base. Afghanistan to Kyrgyzstan. He's on his way back, doing the same route out as he did going in. He doesn't know yet how long until he returns—only that he is returning.

He's made it through.

How do I feel?

I don't know.

Excited? Yes. Anxious? Yes. Relieved? Yes. Scared?

Yes.

Why scared? The past couple of months I've still felt that pulling away feeling. There've been a lot of empty e-mails with the omnipresent "Nothing crazy here" phrase.

I haven't spoken on the phone to him since New Year's. That hasn't helped, either. I still remember the last time I asked him to call and his "not feeling it" retort. I can always tell his feelings from the tone in his voice. I know he has called Angela. I think things are better there. But I think I deserve a call as well. It doesn't have to be long, just a connect. It's always nice to hear his voice. There's a reassurance in the sound of the voice that e-mail doesn't capture and technology can't replace. He needs to consider my feelings as well. Yes, I know he's at war, but if he can call Angela— that on/off romance—why not me? At least I'm always on. I'm the one who's stuck with him through this, not her. Oops. Green-eyed monster's rearing his ugly head again. And I don't care. I'm the one who will be here for sure.

Consequently, my trepidatious state. (Is that a valid word?)

He doesn't have an exact home date yet, but it will be soon.

I'm sure everything is okay. Really.

48

THE LITTLE THINGS I'M...

~Adam~

LOOKING FORWARD TO...

Milk that spoils.

Losing my temper on the highway.

Sharing an orgasm with someone better looking than me.
[Lance: Knowing your ego, is that possible?]

Not needing to have a 9mm on me at all times.

A mattress with a pillow top.

Being able to take a hot shower whenever I want.

Whiskey with a splash of coke.

Not getting excited about seeing a girl go to the bathroom on the thermal camera or 14-power self-stabilizing binoculars.

Not having to shake hands with people who think toilet paper is dirty.

New music.

Grocery shopping.

Chopping vegetables.

Splashing spaghetti sauce on a clean white T-shirt. [Lance: Believe it or not, that is not a positive fashion statement, and probably won't get you dates.] [Adam: I love spaghetti.]

Girl smells.

Not waking up to the Lady Gaga playing loudly in the room next to my own.

A cold beer in a mug fresh out of the freezer.

Lunch.

The smell of spilt gasoline.

The feel of carpet on my bare feet.

Having fewer important conversations with people who can't speak English.

Not having to shave.

Setting my own schedule and having the option to not follow it.

Not smelling Ian's farts.

Motor boating the round fleshy parts of the female anatomy.

Spoons and forks that are not disposable.

Not getting rained on when I have to take a piss.

Blowing bubbles on my niece's belly.

NOT LOOKING FORWARD TO...

Flushing the toilet.

Not having my 9mm on me at all times.

Having to shower every day.

Hangovers.

The way people look at me when I tell them I just got back from Afghanistan.

Getting a real job.

Having to figure out what to wear.

Going places where expletives are not appropriate replacements for adjectives, adverbs, verbs, nouns, pronouns, and all other parts of speech.

Answering questions from people who think it is appropriate to ask, "Did you kill anyone," or "What do you think about...?"

Paying rent.

Hearing people's opinions about "The War," Obama, or Bush.

Doing dishes.

The awkward moment when someone, who wasn't there for me during the deployment, pretends like they care now that I'm back.

Click here for link to photos and/or videos

49

LEAVING ON A JET PLANE NA NA NA NA

~Adam~

Movement was slow, and patience was running thin. Everybody's fuse was getting shorter as time went on. A week-and-a-half or so at Bagram was wearing everyone out. It was emotionally draining—so close to getting home and nothing to do but wait. The small hints of home were more than a little difficult to swallow.

Then, after having our flights canceled, bumped back, and rescheduled, finally our packs were on the truck. Then there weren't enough seats on the plane. So we unloaded and reloaded, and were off.

Again, we found ourselves in Manas enjoying the subtle cultural nuances of beautiful Asian girls speaking Russian and Kyrgyz in that pleasantly hard Eastern European accent. We occupied our days, wrestling for a free outlet to charge my laptop, in the various computer labs and just generally carousing.

* * *

It was in a large tent that had been turned into the local bar named Pete's in which I had my first reset, sitting next to Davis. An Irish beer (I think) brought fermented hops splashing past my lips and down into my belly, granting an old familiar warmth. And suddenly it was like I hadn't been without beer this whole time. [Lance: Muscle memory.] I relaxed and enjoyed the music as the last of the carousing Cavalry soldiers in their Stetsons and spurs (A cavalry tradition is to wear Stetson hats and spurs in uniform, in memory of the days when we really did ride horses into battle.) filed out in their various states of inebriation.

After a few days, we were again boarding. It, of course, wasn't going fast enough. So, one of the captains and I snuck away for nachos and another beer, instead of waiting outside in line.

The flight would have lasted for a while, but I slept the whole way to Germany, where Hunt, Crockett, and I enjoyed a few six packs of local beer and some premixed Jack and Cokes in a can. We stumbled back onto the airplane after a several hour layover, and were off.

"Hey, Joey," I said, kneeling next to his aisle seat.

"What is up?" he responded.

"Not much. Odie is passed out. And I'm bored and can't sleep. So, I figured I'd see what you were up to."

"Well, I do have these," he said, pulling out two cans of Jack and Coke. "If you want one."

"Holy fuck, this is why you are the man," I said, taking one from him.

"I'm not the man, you're the man," he said, pointing his finger at me. "You would be awesome if you could get some cups full of ice."

"Not a problem," I said. I stood up and headed to the kitchen part of the plane, where the dark-skinned, and gently framed, male flight attendant sat. Joey followed me in tow.

"Hey, can we get two cups full of ice?" I asked him.

His eyes shot to the cans in our hands. "You guys aren't supposed to have those on the plane."

"Hmm. It is a good thing we don't, but I just have a thing about chewing ice," I said, stowing the can in my pocket and shrugging. "It helps me sleep."

"Okay, just don't let anyone catch you." He handed us two airline cups of ice.

"I appreciate it man," I said, taking the cups. I handed one to Joey, "You're the man, you know that, right?"

"Oh no, you are the man. I walk in the shadow of your greatness." Joey took the cup from me and headed back to his seat.

"Thank you, sir, you do good work." I smiled and pointed at him with cup in hand.

I poured a glass full of the almost-potent-enough drink and tried to drift off to sleep, but I couldn't get comfortable enough—or drunk enough—to sleep in the aisle seat.

It only took twenty-four-or-so hours before the wheels slammed into the runway with the sudden rush of the air smashing into the rudders as the plane slowed down. "Gentleman, welcome home," the beautiful flight attendant from one of the islands frequented by pleasure cruisers said over the intercom system in her gentle islander accent.

50

ENDING THIS CHAPTER

~Adam~

There is a major misconception that arriving home is like closing the book on a deployment. There is also the misunderstanding that the deployment is never over, that one is unable to completely get out. It is more like ending a chapter, where the events of the previous chapter directly affect the one to follow.

I have learned never to believe anything is going to happen until it is over. This deployment I have decided to close off as I finally fall asleep with Angela's head resting on my chest. My first ended in the airport next to my father, who didn't recognize me even as I sat next to him, and my mother charging me like a Green Bay Packer lineman wearing a "My son is a United States Marine" sweater. My second ended at a house party that Ed threw, doing things I regret with an ex-girlfriend on the bathroom floor. But that is where the confusion really becomes apparent. Although each deployment brings about irreparable change in a person, it doesn't just end abruptly.

I do categorize events in my life by deployments, but that implies that they were separate events in my life, as if I was temporarily beside myself, apart from my actual life and finally able to return once on American soil. I never stopped being me, and borders are manmade. Afghanistan soil feels the same as Iraq's and

America's under my feet. The air enters and exits my lungs in the same way, regardless of where I am geographically, and aside from the different smells.

My return isn't the end of the hard stuff, nor is it the beginning. It just keeps rolling. My first few weeks will be filled with surreal events: finally holding Angela in my arms and kissing her in a completely different way than I rehearsed in my head a thousand times before I stepped off the bus; trying to shake Lance's hand but ending up in one of his Soul Hugs; [Lance: And why would you think or want less from me? It's been almost a year.] and balancing all my other required 'ish social events that I need to attend to; enjoying the way my blue jeans fit and how my shoes slide onto my feet (and still smell a little). Finally, traveling around the country to see my family, who I haven't seen since before I left, and preparing for whatever adventures I am planning next.

All of these will be parts of my life, as the deployment was. The same will be for my fellow Death Dealers and the other members of the Cav. We will still eat, sleep, shit, and fuck the same way we always have, although a little awkwardly at first. We will hopefully have taken a few important lessons from our time spent, tucked wherever we are throughout the country, and apply them to our daily lives, but the basics will remain the same.

We are just people after all.

51

RUSSIAN BEAUTIES AND TORN UNDERWEAR

~Adam~

Indiana welcomed us the same way it released us—with miserable weather. It was always cold, raining, or both. I had activated my phone and was enjoying my newly returned ability to call people on a whim and text message as I pleased.

I called my mom and got a baseball store.

Hmm.

I called my sister-in-law. We talked for a bit, and she gave me Mom's new number.

This time I got Mom. The conversation was neutral. She was excited, but she definitely wasn't as overwhelming as she was my first tour.

I tried Angela. No answer.

Lance. He was working, so I left a voicemail.

I tried Angela again. This time she picked up.

* * *

Every great party night has a horrible party morning, where blood and torn clothing need to be explained.

Hunt had made the right decision, and with the help of Kaitlyn, Crockett's wife, who was frequenting the area to visit him, got a rental car. Tonight, we were off to check out the local strip clubs. By this time Lance had started texting me. "Call me. Call me."

"Can't. Busy."

"Doing what?"

"Strip Club."

After picking up some civilian clothes at the local Walmart and changing in the parking lot, Hunt drove Clemente, Davis, and me to the first club.

Along the way, Clemente asked me, "Did you tell Davis the news about your girl?"

"No," I said.

"What news?" he asked.

"She dumped him," Clemente answered for me with a smile.

"Wow, that is rough," Davis said.

"Yeah, no shit," I said. My mistakes from the first time we were together had brought her to the conclusion that she couldn't go through that again.

Her timing could have been better...

Our military IDs got us through the door of the first club without a cover charge, and the bar was directly to our front, to provide cheaply made drinks.

"Dude, we have to go. This looks like the type of place where you get stabbed in the middle of a lap dance," Clemente said.

"Yeah, I can see the cellulite in that girl's ass from back here," I responded.

We sucked down our drinks and went to the next club.

This one was a drastic improvement. Of course, we noticed that a lot of the girls were foreign.

We found our faces buried between the breasts and thighs of girls from Brazil, the Philippines, Russia, and all over Europe. I got to enjoy bad music, while Hunt kept feeding us shots. It took us a while to notice Davis had disappeared, and by the time we were thinking about going to look for him, he was returning. From the parking lot. He had his reset.

My world was tingling with the familiar sensation of one too many beers and way too many shots while I watched a beautiful girl from Wisconsin gyrate on stage. Her bikini bottom had long tails that glowed neon green in the overhead lights.

"Adam Fenner," I heard the announcer say through my drunken haze. It took me a second to realize that was me.

"Adam is a medic in the Army who just got back from Afghanistan. He is also a pole-smoking faggot," his big voice filled the room, and I pretended to be invisible, while Clemente laughed and pointed at me.

"These mother fuckers," I said to myself, smiling and shaking my head.

I glanced over to my left where the chunky announcer was approaching me in a shirt that was similar to some we saw on the rack at Walmart. "We need you to come to stage three."

"Shit, I'll be called a faggot if I get a lap dance out of the deal," I said, leaving my jacket in the seat and my beer at the edge of the dance floor while I climbed the stairs to meet a young blonde. She directed me to the chair.

Before I knew it, I was seated. My belt was off and around my neck, securing me to the pole. My shirt was off, and she was grabbing at my underwear.

RRRIIIIPPPPP.

The music was too loud to hear, but I felt it.

She tore the band off and somehow got it over my head, throwing it onto the ground.

"Those are expensive underwear you know?" I said, sitting on my hands.

"That sucks for you," she responded with an evil little smirk.

She proceeded to have her way with me on the dance floor, riding me around like a horse and having me do pushups while she was on my back. It was more fun than it should have been. [Lance: Now that is a great visual.] [Adam: Try to keep it out of your next erotic short story.] [Lance: Too late.]

The night began to wind down as I got increasingly wound up. I ended up in a back booth with a beautiful Russian girl. I ran my hands all over her smooth skin, enjoying her small waist and well-defined feminine features.

"Stop biting," she said, stretching out all the vowels as she said it.

"You don't like it rough?" I asked.

"No, I looove it rouuugh."

I smiled and tried to be good, but my hormones were better collected than I was. Eventually, our time was done. I grabbed all the money in my wallet and gave it to her.

I don't remember walking to the car.

Or rolling down the window and hanging my head out to throw up. [Lance: That's my boy. Glad I missed this one.]

I vaguely remember stumbling out of the car, with legs like a newborn deer, and walking to the barracks with my uniform in hand.

Morning came several hours later. I jumped in the shower. My lip hurt, and there was dried blood smeared across my face.

Hmm.

I rushed to the medical station, where I spent the afternoon going through the various medical stations to prove I was fit to the various doctors and psychiatrists. They drew blood, hopefully they didn't smell it, and gave me a few more unidentified shots. This promised to be a long next few days.

My hangover didn't go away until the next day. By that time, I finally had an explanation for my lip and had collected everything that I had lost the evening prior. [Lance: So what was the explanation for your lip?] [Adam: I face planted on the ground outside the barracks.]

The manuscript called me from the bag hanging in my locker.

"Fuck you, I'm hurting," I answered back.

When I was conscious, I was texting with the few girls whose numbers I hadn't deleted. I had two days to get something ready.

* * *

In a small building that looked like a small cafeteria with a well-equipped, but obviously unused, kitchen and an open area for seating, I found myself standing in a line behind Alvanez, waiting to talk to the finance soldiers to make sure that we would get all the money we were owed. He turned to me and stuck his meaty finger into the open space above my U.S. Army name tape. "Where is yours?" he asked, referring to my CMB (Combat Medic Badge).

"I don't wear it," I told him, suddenly feeling guilty.

"Why not, are you one of the cool guys?"

"I--" I couldn't give him an answer. I mumbled for a bit, until we finally changed the conversation to the girls waiting for us in Vegas.

There was a small group of us who had been debating whether to wear our badges. We had been arguing both sides, as a result of who had received it and who had earned it. The requirement to earn a CMB was simple 'ish: perform medical aid while under contact.

Medical treatment in its most basic level could be assessing a casualty, "Hey, are you okay?" That is all it takes. This works for asking someone during a rocket attack on the base, anyone would do, and filing the proper paperwork. But for those of us who knew what it felt like to load friends onto a bird, to see a soldier's blood on their hands, and who have fought the stomach cramps that come with the thoughts of what could have been done better, it felt like a slap in the face when these guys wore their badges. What value did it have if that was all it took to earn it?

Joey argued that us not wearing ours was what reduces the award, by allowing them to shame it, and us not holding our heads high with it pinned to our chest.

I agreed for the time, but still didn't wear it in the face of those who felt that by wearing the badge they were better medics or soldiers.

I held the CMB with a certain prestige. To me this badge didn't simply represent contact with the enemy while being an infantryman or other MOS (Military Occupational Specialty, your job). The CMB represented under-fire caring for one of your soldiers, going into harm's way, and having to think clearly to save the life of a friend or comrade. Medics were like no other medical professional in the world, who would skillfully treat strangers in a variety of situations. A medic had to be able to think clearly and perform to a standard of care in the worst situations on someone close to him.

Joey used to squash the yearnings of young medics as they talked about the CMB that they wanted.

"Okay. Now, pick who will get hurt for you to earn your CMB?" he would say. "Who will wear a Purple Heart to go with your CMB?"

Suddenly, it wasn't just another piece of bling.

As Alvanez, just barely nineteen-years old, still nervous about how to approach a girl and my hero, asked me why I wasn't wearing my badge, it occurred to me that I shouldn't wear that badge for just myself. I should wear it for him, and Alegria, and every one of the other soldiers whom I'd treated when they needed it the most. That badge didn't only honor my actions—it also honored their sacrifice.

52

PHONE CALLS, FAST CARS, AND LIBERACE?

~Lance~

March 23

I was at work. What else was new? It seemed to be all I did now.

I heard the ringer tone I hadn't heard in months. Adam.

Screw work. I answered. "Hey there. Where are you?"

"I'm back in the states. I'm in Indiana. What's up?"

The rush of excitement at hearing his voice was there in mine. I'd wondered how I'd feel. "I'm at work, so I can't really talk. When are you coming home?"

"I don't know yet."

"I'll call you when I'm done."

"Okay."

Later. After work I called but got his voice mail. I left a message, "I'm done with work. You can call me." Then I texted him and told him to call me. He would respond to one of them.

TEXT FROM ADAM: "You're not going to believe where I am. I'm at a strip club."

TEXT FROM ME: "No way. How is it?"

They had a strip club on base? Things had changed in a year.

My phone rang.

It was loud in the background. I heard him say, "Hey, I can't really talk. It's noisy in here."

"I can tell. Okay. Have fun. Call me when you're done."

"I will."

He didn't.

March 24th.

Next day.

TEXT FROM ADAM: "Still recovering from a mother of a hangover."

TEXT FROM ME: "Okay. Call me when you're able."

The next couple of days were brief texts and conversations. Neither one of us could really talk for long, and there was a lot to say. So the conversation was mundane. The meaty stuff would have to wait. He had Army stuff they had him running around doing, and I... what else?... was working. Or rehearsing. I was opening in "The Fantasticks" tomorrow for three days. He'd just miss it. Shit. I would have liked for him to see it.

I wanted to know how the thing with Angela was going. He hadn't said much. I wondered if he was trying to rekindle so that he'd have some girl to come back to, or if it was real. They had broken up originally because there was no spark there, he'd said. How could you manufacture a spark through phone conversations and e-mails? I knew he didn't want to have only me to come home to. He needed his female companionship.

Maybe that's why I felt some withdrawal. I knew that "Don't ask. Don't tell." policy was still in effect. And I knew that his Army buddies called one another "fag" all the time and him especially, he said. He had also said the Army is homophobic, even though gay guys are there. And I'm sure he didn't talk about his gay best friend back home. Probably not wise. I understood that. (I don't like it. But I understand it.) I'm sure his guys would have been all over that. I was merely speculating. Maybe everything was fine between us. I knew he wanted a girl to come back to. And that he was horny.

March 26 Mid-afternoon:

I decided to call Adam's mom.

"Hi, Becky. It's Lance. Just called to see how you are doing?"

"Oh, I'm fine. Things are the same."

"How's Tom?" I always ask this with a little anxiety, hoping he's all right.

"He's holding his own," she said. "I saw your pictures of Richie on your Facebook. It's about time."

"Yeah, I know. I needed to dig them up."

"Richie's good-looking. He reminds me of an actor," she said.

"Well, his cousin is Robert Urich, you know, from the TV shows "Vegas," and "Spenser For Hire?""

"That's who it is. He does look like him. And did Adam tell you who he's related to?"

"No."

"Liberace."

"You're kidding. Hmm. Of all people."

"I know. Isn't that strange? I used to listen to his music all the time. I'm not sure of the exact connection, but it's through his grandmother, Tom's mother. I think he and Adam are first cousins."

"Even stranger," I say, "is that a few years ago, when I lived in L.A., I went to an auction and bought a small crystal chandelier, which hangs in our library. And guess who the owner of it was? Liberace. It's not real ornate, but it's very nice. Now there's an eerie connection. I'll have to bring it up one day in conversation with Adam. That should surprise him. Thanks."

"I'll see if I can find out more from the relatives."

"Great. And I'm glad Tom is holding his own. Talk to you soon, Becky."

It looked like Adam's dad was going to make it until he came home, his grandfather, too. That made me very happy. Sometimes good things do happen for good people.

March 28, 12:00 A.M.:

Adam's ringtone. "Hey. This is late for you," I answered. "Isn't it about three o'clock there?"

"Yeah. I had a thing to do."

"Any word yet? Or are they going to keep you?"

"No. Whaddya think, they'll keep us here forever?"

"Let me know. I can pick you up at the airport if you like."

"I know. I'll let you know."

"All right. Get some sleep. Bye."

"G'night."

This week he'll be home. He sounds fine, but...

I'm borrowing trouble—something I try never to do. So, I won't. He's back. He's safe. Everything will be just fine. I guess this is all part of the process: off to war for a year, second guessing, changes, and feelings. It's probably a universal feeling for all of us back-at-homers.

53

MY BICYCLE

~Adam~

"I don't know if the sinking feeling in my stomach is gravity from the plane landing or the realization that I am about to lead a purposeless existence," I said to Joey as the plane's wheels touched the ground in Vegas.

* * *

It was around 7:30 in the morning when we touched down. It took almost an hour before we were standing in formation in front of everyone's families. The Colonel kept his promise of not making any speeches. "Squadron dismissed," he yelled before the parking lot erupted into cheers. [Lance: I can't believe you denied me the privilege of being there. It would have been great.]

Everyone ran into their families' waiting arms. They smiled and cried as they kissed their wives and loved ones. I met up with Odie, who was giving me a ride to Angela's, who said she would be able to drive me wherever as long as I could make it to her work.

Odie met up with a female companion and played it cool, not showing any emotion. Eventually, after introducing me to his dad, we got our bags and were off.

I dropped my bags and hugged Angela in her office. It was short and cold.

She drove me to Ed's house.

He was sleeping and unable to open the front gate to let us drive in. I jumped the wall and broke into his house. I found his bedroom door locked, where his phone, which was needed to open the gate, was hiding. I knocked. A surprised Ed found me in his hallway.

"What? When? What are you doing here?"

"Can you open the gate for Angela?" I asked.

"Yeah," he rubbed the sleep out of his eyes and fumbled with his phone to open the gate.

Eventually, he went back to bed and Angela left. And there I was. Lance was still sleeping. So, I knew I would have to kill time. [Lance: As if I wouldn't have been up if you had told me. Dick.]

~Lance~

March 29, 12:00 P.M.:

I got up—my sleep-in day—and checked my phone.

TEXT FROM ADAM: "I'm back. I'm at Ed's. Call me so I can come over and get my car. I have errands to do. Wanna do lunch?"

He's home? That asshole! Of course he wouldn't tell me. He didn't want any fanfare or excitement. Low key. I should have known better. But I was hoping. So that "thing" he had to do at three in the morning was getting ready to fly out. My Sherlock Holmes' skills need some honing.

Shit! I have work at 4:00. Too late to call in sick. Lunch is out. If I wasn't so happy to see him, I'd kill him... I still might.

I called him. "Hey, welcome back. You should have told me or warned me. When did you get in?"

"I didn't want to wake you. So, you wanna meet for lunch? I'll get my car?"

His car. Shit! "Give me an hour. How about Denny's by the gym?"

"Okay. I have to wait till Ed's ready. He has to work at three. It'll take him a while to get ready."

"See you then."

I flew out of the house. I was going to surprise him with a factory-fresh, car detailing for his beloved, cherry-red Camaro—the car that no one else would watch for him for a year. I hoped I could get that done fast. Maybe I'd play the "It's for my best friend who just got back today from Afghanistan" card.

I did.

It worked. Record time. The car looked gorgeous. I still had time to fill the tank and meet him.

Meet him.

Here we go.

~Adam~

As everyone woke up, I wrote. When Ed woke up, again, I coordinated him to drive me to Lance. He had work, so it would be short, but I needed to get my car from him to get errands done.

In a Denny's parking lot, Lance was fashionably late. [Lance: If I had had some kind of heads-up, maybe I could have coordinated everything better. I have responsibilities.] He pulled up behind Ed and made his way to my side of the car. Before I was able to get out, he opened the door and pulled me in for one of his Soul Hugs.

Ed left and I jumped into the passenger seat of Lance's mid-sized, bright-yellow SUV and he drove me to my car. The reunion was quick as he finished getting everything he needed for work and headed out.

~*Lance*~

I pull into the parking lot.

He is sitting in Ed's car.

I see his face.

He's home. He's safe.

I park behind him and jump out of the car.

I pull him out of the car before he can open the door himself.

"Hi," I say, a simple greeting.

"What's up?"

His hair is shaggier than before. He's beefier than before, from all the working out. He doesn't have what my friend Clint calls "the 500-yard stare," the haunted look soldiers sometimes have where the eyes focus off in the distance, seeing some past horror.

He looks the same.

We embrace. I kiss him on the cheek and a...

Soul Hug.

It feels right.

* * *

So, I didn't get to meet him at the airport. There wasn't a fanfare of trumpets. There wasn't even a solo of Reveille.

It was the two of us, in a parking lot at the gym.

Best friends.

Back together.

We chatted on the way to my house and talked about... stuff.

"How are you and Angela doing? You haven't talked about her."

"She broke up with me two days ago."

"I guess that's why you haven't talked about her. I'm sorry. Are you okay about it?"

"Yeah. There's nothing I can do. She says she just can't do it again. It's complicated."

Subject change. We'll talk more about it later, I'm sure.

"If you're free tomorrow we could do one of our dinners at Tuscany to welcome you home."

"Sounds good. I'll let you know. Thanks for cleaning my car. It looks great. You didn't have to do that."

"I know that. But I didn't want you to come back to filthy car. I know you love your car."

"Thanks."

"Sure. The tank's full, too."

"You didn't have to—"

"I know. I have to go to work. Call me later."

"Okay."

And that was the first big homecoming day. I sit here and write about what it should have been. I had had this plan of picking him up the airport and having a beer ready for him from a cooler I'd brought, accompanied by a swig of Jack Daniels Single Barrel from his flask, in the parking lot at the airport, as a welcome home. Then, we would go to my house, hang out, and catch up. Make it nice and easy. But that didn't happen. I'd wanted him to ease back in. But he'd wanted it even easier. No fanfare.

It sucked. Elation battling disappointment.

I'd gotten to spend the rest of my evening at work, brooding and having various conversations in my head of the things I would have liked to say to him.

"I can't believe you knew when you were coming back and didn't tell me. You had no one to meet you. You had one of your guys take you to meet Angela, who'd broken up with you, to take you to Ed's, who didn't know you were coming either. You just didn't want it to be me.

"I can't believe you'd do this to me. The one person who kept in touch with you—without your prompting—and cared about you the whole time you were gone.

"It's not fair. I had a nice, quiet, appropriate welcoming in mind. But I'm sure you thought it was going to be something dramatic. Well, it wasn't. I thought about you and considered your feelings. I wish you'd thought about mine.

"Then, to top it off, I get to see you for twenty minutes because I have to work. Because you couldn't let me know you were coming home. This was incredibly selfish of you. You knew what it meant to me. And you denied me the pleasure. This will probably be something I'll never forget."

But...

I didn't say any of that. I may sometime, probably not in such a ranting manner though. Yet, the feeling of disappointment remained. I'd imagined his homecoming in dozens of different scenarios, from simple to lavish. All beginning with me meeting him off the plane. Just that would have been enough for me. I'd wanted to be the first to see him. To have him step off the plane and see my unabashed joy at having him home. I should be grateful he's back and safe. I am. That's what's really important. Isn't it? [Adam: I'm not obligated to dedicate my homecoming to anyone.] [Lance: That was apparent.]

~Adam~

I opened the door to my car, its red paint shined from a fresh wash. [Lance: Yes.] The seat felt as it always had, aside from needing to be readjusted. [Lance: My legs are longer.] It started with a familiar purr. America was slowly proving itself to be like riding a bike. I won't forget how, but I am definitely a little wobbly after so much time spent away, something my transmission took the hit on a few times.

I spent my first night cleaning up the house. I found messes that hailed back to Grant's presence several months ago, before he deployed to the Helmand Province of Afghanistan, according to Ed. I cleaned his sheets, and after having a drink at the local bar, crawled into his bed and fell asleep—the first time in a real bed with sheets in nine months.

The Army was insistent on reminding us that even though we were home, they were still paying us and were ultimately at their mercy, which brought about a variety of mandatory events. The first was moving lockers at the armory. Although it was a menial twenty minutes of my time, it was still my time.

That night I met up with Lance, Richie, and Clint and his wife Casey (D&D friends), and we enjoyed some drinks at the Tuscany. We laughed and goofed around. We fought with the waiter about how many Cuarenta y Tres' to bring us. I'm not the drinker I used to be after all. [Lance: What about all those beers and shots at the strip club?] [Adam: There is a distinct difference between the act of drinking and the ability to handle it.] Our conversations felt like we hadn't stopped having them for nine months, like it had never happened. Here I was, with a collared shirt and skater shoes on, an outfit that I picked (because I don't know how to dress myself). It was as if the whole time I spent in combat boots was a distant memory.

~Lance~

I'd ordered a bottle of Veuve Clicquot Yellow Label to toast his welcome home, after our opening toasts with our usual cocktails: Maker's Mark for me, Jack and Coke for him.

Dinner was great and just right, topped off by a shared Cuarenta y Tres. Things felt right, and I was glad (sort of) I hadn't berated him with my fantasy rages. (In print would have to do.)

There'd been a momentary blip in our lives. A year.

We'd changed. We'd learned. We'd grown. And had come back to square one.

Like we were supposed to.

~Adam~

The following day it was an hour-long ceremony that took us two hours to prepare for. We waited in the back of Convention Center, the single guys talking about failed conquests and the relationship guys still enjoying their post-coital glow.

The Governor and a variety of other statesman (mostly representatives, because if being kept away from our families wasn't bad enough, now these people are too busy to do it themselves and need to send a rep) came to thank us and welcome us home.

A few hours later, we were expected at Freemont Street, where a variety of other events was also planned. The local liquor super-mart was kind enough to donate an open bar. Thank you.

I showed up early in blue jeans and a T-shirt. Apparently, I didn't get the uniform memo. Oh well.

Sandy and Finch received their Bronze Stars with V devices on stage. It was good to see them as well. They were still the same as I remembered them, like brothers always fighting and laughing together, only less wrestling, considering they were both still broken.

I ran into Angela there.

I had seen her earlier in the day, when she was fighting back tears in the back of the Mandalay Bay Convention Center. It was the "wish things could be different" tears. She gave me a few hugs that stretched out longer than even Lance's World Famous Soul Hugs. I smiled and went along with it.

We went out for sushi, then drinks. I walked her to her car. I leaned in for the kiss. This time she didn't shield herself, as she had done when she dropped me off at Ed's only two days earlier.

Reset.

It wasn't the way I expected to end this chapter, but it was, with Angela's head lying on my chest, as we fell asleep. I had made it home.

Every moment felt surreal, like I knew it was happening, but it still didn't feel real. It was as if my last year hadn't happened—but I knew it had. While I was in Afghanistan, I convinced myself that I would never come home, not because I would die, but because the deployment would never end. Now it was as if this was all a dream. I was still expecting to get woken up by mortars while in the bottom floor of the Death Star. And it was because of this pseudo-reality that I found myself not feeling anything toward the world around me.

I had spent a year thinking about seeing Lance, and how a woman's skin would feel against my own. And now, I was experiencing all those things with no feeling of euphoria or jubilation. My heart didn't skip a beat, and I didn't lose my breath.

It all felt...

So...

Empty.

54

THE REST OF THE STORY

~Lance~

I sit here, fingers poised to type, to wrap up the writing. My doubts and trepidations had been assuaged. I would get over my disappointment of his non-existent homecoming. For now, though, I would enjoy his being here.

We'd both been through a lot, neither of us knowing the outcome, taking it a day at a time, and staying in touch as much as we could.

We both learned that we would always be there for one another. Not even a war could break the bond. True friends would always be just that. For no matter the ordeal or the separation, they are always there in your heart. [Adam: That is the kind of talk that will send the rest of my military career up in flames.] [Lance: You just couldn't resist commenting on my happy ending, could you?] [Adam: …]

AFTERWARD

THANK YOU

~Adam~

TEXT FROM SANDIE, TO ME: "Is Deutch shot?"

TEXT FROM ME, TO DEUTCH: "Dude, did you get shot?"

No reply.

* * *

The morning came, earlier than I would have liked. As it had lately, something about America was giving me problems sleeping past eight A.M.

TEXT FROM DAVIS: "He died last night."

* * *

The next day I was in a small basement bar in Slinger, Wisconsin. I had just finished my first Jack and Coke of the evening. I was still getting condolences from people who had read the numerous articles about Deutch on my Facebook page. It had been my attempt to quell the tide of disinformation swirling around the events of his death, for the kids. It did bring me a great deal of unwanted attention.

I was trying to enjoy the pleasant company of a female friend who I had not seen since before I was married, and a friend of hers—without either knowing Susan's scent was on me from only a few hours prior.

I had to find a small quiet corner to talk to a Las Vegas news anchor. He had e-mailed me about my pictures and wanted to ask me about "What kind of a guy he was."

He had interviewed Deutch's local sheriff to see what kind of a deputy he was, and LT COL Cunningham, the squadron commander, for what kind of a soldier he was. But leaning against a laminated wooden booth, across from some chairs that looked like my parents' dining room chairs, in a moderately well lit part of the bar, I talked about the kind of a man I knew him to be.

I was still in shock then. I didn't feel anything because I still couldn't believe it.

* * *

"Have you ever read The Things They Carried?" Joey asked me in the local pancake house after we had just finished flirting with the beautiful young Ethiopian waitress before the funeral service.

"Yeah, but I don't remember much of it."

"He explained in it how to tell the difference between a real and a fake war story," Joey said, sipping on some hot tea.

I looked at him, waiting for an elaboration.

"If a story has a moral to it--" Joey said.

"Then it is a lie."

* * *

I had driven the four hours from my folks' house to the Minneapolis airport the night before the funeral, where I had flown to meet Joey in the baggage terminal of the Las Vegas Airport.

When the plane I was waiting for at Gate Twelve of the Las Vegas airport would finally arrive at eleven in the evening, I would be driving the five hours to meet Susan in Milwaukee. I waited quietly at my gate, the sun uncomfortably warming my skin through the giant airport windows.

Six hours earlier, the Death Dealers were back together again— almost all of us. It had been a month since we had been dismissed, and despite the fact that they started the conversation by insulting my poor choice of clothing, grooming standards, and calling me a fag, it was good to have everyone back.

The SWAT snipers on the roof stood security, while the Patriot Guard stood watch in the parking lot for the Westboro Baptist church.

In the ceremony, I sat two rows back from Deutch's family, watching Clemente's tears gather beneath his chin in front of me— he had flown in from Florida—and Wills' girl wipe the tears off his face, because he couldn't.

Davis, from Kentucky, where he was receiving treatment, and Finch, from New Mexico, where he too was being treated, were pallbearers, with soldiers holding up his left and policemen on his right. Encased in soft fabric, with his legs awkwardly contorted to fit inside the beautiful wooden casket shorter than he was tall, and an American flag draped over the top, they carried him in.

Sergeant Harvey, a dark-skinned preacher well into his fifties and carrying himself better than most twenty-somethings, strolled onto the stage. He didn't set notes on the podium. He didn't need any. He reached deep within himself and spoke.

"It is not the critic who counts, not the man who points out how the strong man stumbled, or where the doer of deeds could have done better. The credit belongs to the man who is actually in the arena, whose face is marred by the dust and sweat and blood, who strives valiantly, who errs and comes short again and again, who knows the great enthusiasms, the great devotions, and spends himself for a worthy cause, who at the best knows, in the end, the triumph of high achievement, and who, at worst, if he fails, at least fails while daring greatly, so that his place shall never be with those cold and timid souls who know neither victory or defeat." Quoting Theodore Roosevelt, his heart guided his speech and washed over the audience of soldiers and police officers from all over the state.

My jaw quivered; it was my hand that wiped the tears from my face as Sergeant Harvey spoke.

"He will always be my little boy," his mother said before dismissing herself from the stage. The tears rolled down my face as I watched her fight to maintain her composure in a massive church filled with her son's family, friends, and peers.

Nye County's Sheriff walked to the podium. He nervously shuffled his note cards. He would not go down in Nye County history as a great orator but as a man who spoke and led from the heart. "I held his hand while the paramedics worked on him. And as they closed the back doors of the ambulance to take him to the hospital—" He paused for a moment and brought his fist in front of his mouth. "Deputy Deutch said, 'It will be all right, sir.'"

I, too, fought to maintain my composure.

As I stepped into the sun, just outside the church, I bumped into SFC Mendoza. He hugged me, his eyes swollen from his own tears. "Glad you made it, brother."

* * *

It was four in the afternoon on Saturday, at gate A12, two doubles of Jack Daniels and Cokes down. With my "Anything that can go wrong will go wrong" hat pulled down over my eyes so the lady across from me didn't see the tears rolling down my cheeks falling onto my laptop as I attempted to push through the worst prologue I could imagine. I remembered the night where we couldn't be there for him—when he responded to that domestic dispute and was shot three times with an SKS.

He died on an operating table with over two hundred of his friends and family sitting in the hospital, while I lay two time zones away on an air mattress in my father's den in Wisconsin. I had fallen asleep, thinking everything would be okay, worrying about Susan who had just come back into my life, and Angela who was having her own drama.

* * *

Well after the services were over, and I could finally sleep, my legs tangled with Susan's, and all I could think to say was, "Deutch, thank you."

* * *

Finally back in Vegas, lying on Grant's blue fleece blanket haphazardly spread across the bed to produce the illusion of a made bed, I watched the fan blades spin, pushing the air gently down onto me, cooling my body from the Las Vegas heat. Grant was in Afghanistan, and I had taken over his room while I tried to purchase a home of my own.

My hands were crossed and my fingers intertwined behind my head on the pillow that I had taken with me to Afghanistan. I tried not to look at my pile of clothes on the floor to my right. I rolled my head to the left. This was where I was piling all the items I would need for my next adventure—my new phone lying next to me with my flight itinerary sitting in my e-mail's inbox.

"I can't believe you are leaving again," Lance had said to me. "You just got home."

I'd smiled.

Africa was calling, a chance for adventure in the villages of Uganda, but this time, on my terms.

GLOSSARY

A/T = Advanced Training, a preparatory training before our pre-deployment training.

AAF = Anti-American Forces, the bad guys.

AAV = Amphibious Assault Vehicle

ACOG = Advanced Combat Optical Gunsight

ACU = Army Combat Uniform

ADA = American Disabilities Act

ADT = Agricultural Development Team, they teach farmers how to more efficiently farm.

AK = Avtomat Kalashnikova, the assault rifle of choice for bad guys because of its low price and ease of maintenance compared to its reliability.

ANA = Afghan National Army

ANP = Afghani National Police

Arty = Artillery (slang)

ASG = Afghani security guards

BAF = Bagram Air Force Base

BDU = Battle Dress Uniform (old style)

Birds = Slang for military aircraft.

b-hut = barracks

C130 = Cargo/troop plan; it is big.

CA = Civil Affair(s)

Camelbak = Known for its backpack pouch to hold water.

CASEVAC = Casualty Evacuation, referred to an improvised evacuation on ground with either a non-dedicated vehicle or on foot.

Cav = Cavalry (slang)

Cheap Times = The hangout for the Death Dealers and SFC Mendoza's office while at COP Najil.

CMB = Combat Medic Badge

COP = Combat OutPost

CP = Command Post

EBR = Enhanced Battle Rifle, slang for Mark 14 Mod 0 Enhanced Battle Rifle

ECP = Entry Control Point, the entrance to the base

EOD = Explosive Ordnance Disposal

ETT = Embedded Training Team, a team established to train local militaries.

FOB = Forward Operating Base

FRACUs = Fire Resistant Army Combat Uniform, pronounced frack-yous

FST = Forward Support Team

HME = Home-Made Explosives

HMMWV = Highly Mobile Multi Wheeled Vehicle, pronounced Humm-vee

IED = Improvised Explosive Device

Illum = The amount of light at any given time, short for illumination and can be a reference to a type of ammunition designed to cast light over an area.

Index = to end an event—only used in training.

IRR = Inactive Ready Reserves, the other part of the contract that every service member signs up for, but often forgets they did sign up for it.

JAF = Jalalabad Air Force Base

KIA = Killed In Action

klick = kilometer (about 0.6 mile)

LN = Local National

LZ = Landing Zone, where aircraft land

M14 = Mark 14, long range 7.62 semi-automatic rifle for the squad designated marksman.

M19 = automatic grenade launcher

M2 = automatic .50 cal machine gun

M203 = handheld grenade launcher attached to another weapon. When this is attached to a weapon, the entire weapon in slang military terms is known as an M203, regardless of the attached weapon.

M24 = Sniper rifle of choice, 7.62 caliber bolt action.

M249 SAW = 5.56 light machine gun for squad.

M4 = short barreled conversion of the M16, 5.56 semi-automatic assault rifle.

M9 = 9mm pistol

MEDEVAC = Medical Evacuation, via a dedicated vehicle air or ground

MOS = Military Occupational Specialty, a service members job

MRAP = Mine Resistant Ambush Protected

MRE = Meal Ready To Eat

MWR = Morale Welfare and Recreation

NCO = Non-Commissioned Officer, enlisted service members who hold leadership positions

NODs = Night Optical Devices

NVGs = Night Vision Goggles, also known as nods

OC = Officer Controller, the person who monitors a training event

OP = Observation Post

PID = Positive Identification, specifically referring to targets to ensure innocent people are not injured

PKM = Pulemyot Kalashnikova, 7.62 fully automatic machine gun, the one the bad guys use.

POO = Point Of Origin

PRT = Provincial Reconstruction Team, a joint service team designed to train and provide for the locals to encourage growth and reconstruction among the local population.

PT = Physical Training

QRF = Quick Reaction Force

RCP = Route Clearance Package

RIP = Relief In Place

ROE = Rules Of Engagement, the law that governs what we do in battle

RPG = Rocket Propelled Grenade

SAW = M249, Squad Automatic Weapon

SFC = Sergeant First Class

SKS = Samozaryadniy Karadin Sistemi Simonova, predecessor to the AK-47, 7.62 Semi-automatic carbine. It's for the bad guys.

SPC = Specialist

SSG = Staff Sergeant

TC = Troop Commander

Terp = Slang for interpreter

UFC = Ultimate Fighting Championship

XO = Executive Officer, pronounced ekes-oh

About the Authors

Adam Fenner has served in both the US Marine Corps and the Nevada National Guard. He has deployed twice to Iraq and three times to Afghanistan. He now resides in Las Vegas and serves with the Nevada National Guard. He is a student pursuing his MBA and is currently working on a dark fantasy series.

Lance Taubold has been a Metropolitan opera singer, Broadway performer and Soap Opera actor. He currently lives, performs, and writes in Las Vegas. He previously released Ripper: A Love Story with Richard Devin, and will soon release an anthology of paranormal romances, **Zodiac Lovers**.

Made in the USA
San Bernardino, CA
01 October 2013